THE GHOSTS OF A WHITER SHADE OF PALE

PROCOL HARUM

THE GHOSTS OF A WHITER SHADE OF PALE

PROCOL HARUM

HENRY SCOTT-IRVINE

OMNIBUS PRESS

London / New York / Paris / Sydney / Copenhagen / Berlin / Madrid / Tokyo

Dedicated to the memory of
Barrie James Wilson
(March 18, 1947 – October 8, 1990)

Contents

Contents

Foreword

In the time I'm thinking about now – the late, waning sixties – there was no better band to slip you into a long night of dreams than Procol Harum, and no better record than *A Salty Dog*. 'A Whiter Shade Of Pale' had been a big hit just two years before, in 1967, and it was one of those songs that changed the whole map. *A Salty Dog*, and particularly its title track, was like a further labyrinthine exploration down that new road. You couldn't know what waited for you around the first turning. Maybe demons. Maybe dragons. Or maybe another new turning.

There was a richness and a mystery about Procol Harum's music that echoed in on you, magisterial melodies and teasing, enigmatic lyrics you could invest with your own fantasies. For me and all my friends who loved the band, and this album, the songs seemed like a challenge. Where would they take you? What would you find? "A sand so white, and sea so blue, no mortal place at all."

The point was not so much what the songs were saying, specifically, as what they were suggesting to each of us, individually, where all those sounds and images would lead us, then leave us. The films of Stan Brakhage, Bruce Conner, Kenneth Anger, Bruce Baillie and others worked the same kind of allusive magic, casting a deep spell that only began with the images on the screen.

Procol Harum's music drew from so many deep wells – classical music, 19th century literature, rhythm and blues, seaman's logs, concretist poetry – that each tune became a cross-cultural whirligig, a road trip through the pop subconscious. For that time, and for this one too – for any, I'm sure – it was great travelling music. I've been on a few journeys myself since the *Salty Dog* days, and Procol Harum has always been with me.

"Your witness my own hand…"

Martin Scorsese
April, 2012

Introduction

Let's face it, Procol Harum's 'A Whiter Shade of Pale' is an odd song. Odd enough that anyone who has been anywhere near a radio, Walkman or iPod in the last 45 years almost certainly would have listened to it.

It entered our lives out of nowhere. To misquote the poet Philip Larkin, it came upon us in the summer of love, between Apollo 1 and The Beatles' eighth LP. It was a tough time to make a debut, because 1967 was a great year for music. Apart from The Beatles there were Otis, Aretha, Dylan, The Who, The Doors, The Kinks, The Animals and Cream. Pink Floyd went quadraphonic, the Stones were busted at Redlands, Hendrix burned his guitar at Finsbury Park and, miraculously, Britain even won the Eurovision song contest that year with Sandie Shaw.

With all this competition, this brand new band with the funny name and even odder song topped the UK charts for six weeks and it soon became a worldwide hit, selling 10 million records and spawning a thousand cover versions. The BBC says it went on to be the most played song in 70 years. It certainly was the most played song during that summer of love, as I bore witness, with any song from *Sgt Pepper* coming a close second.

My own connection to 'AWSoP' (as the aficionados call it) is somewhat nebulous. Apart from (or maybe because of) being one of the nuts who couldn't stop playing the song that summer, it subsequently found its way into my film *The Commitments* and later I had the pleasure of working with Gary Brooker on my film of *Evita*. And, like many others, it was played at my wedding. Except we were in Austin, Texas and it was sung by the great country-blues singer, Toni Price, with the lyrics taped to a mic-stand and the accompaniment on steel guitar.

In *The Commitments*, we were a tad disrespectful. Jimmy Rabbitte, the young band's manager in the story, visits the keyboard player, Stephen, in a church where he is playing the organ. The opening notes of 'AWSoP' ring out and Stephen says, "Great intro, eh?" "Yeah they nicked it from Marvin Gaye," says Jimmy." "He nicked it from Bach," counters Stephen. OK, we meant Percy Sledge, a mistake which we turned into a joke later, when Stephen is in the priest's confessional. Personally I never got the Sledge connection. I was working as a copywriter in advertising at the time and wrote Hamlet cigar commercials, where we used the 'Air On A G-String' music played by Jacques Loussier, so I always assumed it was that. It's not, of course. I was also told it was inspired by Bach's 'Sleepers, Awake'. However, I am reliably informed that anyone who throws their hands at an organ keyboard will come out with something owed to *Orgelbüchlein* – Bach's *Little Organ Book*.

After singing the first verse, Jimmy Rabbitte goes on to say, "Poxiest lyrics ever written." Well, they are vexing, perhaps, or mysterious, elusive, and some think, impenetrable, but frankly, that summer we never worried too much that they didn't make immediate sense. We reacted to the elliptical poetry the same way we did to 'A Day In The Life' – as beautiful words that filled your head with images that just let your imagination fly: the more abstruse, the better. It meant just what you wanted it to mean. Those were the unique times in which the song was born.

That's not to say people haven't racked their brains these last 45 years to offer meaning to Keith Reid's mesmerising poetry. Over the years, people have offered up explanations from drunken seduction, and drug overdoses, to necrophilia, to Arthur Miller's tale with Marilyn Monroe. My favourite was the one about the violated nuns escaping the Nazis. Sounds like a good movie.

As I got older and more pretentious, I could see the influence of André Breton, Lewis Carroll, Chaucer, Milton and Magritte. And less pretentiously, I think, maybe it's a grab-bag of juicy references that Reid had jotted in his notebook – like William Burroughs' 'cut-ups', as practised by Dylan and Bowie. Random thoughts, fragments of ideas, clusters of words, fitted together like a surreal jigsaw and scribbled down into four stanzas that became one of the most beautiful rock songs ever written.

When the seldom-performed third and fourth verses came to light it was hailed by one journalist as, "the most useful piece of clarification since the cryptographers of Bletchley Park broke the Nazi Enigma code during the Second World War". The view was that the last two stanzas explained everything that had gone before, as the metaphors come full circle and the drunken seduction is consummated.

Then I was fortunate to work with Gary Brooker on *Evita*, where he played Peron's Foreign Minister, Juan Atilio Bramuglia. Even if you watch the film with your eyes closed it's impossible not to recognise Gary's extraordinary, unique voice. On the day he finished filming, the crew gathered round for a drink to say goodbye. They peppered him with questions about 'AWSoP' and he sang the final fourth verse, which he said made everything clear. The crew and I stood in a circle surrounding Gary in silence as he finished. All of us, it has to be said, were none the wiser, which for me, is as it should be.

In the final scene of *The Commitments,* Jimmy Rabbitte, looking in the mirror, has an imaginary conversation with Terry Wogan as to what he has learned from his foray into the music business.

JIMMY
Well, as I always say, Terry: We skipped the light fandango, turned cartwheels 'cross the floor, I was feeling kind of seasick, but the crowd called out for more.

TERRY
That's very profound, Jimmy. What does it mean?

JIMMY
I'm fucked if I know Terry.

Sir Alan Parker
June 2012

Chapter 1

Whiter Shades Of Rhythm'N'Blues

The Paramounts 1960–1966

"The Paramounts — one of the best groups to come up for a long time. Put that in the Melody Maker.*"*

Keith Richards

For a band whose repertoire includes many an imaginary tale of seafaring, it should come as no surprise that the roots of Procol Harum lie by the English coast. Though over the years their personnel would ebb and flow like the tide, three of the group's key members grew up to the sound of waves crashing against the shore while the semi-pro band from which Procol developed first stirred amid the heady atmosphere of the seaside.

Basking on the north side of the Thames estuary between Great Wakering and the mudflats of Canvey Island, the Essex resort of Southend-On-Sea has been a holiday destination for East Londoners since the early Victorian era. The town boasts the longest pleasure pier in the world, built in 1830 and stretching out across the sand and sea for over a mile from an esplanade of neon-lit buildings known simply as the Golden Mile. Less than an hour by train from London, Southend-On-Sea has always been a popular destination for day trippers, the Essex equivalent of Brighton and Blackpool, but with a rock'n'roll sensibility; a restrained British version of Atlantic City meets Memphis that is often referred to as 'The Essex Delta'.

Back in the late fifties one of the greatest places to hear rock'n'roll played loud – as it was meant to be heard – was at fairgrounds, and Southend-On-Sea's infamous Kursaal and Peter Pan's Playground were no exception. The brash glamour of the Kursaal boasted two of the largest rollercoasters in Europe, towering high above the waltzers and the dodgems, the candyfloss and the coconut shy, providing the perfect backdrop to a soundtrack of Elvis, Jerry Lee, Little Richard, Buddy and the Everlys. The music was pumped non-stop through cracked speakers at enormous volume on the rides, the 45s were scratched through overuse and you had to shout to make yourself heard above it all – but it was glorious all the same, the soundtrack to an escape from the drudgery of reality, the rock'n'roll roundabout to heaven.

Countless London teens got their first taste of American R&B on day trips to the town's many arcades, cafes, clubs, and bars. By 1963 this vibrant resort had become synonymous with the Britain's burgeoning rhythm'n'blues boom.

According to John Howard, "Southend-On-Sea's social scene post the Saturday morning pictures revolved around the Saturday teenage show at the Odeon cinema, where they played the latest rock'n'roll records, and had live acts like Vince Taylor and Marty Wilde. Then there were the many coffee bars like the Panda, the Shrubbery, the Zanzibar, the Panorama, the Jacobean, the 4Bs, and the Capri – where actress Helen Mirren used to hang out when she was a teenager (then) known as 'Troika'."

At a time in British pop history when virtually every teenager yearned to be in a beat group, the best to emerge from Southend-On-Sea during this halcyon period was The Paramounts, a four-piece that was – unusually for the time – fronted by a piano-playing lead singer named Gary Brooker.

Born May 29, 1945 in Hackney, East London, Brooker spent his first few years in Bush Hill Park, Middlesex, before the family moved back to London, settling in Edmonton. Gary's father, Harry, was a well-known professional musician who played the pedal steel guitar with Felix Mendelssohn's Hawaiian Serenaders but Harry's son's instrument of choice became the piano. Encouraged to start playing when he was five, Gary's first teacher was prone to hitting her students over the wrists with her pen. Nevertheless, Harry Brooker instigated his son's stage debut at the precocious age of seven.

In 1954 the Brookers moved to the Eastwood district of Southend-On-Sea where, within two years, Harry Brooker died. His father might have departed but his inspiration remained and the following year Gary started piano lessons with Ronald Meachen, a teacher who would have a profound influence on his playing. Discarding orthodox methods of tuition, Meachen would steer his pupils through a process of analysing chord structures and scales, encouraging them to investigate 'boogie woogie' styles. The empathy between Brooker and Meachen led to much progress and self-confidence within his star pupil.

"In the late 1950s Westcliff High School for Boys was an evil organisation headmastered by a simian sadist called Henry Cloke," recalls former pupil John Howard. "One day in the Maths class Gary Brooker asked me if I knew Chris Copping, who lived a couple of roads away from me, because he'd heard that Chris had a good musical reputation – Chris attended the *other* Southend-On-Sea grammar school. We both knew that Chris could play a totally accurate intro to Gene Vincent's version of 'Rocky Road Blues' on piano, so I helped the two to make contact. Chris Copping was teaching Robin Trower – then known as Trot – to play guitar; and I remember Robin subsequently got the most amazing electric guitar – the most beautiful one that I'd ever seen."

"My father got it for me," says Trower. Born on March 9, 1945, in Catford, South East London, Robin would prove to be a natural on guitar. "It was a Rosetti, what they call a 'cello' guitar. I was a big Elvis fan. He always had a guitar around his neck. Elvis is what made me want me to play the guitar. I had a (guitar) book and I seemed to pick it all up pretty quick. It only took me a few weeks. As a kid I never practised (laughs). It came naturally. I never actually sat down and tried to work out somebody else's thing from their records. I was more interested in making my own things up. I'd hear guitar and I'd absorb it." (1)

"Rob worked at the Rock Stall outside the Kursaal Ballroom on the seafront," says John Howard. "His dad, Len, was a window cleaner and had the concession on most of the High Street shops. "

"A few of us attempted to form a skiffle group called The Electrics in 1957, adds Howard. "I had maracas, others played guitars, but I was more interested in records. This was put together by a kid called Dave Lewis and included future Paramounts Graham 'Diz' Derrick and Gary Brooker, plus Adrian 'Ada' Baggerley who later joined Mickey Jupp's band The Orioles. We got together regularly at one another's houses, including Gary's place in Eastwood."

The Electrics were all aged 12 and featured Brooker initially playing both banjo and guitar before switching exclusively to piano. For the princely sum of just £1 you could hire The Electrics for weddings and parties. However, the group didn't last long, and while still at Westcliff High School For Boys, Brooker formed his second outfit The Coasters, whose name was inspired not by Southend-On-Sea's location but from the black American rhythm'n'blues combo with the very same moniker. The Southend-On-Sea Coasters, however, mainly played rock'n'roll instrumentals.

'Best band in town' contests were a regular draw at Southend-On-Sea's Palace Hotel just above the seafront, attracting crowds of local teenagers to its dance hall, so it was only natural that The Coasters would pitch themselves against other local contenders. Among these were The Raiders, featuring guitarist Robin Trower and, on bass, another Southend-On-Sea migrant, Chris Copping (born August 29, 1945, Middleton, Lancashire). The Coasters and The Raiders both fancied their chances, but got pipped to the post by a group called Micky Law & The Outlaws.

"The Coasters came a close second, but this result was controversial because some people thought that Micky Law had fixed the votes, which had been counted on slips of paper," says Brooker. "Maybe Micky Law had more pencils than anybody else!"

The evening was not entirely wasted, however, as Peter Martin, the entrepreneur who ran the contest, took note of the talent on display and conceived the idea of putting together a 'supergroup' from the cream of local musicians. Martin named the group The Paramounts and became their manager.

Gary Brooker: "Peter Martin put The Paramounts together by dubious means. He'd already got Robin Trower and Chris Copping from The Raiders, Mick Brownlee, the drummer from Micky Law & The Outlaws, and Bob Scott as lead vocalist. They wanted me on piano." (3)

Copping tells a different story. "Robin Trower and Mick Brownlee both had the original idea of forming The Paramounts together, and as I had started playing with Robin, so I was naturally involved. This was at the end of 1960."

"My favourite band at the time was The Rockerfellas from Romford who played great rock'n'roll," says Trower. "I decided that I wanted to have a band that was modelled on them. They had a piano player. I thought, 'We have to get a piano player'. And the only other piano player I'd seen locally was Gary Brooker."

"Peter Martin got Robin to phone me and asked me if I could come to a rehearsal one Sunday, just to sit in and help out," says Brooker. "I told him that The Coasters were playing that night. Rob said, 'I've spoken to [Coasters' vocalist] Johnny Short, it's OK.' So I went to The Paramounts' rehearsal, and the same thing reoccurred *every* Sunday for a month. Johnny Short assumed I no longer wanted to be in The Coasters, as I'd been missing rehearsals. I thought Johnny Short no longer wanted me! And, suddenly, I was a Paramount!" (3)

The first gig performed as The Paramounts was at the Palace Dance Studio on November 5, 1960, followed by a series of shows at the Cricketers Pub, also in Southend-On-Sea. At all these early dates Bob Scott was the featured vocalist but when he failed to turn up one night Brooker took over, bringing about a sudden and dramatic change in repertoire. With Brooker in the driving seat, the slower Cliff Richard and Elvis Presley covers were replaced by rock'n'roll numbers by Little Richard, Fats Domino, Chuck Berry, and Jerry Lee Lewis.

Fellow piano player John Denton, who was in the year below Brooker at Westcliff High School and was also part of the Southend-On-Sea group scene, recalls, "Back then groups usually only played at dances, rather than at the kind of gigs where you *just* went to see the band," he says. "The first time I saw The Paramounts was at a dance at Leigh Community Centre in Leigh-On-Sea."

Leigh Yacht Club was another early venue. "I remember setting my piano on fire one night at a dance at Leigh Yacht Club," says Brooker. "I left a cigarette on the end, and the celluloid on the keys caught fire and flared. The flames got up to 'A' below middle 'C' before I poured a pint over it!"

In the summer of 1961, now aged 16, Brooker left secondary school and enrolled at Southend-On-Sea's Municipal College to study botany and zoology. Trower had a daytime job cleaning windows, Brownlee became a bricklayer while Copping stayed on at school to take his 'A' levels. It was around this time that Trower's father, Len, bought the Penguin Cafe on Southend-On-Sea seafront. The acquisition followed a local scandal wherein the previous proprietor had been caught pocketing money from the café's Cancer Relief charity collection boxes!

"There were cellars below the Penguin Cafe, full of plastic penguins," recalls Brooker. "It occurred to The Paramounts that this would be a good place to build a club, so we set about burning the penguins, painting the cellar, and building a stage. We bought a piano for £4, and opened up a month later, in late 1961, with a Sunday night show featuring The Paramounts. We called the club The Shades, after Johnny Harris and The Shades, a Southall group, who had recently made several impressive appearances in Southend-On-Sea. Shades was also a new word for sunglasses!" (3)

John Denton: "The Shades was a specialist club, catering for local record collectors, R&B fans and straightforward music fans. They all co-existed without friction in the Coca-Cola, hamburger, and coffee bar atmosphere of the club."

"The Shades did become filled with mods eventually," says Mick

Brownlee. "There were rows and rows of scooters parked outside every night, and crowds of kids racing up and down the seafront on scooters too."

"The Paramounts themselves *weren't* mods," indicates Denton. "But the crowd they attracted included *some* mods…. The Shades… was one of several coffee bars in vogue in Southend-On-Sea."

Before long, The Paramounts extended their Sunday residency to include Wednesdays. "On the nights we didn't play we would go to The Shades to listen to the two well-stocked jukeboxes," says Brooker. "Most of the records in these two machines were the property of Tony Wilkinson, a local R&B collector, who helped us choose our early repertoire of songs." (3)

Record collecting was an ambitious undertaking in the late fifties and early sixties and Tony Wilkinson was a pioneer in the field. While labels such as London-American and Oriole released product domestically, certain American jazz, blues, soul and R&B records were like gold dust and could only be found in a handful of 'specialist' record shops known only to a privileged few. British enthusiasts such as Wilkinson would often pay merchant seamen resident in the Thames estuary to locate these much sought-after American 45s and LPs on voyages to the States.

"I was very lucky!" says Robin Trower. "Tony Wilkinson was importing all these records from Memphis [via Baton Rouge]. I was getting to hear all this stuff that just wasn't available in England."

"I got into record collecting and imported countless rare records from the USA," says Wilkinson. "Rob [Trower] and Gary used to come round to my house and hear these records. Eventually I put this collection in the jukeboxes at The Shades. It was great to hear people play Dale Hawkins' 'Suzie Q' and 'Dr Feelgood' by the original Dr Feelgood!"

"I liked people like B.B. King," says Trower. "I never sat down and worked out what he was actually doing, but I was heavily influenced by him. I also liked Steve Cropper from Booker T. and The MGs, Cliff Gallup with Gene Vincent and Scotty Moore with Elvis, then Chuck Berry and Bo Diddley. Those are the ones that stand out."

On one occasion The Shades regulars discovered that Ray Charles, on tour in Europe, was being broadcast live on French radio from the Paris Olympia. "We got hold of a good radio set, plugged it into the amps, spread the word, and about 150 of us settled down in The Shades to listen to 'The Man'," remembers Brooker. (3)

Len Trower charged one shilling (about 5p today but around 30p in 1961) on the door. "[It was a] dimly-lit cavernous room, formed of two dark areas fronted by a small dancing space and low stage," remembered Denton. "Behind the stage, a zany mural depicted The Paramounts as cartoon replicas. In the two back chambers, youths sipped cola, while girls danced effortlessly to the jukebox playing the sound of 'Thumbin' A Ride'. The dance area was to fill whilst The Paramounts plugged in and commenced to rock. Egg boxes bedecked the walls and ceiling, serving as primitive soundproofing. The cluster of backing vocalist-fans was very effective in this environment, despite the throbbing sound. And the people around the stage were executing what would later be termed 'the Pogo' (some 15 years later)." (2)

Tony Wilkinson: "The Paramounts were the best rock'n'roll band in a rock'n'roll town. There was simply nobody else to touch them!"

John Denton: "This was the most exciting music I'd ever heard. Gary Brooker was playing Jerry Lee Lewis and Little Richard in the true spirit of both men. And he sang their songs better than *any* other British rock'n'roll singer!"

Another Shades regular was John 'Kellogs' Kalinowski who fell in with The Paramounts and became their roadie, spending four years with Southend-On-Sea's finest and thus embarking on a behind-the-scenes career in rock that would sustain him for almost half a century. "Robin offered Kellogs the job as roadie for £4 a week," remembers Brooker. "People always had a roadie, even before the word was invented: someone with a van who would drive the group."

'Pinball wizard' Kellogs, on the other hand, insists that his wages were "four Mars bars a week and as much Coca Cola as you could drink!" His predecessor was 'Greasy' Johnny Bottle, whose credentials for the job were owning a Dormobile and knowing a little about electronics. "He built us a bass amp, made from a radio cabinet of course, which never worked," says Brooker. "In his Dormobile, the manifold heated up, and nobody could sit anywhere near the engine. His party piece was to drive along Southend-On-Sea seafront towards the gasworks; he could get out of his window, whilst the van was moving, go over the roof, in the other side, and back to his driving wheel. It was uphill while he was doing it. Kellogs joined us just before we went on that long British tour – the one that lasted four years!" (3)

The Paramounts started gigging further afield across the south east of England. Brooker recalls the first time he met future Rolling Stone Bill Wyman when The Paramounts were on the same bill as Wyman's pre-Stones group The Cliftons in July 1962. "Four other bands and ourselves played a gig at Greenwich Town Hall in London. It was an old trick by the promoter [to have] a band contest with a small prize. With six bands on, loads of people came to the dance and *he* didn't have to pay." (4)

Around Christmas 1962 Copping decided to leave the group to prepare for a three-year chemistry course at Leicester University and suggested fellow Westcliff High school boy Graham 'Diz' Derrick as his replacement.

By coincidence, Brooker knew 'Diz' from his days in The Electrics. "Diz had shown great musical ability at an early age. Also he was quite independent financially. He had the support of his dad – unlike the rest of us he had both a mum and dad – and if you said to him 'get a bass guitar', one would appear the following day. So Diz got a bass, and his dad put up the money for us to buy a Commer van. We had 'Paramounts R 'n' B' painted on the back." (3)

By the summer of 1963 the Paramounts were all aged 18 and Gary wanted the group to become professional, though this didn't sit well with everyone. Mick Brownlee, who was considering getting married, needed the security of his bricklaying job and quit the group as a result. John Denton recalls that The Paramounts hired various temporary drummers, among them Tony Diamond, who also did service with The Orioles who were successors to The Paramounts at The Shades. When he left Westcliff High School Denton was given the task of booking a band for the end-of-year dance. "I approached The Paramounts and Gary said that they would be pleased to do it, but they didn't have a drummer."

Like many a band of the era, The Paramounts used the classified columns of *Melody Maker* to find a suitable candidate. After the ad ran, Trower decided Barrie James 'BJ' Wilson was the best choice. Wilson, born March 18, 1947, in Edmonton (the same North London suburb where Brooker had briefly lived as a child) was duly enlisted into The Paramounts. Being London based at the time, BJ dossed down at The Shades during his first few weeks with the band. Stan Pearson, a Southend-On-Sea friend of Wilson's, says that BJ's parents did not approve of their son joining a group, feeling that he should "get a proper job", but their position on the issue would change as The Paramounts' career progressed.

With the changes in personnel came a shift in repertoire, seeing the group move towards Ray Charles – 'Sticks And Stones' was a favourite – and, slightly later, to the R&B sound of Bobby 'Blue' Bland. Although in Southend-On-Sea this music was confined to the underground world of The Shades, The Paramounts were not alone in appreciating American R&B. Throughout the UK, in London, Birmingham, Newcastle and – most notably – Liverpool, other groups of their ilk were playing songs they'd discovered on imported American records. It was to burst into the national consciousness in mid-1963 as the first wave of Beatlemania hit Britain like a tornado. Suddenly everybody was singing 'Twist And Shout' or proclaiming "Money, that's what I want."

A turning point in The Paramounts' career occurred on September 5, 1963 when they supported The Rolling Stones at the Strand Palais Theatre in Walmer, just outside Deal in Kent. "[It] was the first time we'd seen the Stones, and they saw us," says Brooker. "In fact we all ended up hiding in the same room because there was a terrible, terrible fight down there between Marines and East End heavies. It was a staged fight. The Marines had to be taught a lesson. Our manager, who ran the dance hall, brought down these heavies from the Krays' snooker hall in London's East End. It was a pretty fearsome battle. 'Our side', if you like, were wandering around looking for somebody to kill with baseball bats and chains in their hands. I remember looking out of the window with Mick Jagger, and we saw one of these Marines run into his car and lock the door. One of 'our boys' just went up, punched the window, which smashed immediately, grabbed him by the ears and pulled him out and kicked the hell out of him. A vicious brutal fight. The Rolling Stones and The Paramounts were both in the same boat there. We became quite close within the space of an hour because we were all scared together."

At this stage in their career the Stones weren't well known beyond London and a few small towns in the south west such as Reading, Guildford, Maidenhead, Windsor and Richmond, where they would sell out any dance floor that they played. "Our manager ran this gig down near Deal in Kent," says Brooker. "I *think* it was that week that the Stones' debut single, 'Come On', was released."

The Rolling Stones' cover of Chuck Berry's 'Come On' (actually released in June) was heading towards the Top 30 and their TV appearances and newspaper articles were generating interest as well as outrage.

According to Robin Trower, the Stones were particularly impressed with both The Paramounts' stage performance and their unique repertoire, which differed from other bands on the R&B circuit at that time. Nevertheless, they were certainly among the ranks of a whole new batch of R&B groups based in the south that included Georgie Fame & The Blue Flames, John Mayall's Bluesbreakers, Manfred Mann (or the Mann-Hugg Blues Brothers as they were initially known) and Chris Farlowe & The Thunderbirds.

Gary Brooker: "Wherever we played we made our reputation. Anyway, we started to spread out in 1963 after having played that gig with The Rolling Stones. Up until that point we didn't know that there were *other* groups playing R&B. The Stones, who really liked us, were still on Chuck Berry, but *we'd* moved on to Bobby Bland and James Brown... The Stones were really knocked out with us because we were doing *real* R&B. And by that I... mean *real* R & B... We were mainly doing the more obscure stuff, songs like 'Further On Up The Road', 'Chills And Fever' and 'Daddy Rolling Stone', and stuff by Hogsnort Rupert. And the Stones said, 'Arr great, never heard anybody do that!' The Stones later came down to Southend-On-Sea to The Shades to see us and I can remember Brian Jones being impressed with the [imported] R&B records on the jukebox."

Within a matter of weeks – thanks to the success of 'Come On' and deft PR moves by their manager, Andrew Loog Oldham – The Rolling Stones would move from clubs and dance halls into theatre tours.

Gary Brooker: "The Stones told Philip Hayward and John Mansfield, who ran the Ricky-Tick clubs, that they should get The Paramounts in. And they said, 'Well let's see them!' And they saw us! So we got *that* circuit, which was down to the Stones."

The Stones even went as far as to cite The Paramounts as 'their favourite R&B group'. In *Melody Maker* (dated March 14, 1964) Keith Richards informed Ray Coleman, "There are two groups in this country that deserve a mention, Wayne Fontana & The Mindbenders are good. And so are The Paramounts – one of the best groups to come up for a long time. Put that in the *Melody Maker*."*

It was only a matter of time before The Paramounts would encounter the influential disc jockey and scene maker Guy Stevens. "Guy Stevens... was 'The Man'," says Brooker. "All he *ever* did was listen to records! We'd go round his place once a week, and by the end of the evening we'd come out with 10 new songs. He showed us a lot of obscure material like 'Chills And Fever' and 'Mohair Sam'. Stevens was the DJ at the Crawdaddy when it was at Richmond [Athletic] Club. I can remember when I first saw him. I saw the Stones at the Crawdaddy and we played there a couple of weeks later. It was one of the most outrageous clubs for rave-ups, because people swung from the rafters there. They got totally carried away with the music."

Born in East Dulwich, London April 13 1943, Guy Stevens played a key role in introducing both musicians and fans to the best R&B music from the US. "He played total out and out rhythm'n'blues from his great record collection," continues Brooker. "He also advised Sue Records

---

* When the Rolling Stones flew into New York's JFK airport for their first American tour on June 1, 1964, they cited The Paramounts and The Hollies as their "favourite British bands" at a CBS and NBC televised press conference.

on what they should release for a long, long time. That's why a lot of records came out here [in Britain] that would never have otherwise come out. Sue Records was in turn to influence a lot of bands at the time ... Guy would say to us, 'Listen to this, yeah? Very rare import'. So we always used to pinch a few of Guy's records and then put some of the songs in The Paramounts' repertoire!"

Another source of employment for The Paramounts was American Air Force bases where the servicemen welcomed what for them was a 'home-grown' repertoire. "Our set was all American rhythm'n'blues," says Brooker. "If somebody 'white' sang a song it was an immediate 'no-no' for us with the possible exception of Bobby Darin, who had quite a lot of soul, and a couple of Dion numbers."

The Paramounts were now gigging four to five nights a week, earning around £30 a show. Kellogs recalls that was the break-even point. "Any less than that and we were in deep financial trouble. So as long as we had enough money to get fuel in the old Commer van to go to, say, Manchester before motorways, we were happy. Then we'd come back to Southend-On-Sea the same night, as staying out in hotels or at Mrs Bloggs' Bed & Breakfast was an extravagance that we could never afford."

For all groups at this level, the natural step was attaining a record contract. Brooker recalls an initial attempt when a London session was apparently financed by a lady from Leigh-On-Sea who had an eye for young men, but nothing came from it. Peter Martin arranged attempt number two, a recording of 'Poison Ivy', the Jerry Leiber and Mike Stoller song originally recorded by The Coasters, along with Bobby Blue Bland's 'Further On Up The Road'. The session was taped at IBC Studios in London on October 18, 1963, with staff engineer Glyn Johns. "Peter [Martin] took it to Ron Richards at Parlophone," says Brooker. "We were against recording a Coasters song, although we didn't mind playing them live. Peter told us to record 'Poison Ivy'. I said, 'That's sacred stuff.' In fact if we'd had the choice, we wouldn't have made a record at all!"

Evidently Richards liked what he heard, for he arranged a further session for The Paramounts on November 1 at EMI Studios, on

Abbey Road, North West London, where they re-recorded 'Poison Ivy' along with a new B-side, a cover of The Drifters' 'I Feel Good All Over', which originally appeared on their 1964 *Under The Boardwalk* album. It was the location where all The Paramounts' recordings would be made.

"We couldn't believe Abbey Road," says Brooker. "When we arrived there for the first session, a man in one of those long brown warehouse coats met us at the side door and helped us in with our gear. A very nice man. It seemed very establishment. Our sessions were always at 11 in the morning. We never recorded at night. You knew you were in a great place where great things happened. It was all *big*. The microphones were huge, the control knobs were huge, and the mixing desk looked like the cockpit of a Lancaster bomber (from World War II).

"We used to get three hours to record two tracks, which involved getting (the right) sound, which was never very easy. Our amps were not in the forefront of technology. We would put down the instrumental track and overdub the vocals. We had no control, but we were allowed to go into the control room to listen to the playback and Ron Richards would say, 'That's a good take boys'. We didn't question it, he was the producer. We never attended the mixes; we'd simply get an acetate a few days later." (5)

'Poison Ivy' was released on EMI's Parlophone label on December 6, 1963. Two weeks later a news feature on The Paramounts in *Pop Weekly* (dated December 21) had Richards talking up the group. "The boys have got a very definite edge to their work. It came through on that demonstration disc they sent me. It's kind of rough and raw, and they can be very exciting indeed!"

The *Southend Star* of December 3, 1963 announced the release of 'Poison Ivy' and promised that The Paramounts would "be appearing on ITV's *Ready, Steady Go!* on December 13 followed by a Manchester TV date later" (in January). On December 16, 'Poison Ivy' was picked as Record Of The Week for ITV's *Thank Your Lucky Stars* Merseyside special which transmitted across the UK on December 21. Liverpool Cavern DJ Bob Wooler awarded the song a maximum of five points and described it as "one of those yeah yeah yeah discs!"

Three weeks later, on January 3, 1964, The Paramounts appeared on ITV's *Five O' Clock Club*. As a result 'Poison Ivy' began to edge its way into the singles charts. On January 17 The Paramounts appeared live on ITV's trendy *Ready Steady Go!* where Gary was interviewed by Keith Fordyce, the show's host. It was "a rather nervous" affair, according to John Denton. The appearance led to 'Poison Ivy' peaking at a UK chart position of 35.

By January 29, The Paramounts had recorded their follow-up single, a cover of Thurston Harris' 'Little Bitty Pretty One' backed with their rendition of Ernie K. Doe's 'A Certain Girl'. This time no TV appearances were forthcoming and the single failed to chart.

Throughout February and March The Paramounts supported The Rolling Stones, John Leyton (of 'Johnny Remember Me' fame) and singer Mike Berry on a long cinema package tour. They were also invited to back up fellow EMI artist Duffy Power on his 1964 single 'Parchman Farm' and its B-side, 'Tired Broke & Busted'. "Those performances were probably closer to capturing [The Paramounts'] live R&B sound than any of their official EMI Parlophone singles," asserts John Denton.

For the third single, released on June 11, the group moved towards a more soulful sound with a cover of Curtis Mayfield's 'I'm The One Who Loves You'. "We weren't aware there was money in songwriting until we came to record our third single," says Brooker. "Ron Richards asked us if we had any new material for the B-side. We didn't and Ron suggested we write one of our own. He said, 'You'll get a little bit more money then'. We told him we'd never written any songs, but he insisted we have a go. Five minutes later we had written 'It Won't Be Long'." (5)

'I'm The One Who Loves You' led to two television appearances in one weekend on ITV: *Ready Steady Go!* on July 24 and *Thank Your Lucky Stars* on July 25, but once again the single failed to chart.

Amidst much touring across England, The Paramounts were booked to support The Rolling Stones at Bournemouth's Winter Gardens on August 23, but they never made it as their Commer van broke down on the way there, according to Kellogs.

October 16 saw the release of The Paramounts' fourth Parlophone single, 'Bad Blood', another Leiber-Stoller song, which had been recorded back on January 15. It was backed with 'Do I', a cover of a Maurice Williams & The Zodiacs song that was taped at Abbey Road on May 14. In an extraordinary move by the ever-vigilant BBC, the single was banned from airplay on the Light Programme because 'Bad Blood' was deemed to be a euphemism for venereal disease.

These disappointments caused some dissension in the ranks and the first to seek employment elsewhere was BJ Wilson, who accepted an offer to join Jimmy Powell & The Dimensions. However, according to Kenny White of The Dimensions, Wilson soon grew tired of his role and quit after only a few weeks to chance his arm as "a professional gambler on the card tables of the French Riviera". The episode is clouded in mystery. "BJ's 'tall tale' about gambling is a myth that he liked to propagate to the amusement of everyone who knew him," says BJ's friend Barry Sinclair.

Meanwhile, auditions for a new drummer took place at the 2I's Coffee Bar in Old Compton Street in London's Soho, the legendary launch pad for the first wave of British rock'n'rollers in the late fifties. Among the hopefuls was drummer/child actor Johnny 'Mitch' Mitchell, who would go on to join The Riot Squad then Georgie Fame's Blue Flames before finding fame with The Jimi Hendrix Experience. Mickey Underwood was the favourite to replace Wilson, but was possibly a little too jazz orientated for The Paramounts. Phil Wainman, who turned up to the tiny 2I's with his own drum kit, was asked by Trower to attend a further audition at his dad's coffee bar in Southend-On-Sea.

Wainman, from West London, was duly chosen and on November 12, 1964, made his live debut with The Paramounts on BBC TV's *The Beat Room* (transmitted four days later). Despite the radio ban, The Paramounts performed 'Bad Blood' along with Bobby Bland's 'Turn On Your Love Light'. No more TV appearances were forthcoming and the single failed to chart.

A fifth Paramounts single was recorded across two Abbey Road sessions on January 29 and February 11, 1965. 'Blue Ribbons' was a cover of a 1963 Jackie DeShannon demo, co-written by the late Eddie

16

Cochran's girlfriend Sharon Sheeley. It was also covered in early 1965 by soul singer Dobie Gray on his album *In Crowders That Go 'Go Go'*. The Paramounts' version of this pop-soul crossover was released on April 23, replete with a full string section, backed with a cover of Johnny 'Guitar' Watson's bluesy ballad 'Cuttin' In'.

From February 21 until March 11, The Paramounts undertook a UK package tour starring Adam Faith, Sandie Shaw and The Barron Knights. As well as performing a brief set, the Paramounts backed the female star of the show. The fact that the former Miss Sandra Goodrich hailed from Dagenham, Essex helped singer and band gel together. "Sandie used to sit beside me on a stool to sing 'Lemon Tree'," recalls Brooker. "We did it as a duet." According to Shaw's autobiography *The World At My Feet*, Gary would ask, "Come here often?" as she sat down beside him on the piano stool. (6) The group also backed former *Ready, Steady, Go!* dancer turned singer Patrick Kerr, who was being managed by Faith and Shaw's manager, Eve Taylor.

Gary Brooker: "Patrick Kerr and his wife [Theresa] were friends of ours. Patrick would demonstrate a new dance each week on ITV's *Ready Steady Go!*. I used to hang around with him, and we used to go to all the TV shows. At one point I'd go every week. I can remember seeing Chuck Jackson. He absolutely blew me away. I recognise some of the things I've seen on the re-runs, and I thought, 'I was there. I remember that.' They were really great shows."

John Denton's diaries recall 'The Paramounts' finest TV moment' when they were invited to appear on *Ready Steady Go Goes Live!* on April 23, 1965 performing 'Blue Ribbons' [transmitted on the actual day of 'Blue Ribbon's release] along with a cover of James Brown's 'Dancin' Little Thing'. "Patrick Kerr's dancers provided some dynamic moves to accompany the boys; with fantastic vocals from Gary, tight drumming from Phil Wainman, and fine guitar work from Robin Trower, the boys really could do no wrong!"

Phil Wainman's overriding memory of his tour of duty is of financially tough times when each member had to contribute £2 a week towards petrol for the band's Commer van. He also recalls a roadie saving cash by "hot-wiring amps into the mains using matchsticks" instead of buying plugs – a move that almost resulted in the band being blown up during rehearsals.

As a band, The Paramounts were, in Wainman's opinion, "on fire! A favourite album was James Brown's *Live At The Apollo*, which we would try and reproduce on stage. This involved rehearsing and then performing a 45-minute non-stop set without any introductions. Gary was a tough taskmaster and any deviation from the original plan where I might inject a drum fill would lead to my getting a small fine, which always went towards more petrol for the van! I remember changing a part of Richard Berry's 'Louie Louie', but Gary never noticed, so I avoided that particular fine."

Wainman released a solo single, 'Hear Me A Drummer Man', and later became a successful producer, making records for The Sweet, The Bay City Rollers, Alex Harvey, and The Boomtown Rats.

By the autumn of 1965 BJ Wilson had returned from his mysterious gambling stint in the French Riviera and rejoined The Paramounts. For the Paramounts it was business as usual with a non-stop whirl of gigs including some backing Sandie Shaw. In her autobiography she writes: "While I was driven in a sleek limousine, they [The Paramounts] crammed into a jolly transit van. I would have done anything to exchange the loneliness and isolation of my world for the warmth and camaraderie of theirs. So I did. After a cold, dreary one-nighter up in Scotland I clambered into their over-crowded tranny for the drive home.

"As we crossed the Highlands, the rusty old van began to belch smoke. Somewhere past Cumbria there was a loud bang and a hiss. The van shuddered to a halt. We all tumbled out into the freezing night to look under the bonnet. The general opinion was that we had run out of water. We looked around in the dark. There were no lights for miles. 'Give it some Coca-Cola!' suggested Gary, and poured a bottle into the engine. We all piled back inside and every so often someone would pop out and top it up with another drink. Just past Manchester we ran out of Coke. All the shops were shut. The roadie Kellogs took command. 'We'll have to pee in the empty bottles.' He disappeared behind the bush and took the first turn. Just before Watford everybody had had a go, but me! I began to panic. There was a limit to being one of the boys, and this was it..." (6)

"Sandie was great," BJ Wilson recalled. "She used to sing lovely, even though it wasn't our kind of music. She'd do things like 'Lemon Tree', 'Long Live Love' and a few groovy numbers like 'The Clapping Song'. We even did 'The Girl From Ipanema', which nobody ever knew the chords to, but we managed to get through it every time." (7)

Gary Brooker: "We were with her for all that period. But with all due respect to Sandie it wasn't really our bag. I mean 'Lemon Tree' is a long way from 'Daddy Rolling Stone'."

Backing Sandie at the Paris Olympia, The Paramounts were augmented by an orchestra. "I liked the sound of the old strings in the background," says Brooker. "Everybody was a four-piece back in those days, and it was nice to have this bit of extra stuff going on."

The Paramounts continued to have their champions. Nicci Rouse, from Chelsea, wrote to the *New Musical Express'* letters page (dated October 29, 1965) stating: "Recently I visited Paris and took the opportunity of seeing the Richard Anthony Show. Although I was disappointed with his performance, which seemed endless, the show was saved by Sandie Shaw. I would also like to mention Sandie's backing group The Paramounts. They were fantastic! These four boys have more talent than any other group I have ever seen or heard. Their talents were being wasted using them as a backing group. Their sound is marvellous, and the drummer is something of a genius. I hope we'll hear a lot more of them."

By September 5, the group had cut their sixth and final single, a cover of P. F. Sloan's demo of his own song 'You Never Had It So Good'. On the B-side was another Paramounts original, 'Don't Ya Like My Love', penned by Trower/Brooker. Released on October 15, the single was admired by The Beatles' NEMS management team, who were now handling The Paramounts' affairs. This led to them being given a place on the bill for the last couple of shows – at the Finsbury Park Astoria and the Capitol Theatre, Cardiff – on The Beatles' December 1965 UK tour.

"The Moody Blues closed the first half of the show," remembers Kellogs. "The Paramounts backed a singer called Beryl Marsden from Liverpool, as well as Steve Aldo from Liverpool. The Paramounts were also given a slot where they could play just two songs. They opened the show each night. Being the 'opening act' you had the dressing room right at the top of the building. And it was quite a long slog climbing the flights of stairs to the top of the Finsbury Park Astoria. But it was thrilling to be on tour with The Beatles. Nobody heard anything when The Beatles hit the stage, only screaming... Before the show I remember that George Harrison – the sweetest man – came all the way up the stairs to the attic to see us. He brought us a gift: a little plastic portable Dansette record player with a blues record by Albert King and a large jazz cigarette for us all to share. I was only 19. Thrilling days!"

The following night, December 12, in Cardiff's Capitol Cinema, as if descending in slow motion into a vast cavern filled with a thousand screaming seagulls, The Paramounts hit the stage, opening for The Beatles on what was to be the final night of their *last* British concert tour, although no one knew it at the time. It marked the end of Beatlemania, the beginning of a new chapter in The Paramounts' career, and the dawn of a new phase in British pop.

The start of 1966 found The Paramounts touring UK clubs billed as 'The Paramounts – Sandie Shaw's backing group' when, in fact, they were no longer her backing band at all. By this juncture they were out of contract with EMI, which had failed to promote their sixth single with the result that their records received hardly any airplay.

On May 23, Robin Trower told the *Bridgwater Mercury's* Michael Guy, "We cannot perform on BBC Radio because we've failed our audition three times. Our earnings have dropped by a quarter and we've had to economise... We're worried that we haven't had a record out since last October, but we've had a lot of troubles lately. We weren't proud of that last disc 'You Never Had It So Good' because it just was not us. But we couldn't do anything about stopping its release as NEMS had the control over what was to be issued. We've since left NEMS. Now we hope to get another single out soon which is more in our style.

There is a vicious circle. You cannot get television bookings unless you have a hit record."

There followed a brief association with the Kinks' former manager/music publisher Larry Page's organisation. According to Robin Trower, "They were trying to turn us into a pop group and it just wasn't for me!" A final Paramounts recording session took place on June 30 at Abbey Road where the group and assorted friends recorded a cover of 'Freedom' by their jazz hero Charles Mingus. It was a last desperate throw of the dice. The Paramounts' days were numbered. A friend of the group, Diane Rolph, remembers Trower becoming "very disillusioned" by this stage.

Robin Trower: "We were still playing clubs nationally and started to play the Flamingo in (London's) Soho. But without the original material being strong enough we really had to stay at that level. I was getting more into the blues – Otis Rush and Albert King – and I really wanted to start writing my own stuff, so I split from the group and formed a trio called The Jam."

The Paramounts' next undertaking was a trip to Germany to back Chris Andrews of 'Yesterday Man' fame, which came about through their association with Sandie Shaw. "It paid us about £30 a gig, so we did that," remembered Wilson. "Robin Trower had quit so we got another guitarist called Martin Shaw and a saxophonist, Jimmy Jewell, and did that tour – just to earn us a bit of money." (7)

Jewell and Shaw, both of whom had been in Jimmy Powell & The Five Dimensions, were forced to double up as roadies. "In the end I refused to roadie," said Jewell, "Especially given the kind of the money they were paying us. Diz their bass player, a nice fella, said he was going to quit after that tour, which is what he did... He later became a professional flautist with orchestras."

Arriving home from Germany The Paramounts went their separate ways. Gary Brooker: "Up until those tours with Sandie Shaw and Chris Andrews we'd breezed along believing in what we were doing. Then we suddenly realised we *weren't* doing what we believed in. We came upon a situation where our repertoire was, in fact, available in every disco in town. It hadn't always been that way. Otis Redding had come from being a sort of 'underground artist' to becoming a public property. Suddenly it wasn't *on* any more. We'd actually lost the exclusivity of the repertoire that we had previously enjoyed in our formative years."

John Denton remains the group's biggest fan and to this day will swear they were as good as any British R&B outfit. "The Paramounts' records should not be compared with the original American R&B and soul tracks of the day. However, they delivered their interpretations of these songs with consummate sincerity and taste, and were excellent pioneers of R&B. These recordings serve as a fine reminder of that period in 1963-65, before rock music started to take itself too seriously.

"I can close my eyes and still picture them all now: Gary, mike stand between his legs, playing that old upright with its Selmer TruVoice pick-ups; the static Rob Trower bent lovingly over his Gretsch, playing perfect solos; the lean Diz gazing impassively, while giving out walking, talking bass; and the youthful BJ Wilson keenly mastering his grey Ludwig set… It's unforgettable." (2)

Chapter 2

From The Paramounts To Procol Harum

1966–1967

"Gary Brooker and Keith Reid are the only people we could ever compare ourselves to! 'A Whiter Shade Of Pale' and 'Homburg' are both like a Dali painting ... Or work by Jean Cocteau... !"

Elton John & Bernie Taupin

If the opening chapter of the Procol Harum story reads as a fairly conventional tale of a talented provincial British R&B band who failed to achieve much because they didn't get the right breaks, then what happened next certainly defies the logical route to pop stardom. From the ashes of one group a new one took flight, but Procol Harum were a million miles from The Paramounts. Soon to include three of The Paramounts' key personnel they played along to an entirely different tune and struck gold with their first single, one of the biggest hits of all time.

Towards the end of the summer of 1966 Gary Brooker disbanded The Paramounts with the avowed intention of becoming a songwriter, a move inspired by his meeting lyricist Keith Reid at the home of mutual friend Guy Stevens in Gloucester Avenue, Camden Town, North London.

The son of Leslie Irving Reid and Milly Hecht, Keith's father was a qualified Doctor of Law living in Vienna before moving to the south east of England where he found work as a tailor. Keith Reid was born on October 19, 1946 at Brocket Hall Maternity Hospital in Welwyn Garden City, Hatfield, Hertfordshire. The family moved to London's East End in the fifties and Keith grew up in a house near to the many World War II bomb sites that still scarred the Mile End Road.

Although not at all religious Keith Reid is proud of his Jewish East London roots, which inspired his interest in writing. "My background for writing songs came from all the reading I did. I lived all my childhood years in the Mile End Road," he says. "I didn't pass my 11–plus exams, which was a great blow to my family. Basically I just didn't like being at school. My mother taught me to read at home from when I was about four. I read constantly and voraciously until I left school when I was 15. I'd just go to Mile End library, because my parents let me use their ticket. I used to go to the children's library first and then upstairs into the grown-ups' library. I'd get seven or eight books out and take them home, read 'em and go back. I really read a lot. I used to read in school all the time. I just used to grab anything off the shelf that looked interesting. I escaped into a world of books." (8)

Keith hated school so much that he didn't even wait until the end of his final term to leave. "My birthday's in October. I remember that I was 15 on a Thursday and I'm not sure I went back to school on the Friday. I just didn't complete the term. I hated being taught. I totally rebelled. I think it was partly because I was expected to succeed and I rebelled against that. My parents, my older brother and my younger sister were all very academically inclined. I just rebelled against the whole thing, rejected it all. It could have left me very badly off. But I always felt that my life was going to begin when I left school and got a job. I always knew that I'd do something in the arts, but I didn't know what. I was interested in music and theatre, but I think basically my love of music and rock'n'roll led to my writing songs."

As well as books Keith would borrow records from the library, including early American blues recordings. "One of the earliest records I remember was an album called *Work Songs From Angola*. For many years I thought it was Angola in Africa. It wasn't until I went to America in about '67 or '68 that I found out that Angola was a famous prison farm in the south! It made a big impression on me this record. Of course I was also very influenced by Bob Dylan. In fact it was Bob Dylan who helped me to find my own voice as a writer."

Among his neighbours was another Jewish boy called Mark Feld, who in the fullness of time would change his name to Marc Bolan. He and Keith become good friends. "We were both 'Original Modernists'," recalls Reid with some amusement. "The term was used shortly before the word 'mod' came into being. I remember Marc and I used to get all dressed up to go out and impress, but ended up round at one another's houses listening to Bob Dylan records. We usually spent Sundays reading *The Sunday Times* inside the Wimpy Bar next to the Whitechapel Art Gallery near to Petticoat Lane market."

Sandra Simons, Keith's girlfriend in the spring of 1966, recalls her first date with Keith: "We went to see 'Little' Stevie Wonder at Klooks Kleek, which was a tiny little club near the railway station in West Hampstead. Only 60 people were there. Keith had big fuzzy hair like Bob Dylan and wore tiny wirey round granny glasses. He kept talking about Dylan. After that he used to send me lyrics he had written. I remember him as a softly spoken, witty, kind man."

Reid: "Once I'd written a few songs I thought, you know, 'Hey, I'm great', and I started going round knocking on doors. I didn't know anybody in the music business at all, not a single person. I was very persistent in those days and I used to go around to all the companies. I'd get hold of people's telephone numbers and call them up and tell them, 'Hey, I'm a great songwriter and I'd like to show you my work.'"

Among Keith's ports of call was the office of Chris Blackwell, soon to become the man behind Island Records. "He listened to me and my work and basically said, 'I've got another chap in an office who'd be interested in you, a bloke called Guy Stevens', he is a sort of A&R man. Chris introduced me to Guy, who took an interest in me and spent about a year introducing me to different people so that I could find somebody to work with... they tried to team me up with Steve Winwood, who had had a pile of my lyrics. I met Steve around the time he was forming Traffic. I remember that Jim Capaldi was there and that Jim obviously thought I was a threat. There was an unspoken antagonism in the air at the time."

Reid became a regular at the Scene Club in Soho's Ham Yard where Guy Stevens was the in-house DJ. Stevens asked Reid to write the sleeve notes for one of his compilations released by Sue Records, the label Stevens oversaw for Chris Blackwell. "There were various people that Guy Stevens tried to team me up with, says Reid. "I remember he also introduced me to Pete Townshend. Pete mentioned me to the guys in Cream [in 1966] when they were looking for somebody, but of course they used Pete Brown."

Pete Brown recently confirmed this. "Yes Jack Bruce met Keith. I do remember that. But they ended up with me. The Cream got a 'White Room' instead of 'A Whiter Shade Of Pale'!"

No one seems to be able to recall the precise date that Stevens introduced Brooker to Reid, but Kellogs recalls the moment exactly. "It was a meeting of minds. You just knew that this would lead to something."

"Guy said, 'Oh this is Keith Reid, he writes words,'" recalls Brooker. "'Gary, you write music'. I said, 'I don't!' He said, 'Well you *could!*' Anyway, Keith gave me this big envelope full of words, which I took away."

Keith Reid: "Guy Stevens was the hippest guy in London at this time. One of his ideas was that maybe I could get together with The Paramounts and write songs with Gary. But The Paramounts split up soon afterwards. [At that point] Gary had given up being in bands to become a songwriter. I had some lyrics, and I gave them to Gary.

The following day Brooker opened the envelope and set to work. "By some coincidence, the next day I had a letter from Keith," he says. "It ended with his quoting a line from the *very* same song that I had written the music for that day ... 'Something Following Me'!"

The next song the pair wrote together was 'Conquistador', which they thought might be appropriate for The Beach Boys. They followed this with 'I Realise', under the alternate title of 'Understandably Blue', which they wrote with Dusty Springfield in mind, but as far as they are aware Dusty never recorded it.

It did lead to an offer for Brooker to join Dusty Springfield's backing band The Echoes. "Either I became an Echo, or Keith Reid and I would become songwriters," says Brooker. "Keith and Guy Stevens had an unspoken plot. They'd decided I was going to sing these songs. But I'd retired! Anyway, in the end I called up some of the old boys that I had had associations with. Some were very kind. Andrew Loog Oldham [The Rolling Stones' manager] supplied his studio for us, having just set up Immediate Records. But he didn't say 'Marianne Faithfull or The Small Faces are looking for something', or anything like that."

One night Keith and Gary were invited to a party at Guy Stevens' house. At the end of the evening as everyone was leaving, Guy turned to his wife Diane and said, "You've turned a whiter shade of pale, I think you better go to bed! Keith must have remembered the line," said Diane Stevens. "This would be around June of 1966."

Keith Reid: "I had the phrase 'a whiter shade of pale', that was the start. And I knew it was a song. It's like a jigsaw where you've got one piece then you make up all the others to fit in. I was trying to conjure a mood as much as tell a straightforward, girl-leaves-boy story. With the ceiling flying away and room humming harder, I wanted to paint an image of a scene. I wasn't trying to be mysterious with those images. I wasn't trying to be evocative. I suppose it seems like a decadent scene I'm describing. But I was too young to have experienced any decadence, then. I might have been smoking when I conceived it, but not when I wrote it. It was influenced by books not drugs... Gary and I eventually decided to form a band, write some more songs and demo them. One of them was 'A Whiter Shade Of Pale'."

Sandra Simons can still vividly recollect the first time she heard 'A Whiter Shade of Pale'. "It was in May or June of 1966 about a year before it became a hit. Keith phoned me up excitedly and played me the original vocal demo of the song down the telephone. He said, 'What do you think?' I replied, 'Great!' And Keith said, 'What a weak watery thing to say'. I always remember that."

Kenny White of Jimmy Powell & The Five Dimensions remembers Gary phoning him up and asking him to come to the Marquee studios in Soho in late November of 1966 in order to demo some songs that he had written with Keith Reid. "Guy Stevens booked the studio. Tony Ollard played bass and BJ Wilson played drums. Both were in George Bean & The Runners at the time. Gary played piano and I played guitar. There was no organ player present. Of the three or four songs that we played I can only remember two: 'Conquistador' and 'A Whiter Shade Of Pale'. Half jokingly Gary said, 'We're thinking of starting a group, would you all like to join?' I remember BJ laughing and saying, 'No chance!' And then everyone just scuttled off and went their separate ways."

The psychedelic-sounding name that Brooker and Reid chose for their new group owed nothing to the mind-expanding drugs that appeared on the music scene in the mid-sixties nor 'the summer of love' that was raging in San Francisco. In fact the pair simply named the group after a cat that belonged to a friend of Guy Stevens. Diane Stevens said her husband had a friend nicknamed Bob, short for 'Bob Hope' [cockney rhyming slang for cannabis or 'dope'], whose wife bred cats. "She had a beautiful Burmese Blue whose name was Procol Harum. Guy suggested that Gary and Keith might consider that as the name for the band. So it became their name."

The name was, in fact, a misspelling of 'Procul Harun' and is often erroneously reported as being Latin for 'beyond these things'. 'Beyond here' or 'far from here' might be more accurate, but even these are not direct translations of procul harun. Harun is an Arabic word of Hebrew descent that means 'light bringer'. Procul means 'beyond' or 'far' in Latin. So Procul Harun possibly could translate as 'light bringer from afar', not inappropriate for a group formed in an era when the search for enlightenment was high on the agenda.

Gary Brooker: "It didn't mean anything! It could have meant Long Red Tail as far as we were concerned. It just seemed to fit because at that stage we didn't quite know what we were either. Back then in

1967 you already had all kinds of band names: The Electric Prunes, The Chocolate Watch Band, The Strawberry Alarm Clock, Pacific Gas And Electric..."

More importantly, Brooker, Reid and Stevens were now immersed in an on-going discussion about the format of the band. "You don't get away from bass and drums," says Brooker. "We wanted a strong electric blues guitar player. The combination of piano and Hammond organ would come from gospel music. A bit of inspiration came from Booker T & The MGs with Otis Redding, as well as from Bob Dylan and what he was doing with his then backing band The Hawks [later to become The Band]. Bob Dylan's 'Just Like Tom Thumb's Blues', recorded live in Liverpool in 1966 as a B-side, was certainly an inspiration. More importantly with the combination of three lead instruments you could have three different solos. It multiplied the possibilities that groups hadn't had up until that point."

In 1966 outfits like Zoot Money's Big Roll Band and Georgie Fame & The Blue Flames featured a Hammond organ played alongside brass instruments, but this brought about a jazz feel, and jazz was never a template for Procol Harum. Dylan's 'Ballad Of A Thin Man', however, certainly served as an inspiration for Procol's 1967 song 'A Christmas Camel', and Dylan's presence would significantly influence Procol's debut single, both lyrically and musically.

Following on from this Guy Stevens assembled several musicians to rehearse in his basement. These included Richard Brown (formerly with The Vogues), organist Alan Morris (George Bean & The Runners), drummer BJ Wilson (now also with George Bean & The Runners), bassist Dave Knights (The Establishment) who had recently auditioned for the Jimi Hendrix Experience, and Gary Brooker on piano. According to Richard Brown the basement was so small and damp that they had to move to a church hall nearby to continue rehearsals. Morris and Knights slept on camp beds in Stevens' basement while the rest of the musicians returned home each night after rehearsals.

Richard Brown: "There were long periods when Dave and I were doing nothing, just sitting around in this damp, horrible basement. We were really just like a backing band for Gary. But then there was the music and the lyrics, this unique astonishing stuff, sung by this fantastic voice, you know. I was amazed that I was actually in a band together with the lead singer of The Paramounts. That was the only reason I was hanging on, because on all other fronts, absolutely nothing was happening." (9)

Wilson split after a couple of weeks to return to George Bean & The Runners, who would appear in the cult 1967 UK movie *Privilege*, albeit without Wilson who was replaced in the embryonic Procol by a drummer known simply as 'Tubs'. In late January Stevens re-hired the Marquee Studios in London's Soho to re-record new demos of 'Conquistador', 'A Whiter Shade Of Pale' alongside 'Something Following Me', and 'Salad Days (Are Here Again)'. Crucially, several acetates were made of these demos – all of which have been lost over time.

Stevens took these demos to Chris Blackwell in the hope that the band could record for Island Records. According to Diane Stevens: "Blackwell didn't think the demo of 'A Whiter Shade Of Pale' was *any* good at all. He turned it down! Guy was so poor at this point that he asked Chris for a staff job at Island Records – even though Chris had just turned down the very record that Guy was touting as a future hit!"*

With Stevens unable to get the backing of a record label, Morris returned to play with George Bean & The Runners, Brown went home to Birmingham, and 'Tubs' and Knights lingered on in anticipation. Meanwhile, Brooker, Reid, and Stevens placed an ad in *Melody Maker*, dated January 28, reading: "Lead guitar, organist, and bass, wanted for Young Rascals/Dylan type sound to develop new material". On the back of this two musicians were hired, bass guitarist David Knights (born June 28, 1945, Tufnell Park, Islington, London) whom Reid had invited to officially audition, and a new guitarist by the name of Ray Royer (born October 8, 1945, the Pinewoods, Essex) who was formerly in the mod group High Time.

---

* The original 'A Whiter Shade Of Pale' acetate allegedly survives as a part of the last will and testament of Diane Stevens who died in 2012. All the original demos are currently 'missing'.

Reid then took the Guy Stevens-produced demos to music publisher David Platz, head of Essex Music. Existing contracts show that Reid had in fact already signed up with Essex Music as a writer as early as September 19, 1966, 'with an advance of £100' and 'further payments scheduled'. Platz was in partnership with record producer Denny Cordell, to whom he played the demos before, in Reid's words, "He tried to 'hawk' our songs around."*

Platz certainly liked the Guy Stevens recordings, as did Cordell. Although he didn't immediately single out 'A Whiter Shade Of Pale' as a potential hit, Cordell's reputation as a record producer was impressive, having already chalked up hits with a roster of successful British groups, including The Moody Blues, Georgie Fame & The Blue Flames, and The Move.

Platz, however, recognised a hit when he heard one, even as a rough demo. He wrote to Gary Brooker on March 7, 1967, stating: "Keith Reid came in yesterday and played me a demo of 'A Whiter Shade Of Pale', and I'd like you to know that we all consider it to be a certain hit. In any event we will do everything possible to exploit the song as soon as the final copy is made."

Though things seemed to be looking up for Brooker and Reid, other parts of the jigsaw needed to be in place before the puzzle was complete and Procol Harum was ready for launching. One particularly important piece arrived via an advert in *Melody Maker* of February 25 which read, 'Hammond organist, harmony vocals, seeks pro group.' The ad was placed by a classically trained keyboard player called Matthew Fisher.

Born in Croydon, Surrey, on March 7, 1946, Fisher – like both Brooker and Reid – showed a precocious interest in music while sharing a similar dislike of school work. "I started piano lessons when I

---

* The first pair of Reid's lyrics to be commercially released anywhere were 'Time Will Tell' and 'You'll Be On My Mind' on AZ Records. The songs were recorded in late 1966 and set to psychedelic music by the famous French pop singer Michel Polnareff. Reid and Polnareff were brought together by Reid's music publisher David Platz. This was a one-off deal.

was about six," he says. "I never practised much, but I liked playing by ear. I also used to play mouth organ around this time. I remember once I'd been slung out of a class for misbehaving and was standing out in the hall. Suddenly I saw the headmistress walking down the corridor and I was terrified she'd ask me why I was standing there. Instead, she asked if I had my mouth organ handy and would I play her a tune?"

Fisher's interest in popular music intensified around the time he turned 16. "A friend of mine lent me his copy of the first album by The Shadows. I was totally knocked out by it and from then on I wanted to play in a guitar group. I started out playing rhythm guitar but soon changed to bass. By the time I was halfway through the sixth form I had all but lost interest in my school work and instead my life revolved around the group and my girlfriend. The band was called The Society Five. The teachers at my school were absolutely appalled when I told them I intended to pursue a career as a musician. In those days it was a bit like saying you wanted to be an astronaut. I didn't heed their advice."

Fisher studied organ at the London Guildhall School of Music, but made his professional debut in 1964 playing an upright piano with The Tornadoes for the far-sighted, but emotionally troubled British record producer Joe Meek. Shortly after this he got a job backing Billy Fury in The Gamblers before finding a job with a young up-and-coming guitarist called Terry Reid, while Reid was still in Peter Jay & The Jaywalkers. Much to the amusement of the band Fisher often added classical organ passages to their live repertoire.

The Jaywalkers played on a high profile concert package tour with The Hollies and Small Faces in 1966. During this time Fisher made a point of asking Small Faces' organist Ian McLagan if he could "try out" his Hammond organ. 'Mac' told Fisher, "They're yelling out for Hammond players. Why don't you buy one for yourself?" Fisher borrowed enough money from his grandmother for the deposit on a Hammond M102, and his career began in earnest.

Fisher was in the midst of a stint with Screaming 'Lord Caesar' Sutch & The Roman Empire when Brooker and Reid answered the ad he had placed in *Melody Maker*. They arranged to visit him at his home in Croydon where they gave him a demo of the song 'Salad Days' and promised him that Procol Harum were "going to be as big as The Beatles". Fisher hated dressing up as a Roman soldier with Lord Sutch while fending off hoards of drunks. "It was definitely time for a change," he says. "Keith and Gary actually signed me up that very afternoon at my home in Croydon. We *all* wanted to do something serious..."

Meanwhile, Guy Stevens was becoming distanced from the embryonic Procol. "Guy Stevens had been out of the picture for some time," says Keith Reid. "Due to his financial circumstances he had returned to work for Chris Blackwell which is how I had first met him. Consequently, Guy wasn't able to concentrate on the development of Procol Harum and had kind of slipped into the background."

In the event, Stevens' fortunes turned from bad to worse. Not only had Platz and Cordell come to the conclusion that he was surplus to requirements, citing a "conflict of interest" as their reason for marginalising him, but sometime that spring, probably during April, he was busted for possession of hashish by none other than Detective Sergeant Jack Slipper, whose career in the force would forever be linked with the Great Train Robbery and the pursuit of Ronnie Biggs. In May Stevens, then involved with Art, an Island signing who later changed their name to Spooky Tooth, would be given a six-month jail sentence, spending that important summer of 1967 incarcerated in Wormwood Scrubs jail north of Shepherds Bush.

With Stevens now edged out, Platz and Cordell formulated other plans for Procol. Cordell set up New Breed Productions – which by July would be renamed Straight Ahead Productions – and formed an alliance with new business associate Jonathan Weston whom he appointed as manager for Procol Harum.

According to Matthew Fisher, "Keith Reid had actually wanted to manage Procol Harum at this stage", but both Platz and Cordell felt that he should "make the creative decisions only, and leave the business decisions to a business manager". As a result Procol Harum signed with New Breed Productions and entered into a separate deal with Jonathan Weston who became their manager at the end of April, some four weeks after Cordell produced a studio recording of 'A Whiter Shade Of

Pale'. Thereafter Keith Reid would become known as 'Procol Harum's co-manager' as well as being their 'lyric writer'.

Not only had he been edged out of the management of the group whose name he coined but, according to Diane Stevens, her husband actually had come up with the all-important phrase that became the title of the song that would transform their lives. "This was something that Guy never really got over," she says. "Especially as he had named the band and coined the famous phrase that inspired Procol's masterpiece..."

Reid, however, disputes this version of the story. "This isn't quite correct," he says. "It is true that 'A Whiter Shade Of Pale' was born during a party at Guy Stevens' house. There was a large group of us sitting round smoking and joking. During the course of much banter, Guy was trying to tell Diane that she had turned very white and he was jumbling up his words. It was this incident that gave me the idea for 'A Whiter Shade Of Pale'. It was much later after... when I had written the whole song that I told Guy about my moment of inspiration. He was of course totally unaware that he had said anything that had inspired me."

Whatever the genesis of the title, Reid produced a set of words around it that almost half a century later continues to confound, confuse and astound.

Though the lyrics defy analysis they rank, without question, among the most memorable ever written. They capture a time – 1967 – and place – London – with exquisite perfection, and as such form an essential component of the soundtrack to a memorable moment in English cultural history, the summer when The Beatles' released *Sgt Pepper's Lonely Hearts Club Band*, the British establishment tried but failed to silence The Rolling Stones by jailing Mick Jagger and Keith Richards when America's West Coast and the British flower power scene ran simpatico.

"It's like a detective story that song," says the film director Alan Parker. "It's so important in all of our lives really. Yet nobody actually knows what the words really mean. Whatever you're doing, whether at a script meeting or together with friends, we'd ask one another, 'What do these lyrics actually mean?' Every five years we'd sit down and have that same discussion!"

The writer himself is eternally baffled by the reaction of men like Parker. "I never understand when people say they don't understand it," says Reid. "'We skipped the light fandango.' That's straightforward. 'Turned cartwheels across the floor.' It seems very clear to me! I used to go and see a lot of French films in the Academy [cinema] in Oxford Street. *Pierrot Le Fou* made a strong impression on me, and *Last Year In Marienbad*. I was also very taken with surrealism, Magritte and Dali. You can draw a line between the narrative fractures and mood of those French films and 'A Whiter Shade Of Pale'." (10)

Gary Brooker: "'A Whiter Shade Of Pale' seemed to be about two people, a relationship and memory. There was a leaving, and sadness about it. To get the soul of those lyrics across vocally, to make people feel that, was quite an accomplishment." (10)

Keith Reid: "We felt we had something very important. As soon as we played it for anyone, we got an immediate response."

In its original form 'A Whiter Shade Of Pale' was almost twice as long as the familiar hit single, with an additional fourth verse that was cut. "Even at four minutes it was long," says Brooker. "Up until that point most singles were two and a half minutes. So we decided to cut down the words." "The fourth wasn't any great loss; you had the whole story in three," re-assures Reid.

Early music paper adverts for 'A Whiter Shade Of Pale' described the song as 'a poem', but Reid is dismissive of this. "I never write my stuff as poems. I just strive to make them poetic. There's a great deal of difference in the words that you write to be sung and the kind of words you write to be read."

A WHITER SHADE OF PALE

We skipped the light fandango
turned cartwheels 'cross the floor
I was feeling kinda seasick
but the crowd called out for more

The room was humming harder
as the ceiling flew away
When we called out for another drink
the waiter brought a tray

And so it was that later
as the miller told his tale
that her face, at first just ghostly,
turned a whiter shade of pale

She said, 'There is no reason
and the truth is plain to see.'
But I wandered through my playing cards
and would not let her be
one of sixteen vestal virgins
who were leaving for the coast
and although my eyes were open
they might have just as well've been closed

In the second week of March, Procol Harum placed another ad in *Melody Maker*, this time to find a drummer. Those auditioned were a varied bunch: Walter Johnstone, of The VIPs (who became Art and then Spooky Tooth), Philip 'Phil The Greek' Andronicus, a notorious 'Soho heavy' and an associate of The Pretty Things who, according to Andrew Oldham, had "never drummed in his life", and the man known only as 'Tubs'. All of these hopefuls were deemed inappropriate by Cordell who was notoriously fussy when it came to choosing drummers.

Keith Reid: "Gary had worked with [former Rockerfella drummer] Bobby Harrison in the past, and we were trying him out. Denny Cordell had already booked Olympic Studios to record 'A Whiter Shade Of Pale' and some other songs ['Salad Days' and 'Alpha']. He had told us he was going to get Mitch Mitchell of the Jimi Hendrix Experience to record with us, which we were excited about, but on the day he said he couldn't get either Mitch or Bobby, so he booked Georgie Fame & The Blue Flames drummer Bill Eyden instead."

Eyden conveniently lived across the road from Olympic Studios in Barnes. Cordell considered him to be a safe pair of hands, having worked with him many times as Georgie Fame's producer. Session engineer Keith Grant made the call to Eyden on March 29, the actual day of the recording. Eyden listened to the original demos, "replicating the drum part played by drummer Tubs on the original Guy Stevens-produced acetate of 'A Whiter Shade Of Pale'," according to Matthew Fisher.

Bobby Harrison (born June 22, 1939, East Ham, London) states that he had "just joined the day before the 'A Whiter Shade Of Pale' recording session", and was in attendance at the session, and had "expected to play". The group would subsequently re-record a couple of alternate, unreleased versions of 'A Whiter Shade Of Pale' with Harrison at Advision Studios in New Bond Street, along with the later issued 'Pale' B-side, 'Lime Street Blues'. This April 19 session was produced by Cordell, with Gerald Chevin engineering.[1]

Bobby Harrison: "As far as I knew they were going to release the version of 'A Whiter Shade Of Pale' with me playing. So when the record came out I was actually convinced it was me playing on it. I thought I was number one in the charts! Then of course I was told it was Bill Eyden, and it felt, well, pretty strange!" (12)

In the event the recording of 'A Whiter Shade Of Pale' that ended up being released featured Brooker on piano and vocals, Fisher on Hammond organ, Royer on guitar, Knights on bass and Eyden on drums. Keith Grant recently claimed that Denny Cordell was *not* in attendance on March 29 at the Olympic 'Pale' session when he taped and created the perfect mix. Keith Grant and Denny Cordell are no longer alive so this particular bone of contention will have to remain a moot point that can be verified only by the musicians who were present. Here, too, there are conflicting conclusions or simply vagueness.

'A Whiter Shade Of Pale' was licensed to Decca's progressive label, Deram, set up in autumn 1966 by the company's ace promotion man Tony Hall, who knew a hit when he heard it. In the case of 'A Whiter Shade Of Pale' it was at Denny Cordell's house where he had been invited for dinner. "I was looking through a pile of white label demos, and I picked out one and put it on," Hall says. "Well I didn't stop playing that demo all night long until about two in the morning. It was 'A Whiter Shade Of Pale'." Hall would later describe the song in his *Record Mirror* column of May 13 as being, "vaguely in the Dylan bag. The most arresting thing about it is the organ figure. It's loosely based upon Bach's 'Air On A G String'."

With the possible exception of wedding favourite 'Jesu Joy Of Man's Desiring', 'Air On A G String' is probably the best known composition by the classical composer Johann Sebastian Bach (1685–1750) and is adapted from a passage in his Orchestral Suite No 3 in D Major. Like many easily assimilated pieces of classical music it has been recorded by all manner of musicians, mostly by classical guitarists, but the best-known popular version is unquestionably that by the French pianist and composer Jacques Loussier, which was famously used to accompany a TV commercial for Hamlet cigars.

"The original Hamlet cigar commercial featuring 'Air On A G String' had always been a big favourite of ours," says Brooker. "When the guy lit up the cigar everything just went cool. Anyway, I sat down one day and tried to play 'Air On A G String'. I just started off with the bass line, and I put in some chords. I think only the first four notes are the same, and then it starts to change. I sang a tune over the top. I thought the in-between part would have some tune, which I wrote... What the bass notes were doing was *very* important to me. If it was an E-chord they played an 'e', and when it went up to an A they played 'a'. I started to find out that the whole nature of a chord changed with the bass note that you had with it. Once I had got this idea that you keep playing these bass chords descending, I just went round and round. I was there. The only problem was I thought, 'How am I going to get the repeated bit at the end of every verse?' I just banged in this triplet, and just changed the tempo of the chords for a bar, then I carried on with the chords again. You just have to flip it around at the end of the last line so that you start again."

While JS Bach's 'Air On A G String' is its most obvious influence, 'A Whiter Shade Of Pale' additionally incorporates elements of Bach's 'Sleepers Awake'. A yet closer melodic influence can be found in the organ choral prelude 'O Mensch bewein dein' Sünde groß' ('O Man, Lament Your Sin So Great'), from Bach's *Orgelbüchlein* (*Little Organ*

Book). The song also borrows ideas from the aching melancholy of 'When A Man Loves A Woman' by Percy Sledge, which itself tips its hat towards JS Bach. Sledge would later cover 'Pale', thus reversing the homage. Denny Cordell later admitted, "I wanted to make Gary's voice sound like a psychedelic Percy Sledge."

The soulful organ playing was very cathedral-like in tone and would earn Matthew Fisher the nickname 'Matthew Celestial Smith' – the 'Smith' part allegedly a reference to organ-playing legend Jimmy Smith. Fisher is unimpressed: "Smith? They just got the name wrong!" he says. "And 'Celestial' was something that I made up afterwards for a laugh as my middle name begins with 'C' for Charles. Anyway, with regard to 'the organ sound', I just had this little preset on my Hammond organ that had a big churchy sound, and I thought that would sound good in a rock band. It just seemed to work."

Fisher considered 'A Whiter Shade Of Pale' to be a suitable vehicle for his unique Bach-cum-Booker-T organ style. "It was entirely my idea to compose a set solo and to give the last two bars a satisfying 'shape'," he says. "What I added was a tune of course... I saw a proof of the [song's] sheet music and the first thing I saw was that the first eight bars were my organ solo. And yet at the top of the sheet music it said, 'Music by Gary Brooker'. Suddenly I realised what I had contributed went way beyond the call of duty... Gary was totally unsympathetic, and I was completely devastated!" (10)

There is a well-known truism in the music business that 'Where there's a hit there's a writ', to which might be added, 'the bigger the hit the bigger the writ'. Many individuals are involved in the hit-making process, from the writers and performers to the record producers and those whose job it is to ensure that records are played on the radio and eventually distributed to the shops around the country. As we have seen, those involved in making 'A Whiter Shade Of Pale' the massive hit it became range from JS Bach through publisher David Platz and producer Denny Cordell to the sound engineer Keith Grant, the musicians in the studio, the lyricist, and many others besides. And one notable individual who could claim a part in its success was languishing in a cell at Wormwood Scrubs.

Originally, however, according to Tony Hall, executive voices at Decca considered the song to be "too dreary, too long, and too slow" and questioned the wisdom of releasing it. "I said, 'You are mad! Bollocks, you're totally wrong'. This is a monster smash!"

Hall arranged to get it played on the pirate station Radio London, at a specific time so that the group could tune in and hear what the disc sounded like through a regular transistor radio. "I told [Radio London boss] Alan Keen that he would get a worldwide exclusive on-air debut of the acetate of 'A Whiter Shade Of Pale', if he would agree to play it at a certain time."

It was a smart move by Hall. The pirates broadcasted from ships anchored in the waters that surrounded the UK and the top stations, notably Radio London and Radio Caroline, attracted millions of young listeners in the days before BBC Radio 1 and independent local radio. Acting on orders from his boss, London's Mark Roman played 'A Whiter Shade Of Pale' on his show *The Roman Empire* on April 17 at precisely 13 minutes and 20 seconds before 4pm from a tiny cabin inside a ship on the stormy North Sea.

Gary Brooker still has a recording of that first radio broadcast. "I got the old Grundig out, and put the microphone near the radio," he says. "My girlfriend Franky [to whom Brooker has at the time of writing been married for 42 years] and I both cheered when the name Procol Harum was first mentioned. The DJ then said, 'I've got this new record here... And I think it's going to sound lovely!' So he puts on 'A Whiter Shade Of Pale' and I think it sounded fine, but I was so euphoric that we were getting airplay on the radio that I got a bit carried away. When the record finished he said something like 'That sounds like a huge hit to me!'"

Roman told his listeners to phone in or to write to Radio London at 17 Curzon Street in London's upmarket Mayfair. Immediately afterwards the station's switchboard was jammed with callers. Needing no further convincing Decca agreed to press up thousands of copies, rush-releasing the single across the globe on May 12. In the second week of its release it stood at number 13 in the UK charts.

On May 12 Procol Harum made their live debut at London's premier psychedelic club, the UFO on Tottenham Court Road. The club's manager, Joe Boyd, had earlier dismissed an approach from Keith Reid who was seeking to further the group's interests. "He said, 'Hey Joe'. 'I was like, 'Do I know you?'" says Boyd. "And he said, 'Yeah, I came to your office!' It was Keith Reid and he was like, 'See what you missed!'"

That same night Procol performed for a second time at the late-night, members-only Speakeasy Club in Margaret Street, near Oxford Circus. "[It was] the day 'A Whiter Shade Of Pale' came out so nobody knew us," Brooker told Johnny Black. "Because we only had ten Brooker-Reid songs, we played those, and then we played a few others that we liked. We played a Bob Dylan song, a Rascals song, and one called 'Morning Dew' that Tim Rose had recorded. Hendrix was down at the Speakeasy watching us playing and he suddenly jumped up onstage when we started 'Morning Dew', grabbed the bass off our bass player, turned it upside down, and joined in. He loved us. He thought we were lovely." (11)

The response to Radio London playing 'A Whiter Shade Of Pale' was immediate. Brooker recalls riding down Oxford Street in a bus and seeing a sign in a shop window that stated, simply, 'Yes we've got it', and another window saying, 'It's in!' "And by the third shop up Oxford Street going on this bus ride I could see copies of our record stuck in the windows. I realised this was what they were talking about. It was very important. So it was there by popular demand, which was great. When it was number 13 in the UK I went to Paris, ostensibly to do a radio interview. When I got off the plane I was met by 100 cheering people. They said, 'Welcome, welcome. We go straight to the radio show'. They said, 'You are number one'. I said, 'Oh really? Number one what?' And so it was number one in France before it was number one here in England."

There was universal agreement among Britain's pop cognoscenti that the record was exceptional. No lesser figure than Paul McCartney subsequently recalled the first time he heard it, at the Speakeasy Club in the company of Animals singer Eric Burdon and Who drummer Keith Moon. "We said, 'This is the best song ever man'," McCartney recalled. (9)

It was a memorable night for the Beatle as earlier the same evening, at The Bag O' Nails Club in Kingly Street, he had met his future wife Linda Eastman for the very first time. Later Paul gave Linda his copy of 'A Whiter Shade Of Pale' as a token of that night.

'A Whiter Shade Of Pale' received its official live debut at the Speakeasy on May 24. *Disc & Music Echo*'s Scene column (dated June 3) reported: "Digging Procol Harum at the Speakeasy last week were all four Beatles, Georgie Fame, Chris Farlowe, Cat Stevens, Andrew Loog Oldham, Eric Burdon, Pete Townshend, Roger Daltrey and Denny Cordell."

Paul McCartney and George Harrison took their partners to watch Procol Harum make their first major UK concert appearance at the Saville Theatre in Shaftesbury Avenue on June 4 where they supported The Jimi Hendrix Experience.

Reviewing this show on June 10, *New Musical Express*' Derek Boltwood wrote: "I am sure that Procol Harum will be with us for a long time – and I think they will not only prove that they are not just a one-hit group, but they will also show themselves capable of producing some really progressive music – they'll have to after 'A Whiter Shade Of Pale', which is surely one of the most up-to-date sounds around."

It took just three weeks for 'A Whiter Shade Of Pale' to climb to number one in the UK singles charts where it remained for six weeks.

"We weren't really ready for such instant success, so I thought we'd better go out and get ourselves some new clothes," says Gary Brooker. "We made an appointment to go to this exclusive boutique called Dandy Fashions in the Kings Road in Chelsea. We rang the doorbell and inside all four Beatles were standing around a harmonium singing 'A Whiter Shade Of Pale' the very moment we came in. Not for us... They just happened to be there singing the song as we came in through the door..."

According to The Beatles' press agent Derek Taylor, "John Lennon played the song over and over inside his psychedelic Rolls Royce Silver Ghost." It probably also inspired Lennon's 'I Am The Walrus' from The Beatles' *Magical Mystery Tour*.

Procol made numerous television appearances on BBC TV's *Top Of The Pops* between May and July with primetime guest spots on BBC TV's *Billy Cotton's Music Hall* on June 18 and ITV's *As You Like It on* June 20, all arranged by 'plugger' Tony Hall.

In the US, where Procol Harum weren't known at all, 'A Whiter Shade Of Pale' reached five in the *Billboard* Hot 100 and stayed in the Top 40 for 10 weeks. The song achieved this remarkable success without *any* American TV appearances whatsoever.

'Pale' became a Top 5 hit in almost every country in the world; in France the single was number one for 18 weeks, while in Venezuela it held the top spot for a staggering six months. 'A Whiter Shade Of Pale' received a UK Ivor Novello Award for Best International Song of The Year and also beat The Beatles' 'All You Need Is Love' in *NME*'s reader's poll for Best Single Of 1967.

Such success did not come without a whiff of envy from other performers. Crooner Englebert Humperdinck was so jealous of Procol's achievement that he refused to speak to the group backstage in the green room at BBC TV's *Top Of The Pops* 1967 Christmas Special. Instead of congratulating the group, Humperdinck, whose schmaltzy ballad 'Release Me' had shamefully prevented The Beatles' double A-side 'Strawberry Fields Forever'/'Penny Lane' from reaching number one earlier that year, angrily blew cigar smoke into Brooker's face before quickly exiting.

Total sales figures for 'A Whiter Shade Of Pale' are difficult to estimate and subject to the influence of those who might have reason to underestimate them in order to reduce royalty payments or overestimate them in order to promote the group's 'legendary' status. Some have suggested that, worldwide, an estimated six million sales had been chalked up by the end of the sixties but this figure must surely include albums tracks as well as singles. In 1978, on its third UK issue Procol were awarded Gold Discs with an embossed plaque that read: 'UK Sales In Excess of 6 Million', but this was surely untrue as according to reliable sources the best-selling UK single of all time is Elton John's 'Candle In The Wind' (1997) with sales of 4.9 million to date. An alleged 10 million copies had been sold worldwide by the end of the seventies, with an estimated 16 million sales to date, according to some sources. It has, of course, appeared on countless compilation albums. There are almost 1,000 cover versions of 'A Whiter Shade Of Pale' recorded in many different languages, and the song has been featured on the soundtrack to numerous movies, TV series and commercials. In the modern digital age it has even become a mobile phone ringtone and a 'Wii' computer game!

Beyond the extraordinary success that 'A Whiter Shade Of Pale' achieved in the summer of 1967 was the inescapable fact that, although – with the exception of drummer Bill Eyden – not strictly the work of session musicians, it had been recorded by a group assembled for the recording session at which it was produced. The six musicians on the record had no history together, none of the experiences that The Paramounts had shared, none of the fraternity, understanding and sympathy that comes from long nights spent in the back of a van traipsing home after an unmemorable gig 150 miles away.

Despite the critical adulation and their commercial success, Procol was inevitably a house of cards and some three weeks into the song's chart-topping run Procol Harum collapsed.

The initial bone of contention was that, without realising what the immediate future would bring, manager Jonathan Weston had put Procol on a UK to-hell-and-back tour, booking the group into venues that might have included London's prestigious Marquee Club, but also a working man's club in Ealing and a village hall in Launceston, Cornwall, where only 50 people turned up and a fight broke out. In between, Procol were appearing on radio and TV as well as doing numerous press interviews.

Fisher claims that as soon as 'Pale' made an appearance in the charts from its first week of release, Weston immediately instructed the Harold Davison agency to line up as many gigs as he could. "Jonathan Weston quarrelled with Cordell about this," he says. "We were travelling around in limousines costing £200 a day to do £60 a night gigs in tiny nightclubs. It all seemed a bit silly really, especially when you are number one in the charts. The promoters must have been rubbing their hands together thinking, 'We've got a number one band for £60!'"

Angered by this, Cordell instructed the band to come off the road immediately, insisting that all future dates be cancelled in order to return to the studio to concentrate on finishing their debut album. The sessions ran into trouble, however, when Cordell decided that Royer and Harrison were working "in the opposite direction" to the rest of the band. According to Fisher, Cordell wasn't very keen on Harrison's drumming in particular. To say that the group was unsettled would be an understatement.

After five abortive recording sessions between May 17 and June 26 Brooker, Reid and Cordell pulled the plug on the album and, as a consequence, the master tapes were filed away with 'never to be used' written on all the tape boxes. Royer and Harrison were then quietly asked to leave the group – while Procol Harum were *still* at number one in the UK singles charts. Manager Weston was also out of the picture.

On July 1, Keith Reid issued a statement via *New Musical Express*: "Procol Harum has terminated its association with business manager Jonathan Weston." Five days later letters were sent by Moody Blues and Move manager Tony Secunda, another associate of Cordell's, on behalf of Procol Harum, to Royer and Harrison officially terminating their roles with the band. As a direct consequence of this Procol Harum were unable to appear live on *Top Of The Pops* that week (an earlier taped insert was used). The official story was that "Gary Brooker has been ordered seven days rest", according to *New Musical Express* on July 8.

During the enforced absence a plan was hatched to enlist former Paramounts Robin Trower and BJ Wilson. Brooker telephoned Trower asking, "Wanna join a band that's number one?" even tape recording the conversation for posterity. Brooker then placed a similar call to Wilson.

Southend-On-Sea musician Will Birch, who shared a train journey with Trower into London's Fenchurch Street Station on July 11, recalls Trower telling him: "I'm going to rehearse with Procol Harum in Hammersmith. We're practising a new follow-up single called 'Homburg Hat'."

By July 15 Procol were back on the *Melody Maker* front page with the headline 'Procol Split Up – Two Quit' above a report that stated both Royer and Harrison had been officially 'fired' and that Secunda had been duly hired as Procol's co-manager and spokesman. Three days later, in the *Daily Mirror*, James Wilson reported that, "Two former members of Procol Harum claimed last night, 'We didn't quit. We were sacked.' Yesterday their solicitors said, 'Far from leaving of their own accord, both were sacked by people who we know had no right to do so. We plan to take an injunction stopping the group from using the name Procol Harum.' A spokesman for the group, which has replaced Royer and Harrison, said, 'I think the root of all this is that there is a lot of money involved. He added, 'Both boys will get every penny that they are entitled to. If their hit record makes £50,000 in royalties – and we are not definitely sure yet – they will each get a fifth.'"

According to Fisher, a settlement with Royer, Harrison and Weston was made on the steps of the court. "So it got *really* close to going to court," he adds.

Robin Trower: "I remember Gary told me that he saw Mick Jagger at the time that all that was going down, and Jagger said to him, 'You've blown it!'"

Jagger, currently awash in his own legal battles in order to keep himself and Keith Richards out of jail over drugs charges, was wrong, but trouble was now brewing for Procol from another of the musicians who'd been involved in the recording of 'A Whiter Shade Of Pale'.

Dissatisfied with the 1967 Musicians Union rate of 15 guineas (£15 and 75 pence), Bill Eyden decided to seek a share of the royalties, but it seems that his motivation was partially stoked by the press. "The press got onto it and came round," said Eyden, who died in 2004. "Denny Cordell had put them on to me, telling them the other guy [Bobby Harrison] was getting all this money, and I wasn't. They start asking questions, and you start thinking, 'Crikey, yes, why aren't I getting a rake-off?' I felt pretty sick. You can go in for a session where all the music's written out, but if you're called in *and* you make something of it, that's different. That record definitely has the Bill Eyden feel. The drumming is an integral part." (12)

The following week brought more problems when *Top Of The Pops* producer Johnny Stewart banned the promo film for 'A Whiter Shade Of Pale' because it contained images of the Vietnam War. Shot in two locations – Witley Court, a mansion house in Worcestershire, and the Saville Theatre in London – it was directed by Peter Clifton. A replacement promo featuring Trower and Wilson was shot in and around London and made available to Scopitone film-loop jukeboxes globally.

The *New Musical Express* of August 12 reported: "Procol Harum announced on Wednesday that it had reached an amicable settlement with guitarist Ray Royer and drummer Bobby Harrison, ending the dispute which followed their departure from the group last month. Royer and Harrison – who will not be returning – had previously claimed unjustifiable sacking, and maintained the group was not entitled to use the name Procol Harum without them."[2]

Clearly the 'old pals' act involved in the enlistment of Trower and Wilson would not look good in the media, even if the new recruits were to prove far better musicians than their predecessors. However, the whole debacle did help to dispel the tag of 'session group' given to Procol by *The News Of The World*. In the same year that The Monkees were slammed for being 'manufactured', this slur did nothing to further Procol's image as a solid unit.

During the last two weeks of July, the new look Procol Harum returned to Olympic Studios to re-record tracks for their debut album under the supervision of Denny Cordell. Rush released in the USA in August on Deram and distributed by London Records USA via the Richmond Organisation, the eponymous album reached number 47 in *Billboard*. By September the record would be issued across most of the western hemisphere on many differing labels.

In the latter half of 1967 the group made a dozen trips across the English Channel to appear on French TV. In ultra-stylish Paris they were considered to be 'a British phenomenon', and performed to 20,000 fans at the Châtelet Music Festival. The band also headlined at the Bilzen Jazz Festival in Belgium which was filmed at the end of August. Live on camera, manager Tony Secunda announced that Procol's follow-up single, titled 'Homburg', would be "even bigger" than 'A Whiter Shade Of Pale'.

Towards the end of the summer Secunda decided the group's sartorial image needed a spring-clean and proposed they kit themselves out in psychedelic tunics designed by the Fool, a Dutch fashion team whose brief association with The Beatles would end in red faces all round. Commissioned to produce designer clothes for the Fab Four's short-lived Apple shop in Baker Street, the Fool turned out to be one of many who would separate The Beatles from their cash in 1968. These Procol costumes were even more eccentric than the Chinese tunics that Brooker had previously purchased from Dandy Fashions for his earlier TV appearances.

While Fisher describes the clothes as "kind of psychedelic military", Brooker says: "They were more like something from outer space. They were terribly brilliant colours of silks and satins, multi coloured, mind expanding, psychedelic. We went and tried 'em on and thought, 'We can't wear these!' And then we went, 'Oh all right!' Of course some people were totally unimpressed."

The issue of the costumes turned to farce in Paris on September 25 as Brooker recalls: "We played at the Paris Olympia in the Fool costumes and we had to do a runner. The cars didn't arrive. So Matthew Fisher in his own way said, 'I think I'll walk, it's not far.' I don't think he realised what he had on. Eventually we got our cars. Saturday night streets. Packed out. Midnight. All sorts out. The middle of Paris. After about 10 minutes driving in the car we spotted Matthew standing on a corner twiddling his moustache, dressed in a lime green cape, cerise knee length trousers and a pair of velvet boots, just hanging around there. I mean he was bound to get into trouble dressed like that. So we opened the car doors, and pulled him in!"

Tailoring was evidently not the Fool's strongest point – Trower's costume was far too large and Fisher's was also a bad fit. In the end

Secunda had a confession to make: "In fact these were costumes that The Move previously rejected."

Procol Harum's follow-up to 'A Whiter Shade Of Pale' was abbreviated from 'Homburg Hat' to 'Homburg' and issued in the UK in the late autumn of 1967 on the recently revived Regal Zonophone label and distributed by EMI Records, which licensed the imprint from Straight Ahead Productions' David Platz and Denny Cordell.*

There were certain similarities between the two songs; Brooker's unmistakable voice, a broadly comparable tempo, Brooker's predominant piano instead of Fisher's Hammond organ, and lyrics which again didn't make much literal sense but hinted at something deep and meaningful in a rather absurdist, surreal fashion.

Interviewed by DJ Brian Matthew for the BBC's World Service, Brooker gave some surprising answers.

Brian Matthew: "The new record 'Homburg'… do you think there's any danger you're going to be accused or criticised for producing very much the same sort of sounds?"

Gary Brooker: "Well I hope we are, 'cos it is the same… same people… more or less… so it's going to be the same sound. If they don't say things against it I shall be very disappointed."

Brian Matthew: "Don't say things *against* it? Why do you want them to do this?"

Gary Brooker: "Well, there are probably about one million people who want this one to miss."

Brian Matthew: "Yes?"

Gary Brooker: "Yeah. 'A Whiter Shade Of Pale' was too big for a lot of people. And if they don't say things against it, then I'll lose my faith in them."

Brian Matthew: "Ha ha ha. That's a *splendid* answer. I'm sure they're all going to be wrong. Anyway, can we hear a performance of it now? The great new winner for Procol Harum, 'Homburg'."

---

* 5: Gary Brooker's father played the pedal steel guitar in Felix Mendelssohn's Hawaiian Serenaders who also originally also recorded on Regal Zonophone back in the 1950s

Still kitted out as psychedelic caped crusaders, Procol Harum performed 'Homburg' on *Dee Time*, the BBC's Saturday night primetime chat show hosted by Simon Dee on October 14. This was followed by an appearance on *Top Of The Pops* and a BBC TV children's programme called *Crackerjack* which was watched by an estimated four million people. Hosted by two comedians, Peter Glaze, who was short and fat, and Leslie Crowther, who was tall and thin, *Crackerjack* was televised 'live' in front of a studio audience of 500 screaming children. Glaze and Crowther wore Homburg hats and long overcoats during Procol's performance. Crowther quickly removed Glaze's hat while a bemused Brooker sang the line, "You better take off your Homburg 'cos your overcoat is too long".

Disc & Music Echo's influential singles reviewer Penny Valentine described 'Homburg' as being "even better than 'Pale'", adding: "Now the main instrument is a cool piano with the famous organ tucked firmly in the background and out of the way. The piano opens with gentle spring sounds as Gary's voice comes cracking in with words that are even more evocative than 'Pale'. The words will remind you of wet leafy roads and tramps, and are vaguely reminiscent of Samuel Becket's *Waiting For Godot*."

Also impressed was a singer, songwriter and pianist then on the cusp of changing his name from Reginald Dwight to Elton John. In a 1989 interview Elton recalled the line "The mirror upon reflection has climbed back upon the wall", perceptively describing it as "like a Dali painting". (13)

'Homburg' failed to match its predecessor, but still reached number six in the UK charts, number one in Italy, where it sold 300,000 copies, and 34 in the USA. This prompted further encouragement from *Disc & Music Echo*, which, on October 21, announced 'Procol Crash States' on its front page, accompanied by another picture of the group in their garish Fool costumes.

Meanwhile, the Italian rush-release of Procol's debut album was issued in a candyfloss pink and white sleeve. The LP included, rather oddly, an early version of 'Shine On Brightly', which was sung in Italian, and called 'Il Tuo Diamante'. The song became Procol's third hit single, leading to an appearance on primetime Italian TV (RAI) miming along to this and their two previous hits. Procol had hoped to see the UK release of their album in the record shops for Christmas, but EMI inexplicably delayed it further until the end of January 1968.

On October 25, Procol Harum crossed the Atlantic for the first time. The toast of East Coast America, they played at the Village Theater in New York's Greenwich Village before flying to the West Coast for a short residency at Hollywood's Whisky A Go-Go. A trip to San Francisco took in three dates with Pink Floyd at Bill Graham's Fillmore and Winterland theatres followed by three dates supporting The Doors.

Robin Trower: "You can't imagine how exciting it was to be there. All the music that we loved was coming out of America. And we were suddenly there. It was just great!"

Gary Brooker: "Bill Graham… used to put you on a bill you couldn't really argue about. Who was the best? It didn't really concern us. We were just *privileged* to be on the same bill as some of those bands, people like Pink Floyd and The Doors. And there were a lot of bands that we were on with that have simply disappeared from memory like HP Lovecraft, and Pacific Gas And Electric."

Robin Trower: "Our first show was in New York. I was a little bit daunted by it. New York had a real feeling of violence about it, which I hadn't come up against before. All through the night you'd hear cop cars, sirens, guns going off. Kinda puts you on the back foot a little bit." (1)

Gary Brooker: "San Francisco for two weeks at that time was good for us, but the Summer of Love was over. People were starting to die from taking too much speed. It was a bad scene. The love had gone. People were starting to say, 'No, it was real nice here a couple of months ago, but now it's getting ugly!'"

The gap between the idealism of the hippies and the iron fist of America's political right turned ugly, and one area where this was most visible was outside the concerts at which Procol performed.

Robin Trower agrees, "You got to remember with long hair, especially in the sixties, you were looked at in an aggressive manner, which was quite intimidating."

51

"Those were very different times in America," says Keith Reid. "People abused you if you had long hair. Young people were being drafted to fight in the war in Vietnam. And a lot of people were very unhappy about the war. It was a very political time."

1 Two of the 'A Whiter Shade of Pale' alternates with Bobby Harrison on drums were finally issued in 1997 on *Procol Harum's* 30th Anniversary Boxed Set via the Westside label. The recordings were later used in court in 2005 in the 'A Whiter Shade Of Pale' songwriting accreditation claim brought by Mathew Fisher against Brooker-Reid/ Onwards Music Ltd.

2 Royer and Harrison went on to make a 'cult album' as a four-piece under the name Freedom shortly after their departure – the soundtrack to Italian film maker Tinto Brass' movie *Nerosubianco* (the English title was *Black On White* and in the US *The Artful Penetration Of Barbara* aka *Attraction*). Freedom didn't just play on the soundtrack – they also appeared in the film performing their own music, in one scene perched in the branches of a giant tree. It's one of the most 'out there' swinging sixties films ever made. Harrison would later form The Bobby Harrison Band and then Snafu during the mid-seventies.

Chapter 3

Two Regal Albums
1968

"Shine On Brightly was a real heavy influence when writing Tommy."
Pete Townshend

"I can tell you Procol Harum was a pretty happening album!"
Jimmy Page

In keeping with many late sixties innovative album sleeves, the cover for Procol Harum's eponymous debut LP was eye-catching. However, instead of swirling Day-Glo colours and lysergic-influenced imagery, it featured a simple but striking monochrome woodcut image, a hippie take on 'Art Nouveau' in the manner of Aubrey Beardsley – according to the artist Dickinson – showing a dreamy-looking girl in an ankle-length white dress whose long dark hair intermingled with the leaves and branches of a tree. Though uncredited on the sleeve, the artwork was created by Keith Reid's girlfriend who was known simply as Dickinson.

The reverse of the album sleeve featured a one line note which advised: "To be listened to in the spirit in which it was made". This was because the album had been recorded almost 'live' at Advision Studios in London's New Bond Street. The sessions involved about six takes for every song. Each channel of the four-track tapes featured two musicians performing 'live', making any overdubbing somewhat difficult. In the light of this, former drummer Bobby Harrison's claim that he and former guitarist Ray Royer "must have been on three-quarters of the issued *Procol Harum* album" actually beggar belief.

According to Kenny White, "What you hear on the album is what was recorded at Advision with Trower and Wilson. There is only one truth and that is 'the truth'. I know. I was there. The album was recorded in two 12-hour sessions over two days in July starting at 7pm in the evening and ending at 7am in the morning. I had my head resting next to Robin Trower's Marshall amp for hours. I just couldn't get enough of what he was doing. His playing was fantastic as was BJ's drumming. They gave the best performances of their entire career on that album. They all did!"

For the purposes of research and in order to seek out 'the truth', the aborted Olympic sessions from May and June 1967, featuring Harrison and Royer, were accessed from the vaults for the first time since 1967 in order to see if Harrison's claims could be substantiated. The earlier sessions engineered by Eddie Kramer continually break down and bear no similarity in terms of guitar parts nor percussive parts to the wholly re-recorded versions featuring the new line-up, whereas the Advision masters feature Trower's blues riffs sounding exactly as we have come to know them. By comparison, the earlier Royer sessions offer a few nice arpeggios and licks but they bear no resemblance whatsoever to the work undertaken by his successor. Harrison's drumming is perfunctory at best and, stylistically, a million miles away from the unique drumming of BJ Wilson as featured on the released album. [*See Appendix #1*]

'Conquistador', the song that Brooker and Reid had intended for The Beach Boys, opens the album. Inspired by Cervantes' *Don Quixote,* the tale of a rusty old retainer was revisited in a later Procol Harum B-side entitled 'In The Wee Small Hours Of Sixpence'. 'Conquistador' was considered as a potential single, but this plan was shelved until the band re-recorded the song live in November 1971 with the Edmonton Symphony Orchestra.

'She Wandered Through The Garden Fence' was also a strong contender for single release, but the lines "Threw me down upon my back, strapped me to her torture rack," might well have raised eyebrows at the easily offended BBC. First performed by the band on a French TV chat show, fellow guest actress Susannah York was seen to smile when Brooker sang these particular lines. While the opening three notes stem from 'To A Wild Rose' by Edward Alexander MacDowell and the organ solo is based on Clarke's 'Trumpet Voluntary', there's an underlying humour to the track, the spirit of Joe Brown or even George Formby.

'Something Following Me', the first song that Brooker wrote with Reid, has a Dylan-inspired lyric that tells of a man being followed by his own tombstone, while 'Mabel' – "Please get off the kitchen table" – has a distinct Lovin' Spoonful influence. Brooker plays a celeste in this uptempo fusion of John Sebastian-meets-Dylan's 'Rainy Day Women Parts #12 and #35'. The percussion is played by African musician Rocky Dijon (who went on to provide congas for The Rolling Stones on tracks like 'Sympathy For The Devil') while the violin part was contributed by either John Stein or Wilhelm Martin from Denny Laine's short-lived Electric String Band experiment.

'Cerdes (Outside The Gates Of)' is a tale alluding to all kinds of myths and those that propagate them; perhaps even Procol's gothic-blues take on Dylan's 'Gates Of Eden'. Brooker wrote a great opening bass line for Dave Knights that sounds sublime on the 1997 CD digital remaster.

'A Christmas Camel' is again most Dylan-like lyrically, the piano chords reminiscent of 'Ballad Of A Thin Man'. The lyrics to uptempo period piece 'Kaleidoscope' were allegedly written by Reid as a potential theme song for Jack Smight's 1966 Hollywood feature of the same name.

'Salad Days (Are Here Again)' first featured in the seldom seen *avant-garde* feature *Separation*, written by and starring the late Jane Arden.

The movie was directed by Jack Bond, who went on to direct several excellent arts documentaries for both the BBC and ITV.*

'Good Captain Clack', first released as the B-side to 'Homburg', was allegedly about "an Australian friend called Peter Clack" [as Reid later revealed in the 1970 Australian documentay *The Procol Harum*]. The line *"still scowling black"* could be taken as Reid at his most mischievous. When asked if the "Australian friend" in question was film-maker Peter Clifton (who shot the promo for 'A Whiter Shade of Pale') Reid emphatically denied this. Fisher had previously played a season at Butlin's holiday camp in Minehead, which might have contributed to the organ style he uses here. Musically it's reminiscent of 'Tommy's Holiday Camp' by The Who, which it potentially inspired, and would have perfectly slotted in to the Bonzo Dog Doo-Dah Band's repertoire.**

'Repent Walpurgis', credited to Fisher, was an instrumental epic used to close Procol's live shows from the time. A few themes were 'borrowed'; a clever derivation of a chord sequence from The Four Seasons hit 'Beggin'', with Brooker inserting Bach's 1st Prelude (from Book Number One of the 48 Preludes and Fugues) alongside a clever nod to Tchaikovsky's 1st Piano Concerto amid the body of the composition.

"Frankly the piece owes an awful lot to Rob's guitar playing," says Fisher, a view Brooker concurs with. "Yes, Rob was a very emotional soloist – and those solos really went somewhere".

With Trower's blues-drenched guitar and Wilson's inventive percussion placed very much at the forefront, *Procol Harum* was recorded on four-track by producer Denny Cordell and engineered by Gerald Chevin in July 1967.

Following on from the technological advances of recent groundbreaking albums – The Beatles' *Sgt Pepper* being the most obvious

---

* The film was released in England in July 1967. It also featured the 'Separation' theme written by Matthew Fisher, which he would later re-record for his début solo album *Journey's End* in 1972.

**The Bonzo's Viv Stanshall was also from Southend-On-Sea, like Brooker and Trower.

example – Procol's debut met with some criticism for sounding rather thin. Unusually it was only available in mono in Britain.

Matthew Fisher: "The first album wasn't in stereo because the producer didn't like stereo at the time. Denny was kind of like Phil Spector with a back-to-mono viewpoint."

In Cordell's defence, mono was still the dominant format in British households with stereo not fully taking over until 1968 – the same year that albums first overtook singles' sales. Omitting both 'A Whiter Shade of Pale' and 'Homburg', *Procol Harum* failed to chart in the UK when first issued. However, in the spring of 1972, after being re-issued and re-titled *A Whiter Shade Of Pale* coupled with 1969's *A Salty Dog* it reached a UK chart position of 27, earning Procol Harum two Gold Discs in the process.

On January 16, 1968, Procol belatedly showcased their debut album at the Speakeasy Club followed by a gig at the Saville Theatre, supported by Fairport Convention. A week later Procol performed alongside The Moody Blues, Brian Auger & The Trinity and Long John Baldry at the Midem Festival, the big annual music biz event in Cannes, topping the bill in a concert televised for French TV transmission on March 1. Their 15-minute set featured 'A Whiter Shade Of Pale', 'Kaleidoscope' and 'Repent Walpurgis'. Dressed from head-to-foot in a black gothic-looking monk's robe, Fisher's face was hidden from view by a hood. He wore the outfit to draw attention to the fact that whenever he appeared on television, the cameras only ever seemed to focus on his hands playing the keys.

Matthew Fisher: "Tony Secunda was winding me up about this. And I remember not feeling very well that day. I think that was probably the last time I ever wore the monk's cape."

A mini tour of England was interrupted by a weekend in New York where Procol headlined over Moby Grape at the Anderson Theatre on February 10 and 11. After returning to London to record a session for John Peel's *Top Gear* on St Valentine's Day, Procol then played the Mayfair Arts Ball on February 20, supported by Chris Farlowe & The Thunderbirds, J D Bachus & The Powerhouse, and The Sect. A German tour with The Bee Gees followed in March, and on March 24, the band were part of a multi-artist, charity show organised by the *Daily Express* at London's Wembley Empire Pool featuring The Spencer Davis Group, The Move, The Easybeats, Cat Stevens, and Simon Dupree & The Big Sound.

Procol Harum spent much of the year touring the US and recording their second album, which had a bigger budget as a direct consequence of Tony Secunda securing a five-album deal with Herb Alpert's A&M Records Inc. in the USA. Secunda went into characteristic overdrive, feeding the press stories such as *Disc & Music Echo*'s report that Procol Harum were "to debut on three networked American TV shows, *The Ed Sullivan Show, Hollywood Palace* and *The Smothers Brothers Comedy Hour*". These high profile appearances failed to transpire, apparently because Secunda demanded huge performance fees.*

According to Keith Reid, "Tony Secunda told *Paris Match* to 'piss off' when they came over to England to do a special feature on us. It would have been a front page story printed in both French and English, and sold globally!"

These errors of judgment by Secunda led to inevitable tensions, resulting in a parting of the ways midway through Procol's second American tour in June 1968, but "the contractual break would be almost a year later", Brooker revealed to *Rolling Stone*'s Andrew Bailey in 1971.

Keith Reid: "When we were in the USA in 1968 we went to see Albert Grossman [Bob Dylan's then manager]. There was a possibility of him managing us in the USA. He played us a tape of this new group he was managing called The Crackers, which is what The Band called themselves then. This would be *after* we had recorded *Shine On Brightly*." (14)

Matthew Fisher: "Yes there was always talk of that. But when we did finally meet [Grossman], he didn't seem very interested in us at all!"

Procol entered into yet another management deal, this time with a former associate of Frank Zappa called Bennett Glotzer, and Ronnie Lyons who, according to Reid, "tour managed Procol throughout the

---

* Procol eventually made their American TV debut on The Smothers Brothers show in early 1970, some 18 months after Secunda's departure.

latter half of 1968 and all of 1969." This resulted in further gigs booked on America's East and West Coast as well as in the Midwest. During the summer and autumn, Detroit's legendary Grande Ballroom became Procol's favourite American residency next to San Francisco's Fillmore West. It was here that they met White Panther founder and manager of the MC5, John Sinclair, who had set up the White Panthers in support of the Black Panthers during the Detroit riots across 1967. Sinclair's fellow Grande Ballroom cohort Russ Gibb promoted the Oakland University Pop Festival at Baldwin Pavilion on September 1 where Procol shared billing with acts as diverse as Howlin' Wolf, Pink Floyd, The MC5, and Iggy Pop's 'Psychedelic' Stooges.

Procol played a two-night stint at New York's Fillmore East on the same bill as Country Joe & The Fish and Ten Years After later that month. They also headlined a coast-to-coast tour with Santana, which they interrupted to attend the San Francisco Pop Festival during the final weekend of October, appearing alongside The Chambers Brothers, Deep Purple, Canned Heat and Creedence Clearwater Revival.

The Santana shows in particular caused Fisher to tire of the non-stop grind of life on the road.

"We played with Santana dozens of times. They were opening up for us out there," says Brooker, "but I don't think anybody ever really knew them. I mean Matthew hated the organist and he hated Carlos Santana. Fisher would never come out of his room. Trower didn't like anybody, and Reid never spoke to a living soul! BJ Wilson got on well with them. I used to have a drink with the organist and the drummer. But we were on with so many bands, and sometimes they were shy of talking to us as well."

Trower: "Santana? The original band were *fantastic*. What was unusual about them was you felt they were all *real* musicians as opposed to rock musicians. They were progressive. You could imagine them being jazz players who were all formally trained musically as opposed to being like us with a harder background in rock, blues and soul."

Procol's extensive American touring continued to the end of the year with a show featuring Love and Chicago Transit Authority at LA's Shrine Exhibition Hall on November 9, and then the Kinetic

Playground, Chicago on November 27 and 28 where they shared two nights billing with The Grateful Dead before returning home to England for Christmas. The arduous US touring schedule resumed on December 28, when the group took the stage at the Miami Pop Festival in Hallandale, Florida, playing to a crowd of 100,000 on a bill that featured, among others, Chuck Berry, The Turtles, Fleetwood Mac, and Canned Heat.

On New Year's Eve 1968 Procol arrived at Cocoa Beach in Florida for a small, but special gig. Among the US crew for that night's show was one Gil Henry who was working for the American concert promoter Howard Stein. "The actual show was in Merritt Island at a converted skating rink," says Gil Henry. "When Procol Harum came on it was crazy. There was a crowd of about 2,500 people packed into this little rink and the stage was a dismal excuse for a performance platform...

"Gary wore his stars and stripes hat that reflected the American flag. He played magically, as did Matthew Fisher. The sound produced by Trower's guitar was mesmerising: the crowd was speechless. When a song was over it was like dead silent: you could hear a pin drop, and then a thunderous roar of applause vibrated throughout the old skating rink. The people were dumbfounded by the sound that they heard that night. One reason for that was that they never really thought that a band could sound so good in that old skating rink, but they did and it was pure harmony. All of the instruments melded together and created that early Procol Harum sound that was *so* unique.... They played all of the hits and many songs that weren't so well known...

"When it was time for the band to finish, the crowd would have no part in letting them leave just yet, so they came back out on stage and finished with 'A Whiter Shade Of Pale' and 'Repent Walpurgis'. It was truly a magical show. I can still see the looks on the faces of people that I grew up with. [They were] totally awestruck by what they had just experienced. To this day everyone I talk to remembers that show as the best rock show they ever saw. And I'm one of them!"

Procol's second album, *Shine On Brightly,* was released in the run–up to Christmas of 1968. It was a hugely ambitious album that was once again credited to their producer Denny Cordell. Cordell had in truth lost interest in Procol Harum during the recording of *Shine On Brightly* and diverted his attention to protégé Joe Cocker, even poaching Wilson and Fisher to play on Cocker's album *With A Little Help From My Friends*, the title of which became a massive global hit. Not leaving them entirely to their own devices, Cordell arranged for two creative talents to share the reins, namely the uncredited engineer Glyn Johns (who also, notably, worked on the Rolling Stones' *Beggar's Banquet* at Olympic Studios that year) and the 'assistant producer' Tony Visconti.

Matthew Fisher: "Denny Cordell… went off to the USA to work with Joe and left Tony Visconti to look after us. Having started work on the album, Tony continued to stick around after Denny came back, so you could argue that much of the album was co-produced by Denny and Tony." (15)

Keith Reid: "Denny became less and less involved. He wondered what on earth we were doing, and left us to get on with this strange psychedelic record!"

"Denny was going through a very insecure phase at that time," Visconti recalls, "having business as well as marital problems, so a lot of the time on those Joe Cocker, Move, and Procol Harum things Denny just wasn't there. I was always obediently in attendance, because I was his apprentice. So there's a lot of me on those albums. I produced two tracks for *Shine On Brightly*, namely 'Magdalene (My Regal Zonophone)' and 'In Held 'Twas In I's second piece entitled "Twas Teatime At The Circus." * (16)

Shine On Brightly is perhaps Procol's *tour de force* – Brooker's very British take on 'blue eyed soul' features strongly alongside Fisher's evocative Hammond organ and Trower's unique and emotive guitar-playing, while the vastly underrated rhythm section of Knights and Wilson provides the ideal platform, taking Procol's second album into the realms of excelsis.

★ The original tape box for 'Wish Me Well' credits Visconti as 'producer' alongside the working title 'The Gospel According To ….'

The opening track, 'Quite Rightly So' had already been premiered in March as a standalone single (backed with 'In The Wee Small Hours Of Sixpence', it stalled at a disappointing UK chart position of 50). The song was allegedly based upon a letter that Reid wrote to the singer Sandy Hurwitz, whom he dated when Procol débuted in New York in the autumn of 1967. The song has also been reported as being about the Velvet Underground's muse and chanteuse Nico, who Reid allegedly met around the same time.

The hallucinatory nature of the lyrics to 'Shine On Brightly' are part and parcel of one of Brooker-Reid's finest compositions, taking the listener on a surreal journey along a pathway to madness. To hear the song in its full stereo glory was part of the process.

Matthew Fisher: "We were happy with *Shine On Brightly* in that it was mixed in stereo. If it wasn't for me and Rob Trower, *Shine On Brightly wouldn't* have been in stereo. We'd be in the studio and Traffic or The Small Faces would be in the studio next door recording in stereo and I'd go, 'Hey they're recording in stereo, why not us?' And [Denny Cordell] just dismissed it. We all kept going on at him until he finally relented and recorded the album in stereo. The producer wasn't happy working in stereo. *He just wasn't into it.*" *(15)

Gary Brooker: "Glyn Johns was responsible for the stereo mix of that song ['Shine On Brightly'] ...There were probably some psychedelic drugs involved in that one. It was very hard to avoid that in America at the time. I was there – like everybody else ..."

'Skip Softly (My Moonbeams)' often featured playful experimentation from Brooker when performed live at the time, as evidenced by a surviving tape from a 1968 Fillmore West show which features a segue into Richard Strauss' 'Also Sprach Zarathustra', the famous closing theme to the 'star child' sequence in Stanley Kubrick's *2001: A Space Odyssey*. There are also hints of Khachaturian's 'Sabre Dance' in the organ figure towards the close of the studio version. A radical

---

★ 4: In the light of Cordell's distaste for stereo, and in keeping with the demands of the public, a mono version with a different mix was also issued in the UK on EMI Regal Zonophone alongside the stereo release.

interpretation of 'Sabre Dance' was taken to number five in the UK charts by guitarist Dave Edmunds' band Love Sculpture in November 1968, but it appears Procol beat them to it.

'Wish Me Well' is a fine example of a Procol blues with strong performances from Brooker, Wilson, and Trower, who delivers some heavy duty lines. "'Wish Me Well' was intended to be a gospel song," Reid recalls. "I remember us doing that at Olympic Studios with some of the guys from Traffic coming in to do handclaps and stuff while Robin and Gary sang it as a duet.

"Gary and Steve Winwood both looked to Ray Charles as their main vocal influences. There was also the organ playing which both bands featured. But I think Matthew Fisher played a Hammond B3 while Steve Winwood played a smaller L100. So there was a difference in the sound, but there was a similarity [between Procol Harum and Traffic] because of the shared interest in blues and R&B. Most English musicians from that period had the same influences." (17)

'Rambling On' is a tale about a man who dreams of "*flying up in the sky*'" after seeing the mid-sixties *Batman* movie, with Reid describing his words as "a flight of fancy, nothing more, nothing less!"

"The song's piano chords borrow from Holst's 'Mars' from 'The Planets Suite'," Brooker points out, "and serve to counterpoint Robin's guitar work."

'Magdalene (My Regal Zonophone)' opens the album's second side. Originally recorded as an alternate version in early 1967, the song was written after "a stoned evening sitting around the piano" when Brooker and Reid felt like doing something in a Salvation Army band style.

The remainder of the second side was dominated by an ambitious, 17 minute piece given the lofty title 'In Held 'Twas In I' which incorporated five different themes – 'Glimpses Of Nirvana', ''Twas Teatime At The Circus', 'In The Autumn Of My Madness', 'Look To Your Soul' and 'Grand Finale'.

Matthew Fisher: "I remember Keith approaching me with regard to an idea he and Gary were working on for a long track that would take up most, if not all, of one side of the album. I think the inspiration for this was *Sgt. Pepper*, the way the tracks ran into each other. Originally there was no title and we used to refer to it as 'The Great Work'. The title 'In Held 'Twas In I' was my idea: i.e. to take the first word of each section."

Keith Reid: "It was originally called 'Magnum Harum'! Matthew wanted to get involved in the writing of the album. We had a few pieces that we were working up, which eventually became 'In Held 'Twas In I', and as it was unfinished we felt that it was a good way of getting Matthew in on the writing side of things."

'Glimpses Of Nirvana' begins with Brooker reading aloud a tale about a visit by a pilgrim to the Dalai Lama and his quest to find the meaning of life.

Keith Reid: "It's very funny. I met somebody in the Baghdad House, a café in Fulham Road in London, who was an American writer involved with The Beatles. I went there with him and he told me this story about how the Dalai Lama will only tell a young disciple about the meaning of life after he's spent five years in meditation. Eventually the pilgrim returns to the Dalai Lama and says, 'Well father, what is the meaning of life?' and the Dalai Lama replies: 'Well my son, life is like a beanstalk — isn't it?' Gary reads out his answer at the beginning of the record. We started with the story and then Matthew and Gary wrote a bit of music." (17)

Matthew Fisher: "At the first communal writing session they'd got as far as 'Life is like a beanstalk — isn't it?' They needed a link between that bit and the slow theme that follows soon afterwards. I supplied the link. I wasn't very involved in the next bit or two, and my next input was the idea of the clock chiming after, 'It all works out'. I believe it chimes 13 times."

Tony Visconti: "On 'Twas Teatime At The Circus' I joined the band in the studio to scream and shout as a part of the crowd." (18)

Matthew Fisher: "For 'Teatime At The Circus' I supplied the music for '*And though the crowd clapped furiously they did not see the joke*', together with the little riff that precedes it."

Keith Reid: "I was quite pally with Jimi Hendrix at the time, so I had this line which went '*Twas tea-time at the circus, King Jimi was there*', which was all about Hendrix. We put that to music and we just kept on going with absolutely no idea where we were headed until we finally got to the end!"

The next segment, 'In Autumn Of My Madness', was predominantly Fisher, who also played acoustic guitar.

Matthew Fisher: "I remember Franky [Gary Brooker's wife] was most upset that Gary did not replace the piano [part] that I'd played on the basic track. She felt it was totally unacceptable for a Procol recording not to include Gary! The bit after 'Autumn…' was basically down to Rob Trower, although he never claimed a credit for it. It leads into a reworking of the slow theme … which this time includes some weird chords that Gary and I worked out … Then comes 'Look To Your Soul', which was written by Keith and Gary."

Fisher was also mainly behind the opus 'Grand Finale'. "Of course I had a little help from Haydn," he adds wryly. "Although Rob's guitar solo is played over the chords used earlier behind Keith's soliloquy, *'Held close by that which some despise…'*, so I suppose Gary could claim that bit. There are two pianos on this track: a grand piano played by Gary and an upright played by me. My piano is the one that plays the solo when the choir enters. I also do that insane run at the end of the guitar solo.

"Although all of 'In Held…' had been thus far recorded at Olympic Studios, we had to take the 'Grand Finale' off to Advision to add the choir, as that was the only 8-track studio available at the time. The 'choir' consisted of various friends, relatives and band members who could either read music or were otherwise capable of learning a part. I think while we were at Advision we also recorded the kettle drums at the end. We then took it back to Olympic to join it up to the rest of the mix."

Having recorded all of the parts in stages a considerable task was involved in editing all the elements together to produce one continuous whole.

Keith Reid: "It was Glyn Johns who matched it all up and made it sound like a unified thing… He was definitely responsible for making it sound as if it had been done at one place and at one time, instead of being separate pieces recorded over several sessions." [See Appendix 4]

The end product was both startling and imaginative, though very much a product of its age when people of a similar mindset were searching for enlightenment. It should therefore come as no great surprise that the album sold more copies in California than in any other part of America, according to sources at A&M Records.

Gary Brooker: "'In Held 'Twas In I' was a different concept... It was recorded at a time when people did have their minds expanded. You didn't have to take psychedelic drugs for your mind to expand, and your horizons to reach out a bit. 'In Held 'Twas In I' started out with talking, then some chanting, followed by some singing. And that was quite mind expanding in itself."

Veering into the realms of Eastern mysticism, which swayed so many in 1968, Reid's lyrics for 'In Held 'Twas In I' contained notions of self doubt alongside wit and wisdom. They were full of profundities, not least, *"The lesson lies in learning, and by teaching I'll be taught."*

Procol's grand experiment did not go unnoticed by other musicians. In an interview with *International Times'* Barry Miles in 1969, The Who's Pete Townshend said that 'In Held 'Twas In I' "was a real *heavy* influence when writing *Tommy*."

Gary Brooker: "We [later] bumped into Pete Townshend in a Los Angeles hotel when touring America. Keith Reid and I spent a pleasant afternoon with him. [Pete] told us that the concept of 'In Held...', of five pieces tied together, that particular concept had given him the idea towards doing *Tommy*... except he had a big proper story. Anyway, he did say that it helped him to form the idea for *Tommy*, which was very nice of him. I might add that whilst we were chatting with Pete, Keith Moon and BJ Wilson managed to disappear for the entire afternoon only to end up getting themselves arrested for indecent exposure!"

The British sleeve for *Shine On Brightly* featured a painting by George Underwood, an artist and former musician who was a close friend of the still largely unknown David Bowie and who had been recommended to Procol by Tony Visconti. Underwood had provided the striking artwork for Visconti discoveries Tyrannosaurus Rex's 1968 début album, *My People Were Fair...* The artwork neatly depicts the lyrics by showing a "Prussian blue electric clock"; a "chandelier in full swing", "fat old Buddhas carved in gold" and "some sign post that is not there".

In America the powers that be at A&M deemed the image to be offensive and their art department replaced Underwood's lavish painting with a hideous green tinted gatefold sleeve featuring a shop dummy placed next to an upright piano in a cactus filled Californian desert. This particular cover was the work of art director Tom Wilkes and photographer Guy Webster. At the same time, Wilkes concocted the original controversial graffiti-laden toilet cover for the Rolling Stones' *Beggars Banquet*, which also caused record company ructions, forcing the Stones to back down with a more austere sleeve.

Shine On Brightly reached a number 24 *Billboard* chart position, having been released in September 1968 to tie-in with Procol's American touring schedule. When later released in the UK (December) it received universally excellent reviews in the music papers, yet conversely it failed to sell in great quantities. While this seemed an injustice at the time the band members consider the album to be among Procol's finest achievements.

Robin Trower: "When you consider all of the strong contributions that we all made in Procol Harum, *Shine On Brightly* turned out really well, and it deserved to!"

Chapter 4

Indecision & A Salty Dog
1969

"A Salty Dog is their masterpiece."

Jimmy Page

Although commanding the respect of their peers Procol Harum remained haunted by the ghost of 'A Whiter Shade Of Pale'. As a result they ignored British audiences for almost 18 months, not returning to the British stage until the autumn of 1968. However, they remained uncertain about the *right* location for the recording of their next album. So once again they hesitated...

As the turbulent sixties drew to a close, 1969 saw debut albums from British artistes Elton John and King Crimson, both of whom utilised writers that, like Keith Reid, delivered lyrics that were later set to music. Bernie Taupin provided songs for Elton John while Pete Sinfield wrote the words for King Crimson. Sinfield cited *Shine On Brightly* as being an "influence" when writing 'Epitaph', and Taupin 'A Whiter Shade Of Pale' on 'Grey Seal'. This was noteworthy praise from Procol's contemporaries.

Over in America Procol's strong reputation was consolidated by the effort they put into touring there. The 'new' American music press, epitomosed by *Rolling Stone* and *Crawdaddy,* was staffed by knowledgeable journalists with a literary bent. These writers gave in-depth analyses of the music scene and its associated counterculture, and were clearly at odds with the British pop papers that, with the exception of *Melody Maker,* still tended towards trivia.

Possibly acknowledging that to be identified with the American counterculture might be to their collective benefit, Procol chose to record their third album at Wally Heider's studio in Los Angeles in the autumn of 1968. Three songs were recorded by Heider: 'Pilgrim's Progress', 'Long Gone Geek' and 'Stoke Poges'. The latter was a Matthew Fisher instrumental, possibly planned as a follow-up to 'Repent Walpurgis', serving as a potential album closer for *A Salty Dog.* Eventually the song was deemed unworkable and dropped. "I don't think 'Stoke Poges' was very good at all," opined Fisher. "In fact I gave away the acetates." *

While in LA, Gary Brooker was contacted by Ron Richards, who had formerly produced The Paramounts. Richards offered Procol Harum the opportunity to work at EMI's Abbey Road Studios, utilising the latest eight-track technology, and Procol Harum quickly headed back to Blighty.

Matthew Fisher: "We'd never been terribly happy with the sound on the first two albums that Denny Cordell produced. So when we got a chance to choose a studio we liked, we chose the place where The Beatles recorded, which was, of course, Abbey Road!"

Following the release of *Shine On Brightly* Fisher's mounting creative frustration was a problem that now needed to be addressed. "I was getting fed up with being on the road and staying in hotels," he says. "I wanted to spend my time in the studio. So on one of the various occasions that 'I'd left Procol' they persuaded me to come back with the proviso that, '*If* you come back, we'll let you produce the next album' which was *A Salty Dog.*"

---

* A Procol Harum multi-track featuring a live performance of 'Stoke Poges' recorded at San Francisco's Fillmore West from November 1, 1968 has yet to surface. Perhaps it was deliberately lost?

With Fisher at the helm and engineer Ken Scott (who had recently worked on The Beatles' 'White Album') ably assisting, production on *A Salty Dog* began in earnest.

Robin Trower: "My overriding memory of those sessions is [of] 'A Salty Dog' for which Gary wrote the music as well as the orchestration. I remember the first time he played it to me, I was just blown away. It turned out really well. It's *such* a beautiful song. It's his masterpiece really."

Matthew Fisher: "'A Salty Dog' has excellent orchestral scoring. In March 1968 we toured Germany with The Bee Gees, who were backed by an orchestra. I remember the viola player giving Gary a few pointers when he was writing 'A Salty Dog'. It turned out to be his masterpiece. I think its Procol's *Citizen Kane*!"

Having had no classical training whatsoever one wonders just how Brooker was able to write such a beautiful and complex score, yet make it weave and flow with such simplicity.

Ken Scott: "My one recollection of the string [overdub] sessions was of Gary conducting 'A Salty Dog'. The orchestra were *very* taken aback by a rock'n'roll longhair leading them."

The basis for Keith Reid's lyrics was widely reported as having been inspired by a line of graffiti that was carved deeply into a bar–room table in Philadelphia. Reid gives the correct version: "In Cleveland, I saw written on a dressing room wall the words, 'Great god skipper, we done run aground.' It's amazing how ideas for a song come about. It all began there really."

American college graduates have since written theses about 'A Salty Dog' which is now seen by many as a modern day equivalent of Coleridge's *The Rhyme Of The Ancient Mariner*. Except in Reid's world the ships don't 'run aground', they 'run afloat!'

A SALTY DOG

All hands on deck, we've run afloat!' I heard the captain cry
'Explore the ship, replace the cook: let no one leave alive!'
Across the straits, around the Horn: how far can sailors fly?
A twisted path, our tortured course, and no one left alive

We sailed for parts unknown to man, where ships come home to die
No lofty peak, nor fortress bold, could match our captain's eye
Upon the seventh seasick day we made our port of call
A sand so white, and sea so blue, no mortal place at all

We fired the gun, and burnt the mast, and rowed from ship to shore
The captain cried, we sailors wept: our tears were tears of joy
Now many moons and many Junes have passed since we made land
A salty dog, this seaman's log: your witness my own hand

'A Salty Dog' is undoubtedly Procol's tour de force and it seemed that everybody connected with it received recognition of some sort, even the humble roadie.

Kellogs: "I remember standing on a chair in the studio in Abbey Road, I was up close against a microphone to play these two notes on this Bosun's Pipe on 'A Salty Dog'. When the record came out I got a credit, 'Kellogs – Bosun's Whistle and Refreshments'. When we went to America, a lot of people would come up to me and said, 'Hey man, are you Kellogs with the refreshments? Hey, I know what you mean by 'refreshments', man. Have some of my shit, man!' It served me in very good stead. I never lacked for the essential herbs of the day, due to that little credit... In truth what I'd *really* done was go across the road from the studios to get the band cups of tea, and plates of egg and chips!"

Over the years, 'A Salty Dog' went on to inspire several interesting cover versions. Artists as diverse as Billy Joel, Sarah Brightman, Marc Almond and Jan Akkerman (formerly of the Dutch group Focus) have all recorded the song with varying degrees of success. Almond's version was released in 1986 as part of *A Woman's Story*, a collection of cover versions aptly sub-titled 'Some Songs To Take To The Tomb.'

"When we first got to Abbey Road," Fisher recalls, "there were a lot of instruments lying around, including a large mellotron, which we didn't use, the harmonium used by The Beatles on 'We Can Work It Out' and an upright detuned piano. It was rumoured that this was the piano used by Russ Conway on his hits of the late fifties. I think Gary tried the piano out and decided that it was the right sound for 'The Milk

Of Human Kindness'. I think this was just an instant reaction to the sound rather than anything more pre-meditated."

While maybe not Russ Conway, Brooker's honky tonk piano style on 'The Milk Of Human Kindness' certainly has echoes of The Band about it. The American music writer Paul Williams, founder of *Crawdaddy* magazine, alluded to The Band's *Music From Big Pink* in his liner notes for Procol's second album, *Shine On Brightly*, in which he staked a big claim when suggesting that The Band had been "influenced" by Procol's debut album – a claim later refuted by Robbie Robertson. If truth be told, the influence was surely the other way around. Brooker had seen Bob Dylan on stage as early as 1966 on Dylan's controversial 'electric' tour where he was backed by The Hawks, The Band's original name.

Rumours abound that Procol jammed with members of The Band and Van Morrison's group while rehearsing songs destined for *A Salty Dog* at Garth Hudson's house in Woodstock – a story that Fisher refutes. However The Band's distinctive sound would clearly serve as an inspiration on Brooker and Procol Harum from that point onwards.

'Too Much Between Us', co-written by Trower-Brooker-Reid, is a delicate acoustic collaboration featuring Brooker's voice at its most sensitive, clearly displaying his versatility as a singer. Reid's lyrics feature the line, '*There's too much sea between us*' and with 'Too Much Between Us' being one of four compositions on the album alluding to water, some music writers mistakenly reached the conclusion that *A Salty Dog* was a concept album about the sea. Albums such as The Pretty Things' *S F Sorrow* and The Who's *Tommy* were released around this juncture, and possibly played a part in such erroneous thematic assumptions.

Co-written by Brooker and Reid while Procol were staying at Woodstock, 'The Devil Came From Kansas' was rehearsed on the Hohner Pianet that Brooker took on tour with him for composing (and the same piano he'd used since his days in The Paramounts) and became a live standard at many Procol shows of the period. The studio recording featured un-credited backing vocals from Brooker's wife, Franky, and Keith Reid.

"'The Devil Came From Kansas' came about because I've always liked Randy Newman," says Reid. "I bought his first album, which featured a song called 'The Beehive State'. It had a line about a corrupt senator from [Kansas]. That inspired the song."

THE DEVIL CAME FROM KANSAS*

The devil came from Kansas, where he went to I can't say
Though I teach I'm not a preacher, and I aim to stay that way
There's a monkey riding on my back, been there for some time
He says he knows me very well but he's no friend of mine

'Boredom', credited to Fisher, Brooker and Reid, is an uptempo number featuring a marimba, discovered in the instrument cupboard at Abbey Road. As The Beatles had discovered, this mythical cupboard full of strange and unfamiliar instruments helped to enlarge many a record's sonic palette. "EMI always had lots of interesting things lying around," says Ken Scott, "and as more multi-tracks for recording became available, it allowed for more musical experimentation ..."

Matthew Fisher: "The cupboard was full of all kinds of goodies: wooden blocks, tambourines, xylophones, glockenspiels, marimbas, and flutes. [For 'Boredom'] Rob chose the tambourine with sleigh bells to play. I played acoustic guitar on the basic track. I think it was my idea to add the marimba and recorders. The recorders would have been taped on a different day, since they didn't come from the Abbey Road cupboard. They were brought in by me and Gary. I brought in a treble recorder and Gary a descant. I think the idea of the recorders was influenced by my enthusiasm for a track [released in 1958] called 'Tom Hark' by Elias & His Zig-Zag Jive Flutes."

As with 'A Salty Dog', 'Boredom' brought forth several cover versions; the first by Mitch Ryder on his 1969 album *The Detroit Memphis Experiment*, featuring Ryder playing alongside Procol's Stax

---

* The earliest British cover of 'The Devil Came From Kansas' was undertaken in 1969 by Glaswegian blue-eyed soul singer Frankie Miller and his first band The Stoics. This led to a lifelong friendship between Procol Harum and Frankie.

Records heroes Booker T & The MGs. Progressive rock outfit Tea & Symphony recorded an impressive version for EMI's Harvest label in 1969, while folk duo Tir Na Nog provided an acoustic interpretation in a live setting. The Beatniks, an avant-garde Japanese band, also put their stamp on it.

A 12-bar blues, inspired by his lifelong love of Muddy Waters, 'Juicy John Pink' was Robin Trower's first composition for Procol Harum. "Robin came up with the music for 'Juicy John Pink' and it just sounded like an early blues," says Brooker. "I wasn't really a writer at the time," Trower adds, "I was just lucky to come up with some ideas."

'Juicy John Pink' was recorded at the Rolling Stones' original rehearsal space – now the headquarters of *The Stage* media newspaper – in Bermondsey Street, South East London

Gary Brooker: "Ian Stewart, who was The Rolling Stones' piano player cum roadie who looked after everything for the Stones, said, 'You can produce this here. All you need is a couple of mics.'"

With the railway arches near to the studio providing a haven for the numerous meths-drinking tramps living underneath, a clue emerges as to who Reid's 'Juicy John Pink' character could be. Brooker sings in character, "*Well I opened my eyes this morning, I thought I must be dead!*" 'A Salty Dog' indeed!

'The Wreck Of The Hesperus', sung by Fisher who composed the melody, was Procol's second song to feature a full orchestral accompaniment. Matthew Fisher: "With 'The Wreck Of The Hesperus', I was thinking of Phil Spector meets Tchaikovsky. I do remember I was looking at the scores of Tchaikovsky's Sixth Symphony and working out how he did *this* or how they got *that* effect. I think 'The Wreck Of The Hesperus' had some post production in New York at Phil Ramone's A&R Studios, which used to be CBS Studios. I think it was *only* my stuff we worked on there. I suppose I was more sensitive about what was wrong with my songs, so I guess more time was spent getting [things] right."

'All This And More' proceeds at a stately pace with Brooker's impassioned vocals and regal piano juxtaposed against Trower's chugging bluesy licks. Matthew Fisher: "Gary announced that he'd also done a small arrangement for trombones for the end of 'All This And More'. I think this was a try-out, but everybody liked it so it was used."

The punning title of 'Crucifiction Lane' (Trower/Reid) came from a Bermondsey street called Crucifix Lane, adjacent to where The Rolling Stones' rehearsal studio was located. This was another of the album's songs to make reference to 'the sea' – the line "*And if the sea were not so salty*", sung, unusually, by Trower in a rather bluesy mid-Atlantic vocal style perhaps with Otis Redding in mind.

For 'Pilgrim's Progress', Fisher composed the melody as well as singing and playing virtually every instrument including the Phil Spector-like bells at the end. The song's haunting hymnal quality was inspired by The Bee Gees but Fisher now feels the vocal should have been handled by Brooker.[*]

Interestingly, recently discovered EMI studio tapes for alternate versions of 'Pilgrim's Progress', 'The Wreck Of The Hesperus', and 'Boredom' cite Ron Richards as 'producer'. So was Richards asked to produce 'A Salty Dog' at some stage? "There was never a possibility that Ron Richards might produce *A Salty Dog*," Reid insists, "It was never *ever* discussed."

Ken Scott: "... [as a producer] Matthew Fisher was always very easy to work with. They all were. Very enjoyable sessions all round. Matthew felt, not unsurprisingly, more like a member of the band than a producer."

It's to both Brooker and Fisher's credit that *A Salty Dog* ended up becoming a genuine product of group unity. Each artist was given a 'director' role for his own song: Trower oversaw the recording of his own compositions while Fisher paid attention to his. By mixing and matching – Brooker and Trower on 'Too Much Between Us' and Brooker and Fisher on 'Boredom' – Procol had discovered a new winning formula.

---

[*] Ironically Gary Brooker would continue to sing 'Pilgrim's Progress' up until 1973, some four years after Fisher's departure from Procol Harum. He delivered a particularly good version during the band's appearance on the *Beat Club Workshop* TV show, transmitted in Germany from Bremen on Christmas Eve 1971.

Oddly one great song, 'Long Gone Geek', was omitted from the running order, and instead became the B-side to 'A Salty Dog', perhaps because 'Geek' was the only good recording from the earlier and otherwise aborted Wally Heider sessions. Reid's lyric, written before his first trip to the USA in autumn 1967, concerns a gun toting tabby cat, while Brooker's shout of "Procol Harum" off-microphone near the end makes cryptic reference to the Burmese Blue cat that originally inspired the band's name. Reid gleaned the word 'geek' from Dylan's 'Highway 61 Revisited' and the 'Pinstriped Sweet' character, "*the convict in Cell 15*", was already familiar from Brooker's final yell in 'Lime Street Blues' (the B-side to 'A Whiter Shade Of Pale'.) "Musically, 'Long Gone Geek' was a Small Faces-influenced piece," Fisher admits.

Continuing in the tradition of memorable Procol album sleeves, the cover for *A Salty Dog* was designed by Keith Reid's "muse", his girlfriend Dickinson. Essentially a parody of the old Player's Navy Cut cigarette packet, the painting of the bearded sailor framed by a life belt is now rightly regarded as one of rock's most iconic sleeves and continues to feature in numerous anthologies of album covers to this day.

While the sleeve continues to have a longevity of its own, the album itself deserves to be rehabilitated as it is every bit as magnificent as any of the great late Sixties albums that continue to be lauded in polls and retrospectives. Still sounding as crisp, clear, and emotive as the day it was issued, the music has a timeless quality to it yet it is somewhat overlooked in rock's annals. *A Salty Dog*'s strength resides not only in the power of its highly melodic compositions, but also in the passionate performances in evidence from everybody involved.

If anything Procol Harum's third album deserves to be heralded as one of the finest ever to be produced in a British recording studio. Following unanimous critical praise from the UK music press, and in recognition of the vast contribution that any engineer makes to a great record, *Music Week* cited Ken Scott as being 'The Best Studio Engineer Of 1969'.

Ken Scott: "I received no award for *A Salty Dog*. Now I must emphasize that that doesn't mean that one wasn't given. EMI Studios, at the time, didn't want engineers to get *any* form of credit for their work, hence no awards. I can't honestly say that it affected my career one way or the other. The title track, however, is still one of my favourite recordings, and, in my mind, one of my best."

In recognition of its epic nature, 'A Salty Dog' was released as a British single a month ahead of the album's June 1969 issue, but it was far from plain sailing when competing against the bubblegum pop of Clodagh Rodgers and Tommy Roe, and it ran aground at number 44. The album met a worse fate by failing to chart despite every review speaking of the album in glowing terms – *Melody Maker*'s Chris Welch described it as 'Procol's finest hour'. Inevitably *A Salty Dog* fared more successfully across the Atlantic, reaching 32 on the *Billboard* Hot 100. [Reissued in early 1972 as a 'double' with Procol's debut album, *A Salty Dog* eventually reached a UK chart position of 27]

The live debut of songs from *A Salty Dog* took place at the massive Palm Springs Festival in California on April 6, 1969.

Matthew Fisher: "We sat down on stage, I turned on the Hammond, cranked it up, pulled out the pedal drawer bar, and there was this horrendous hum! I looked round and there was some prat with his foot on one of my pedals. So I went, 'Fuck off'. He looked like some old tramp who'd just wandered onstage. Then the guy who was originally going to announce us goes on to introduce the prat who'd been standing on my bass pedal as 'Doctor Timothy Leary'!"

Gary Brooker: "Doctor Timothy Leary had this little phrase, 'Turn On, Tune In, Drop Out!'... But when he introduced us he'd invented this *new* phrase. So he shouts out, 'Keep Doing It. Keep Smoking It. Get It On!' The audience became so wild and unruly that police helicopters and riot police were brought in to disperse everyone during Ike & Tina Turner's electrifying performance shortly afterwards."

Having not played a major gig in Britain since early 1968, Procol finally returned home amidst much speculation as to whether they'd actually turn up to the Camden Fringe Free Festival on Parliament Hill Fields, in London's Hampstead Heath, on Sunday, May 18, where they topped the bill over Soft Machine, Yes and Blossom Toes.

"When you've not played a gig in your home country for that long at that stage in your career," said Brooker. "It means a lot to play to a large audience that you *hope* will appreciate you."

The tiny concrete stage was surrounded by a sea of photographers and among the crowd was future BBC Radio 1 DJ Bob Harris who later noted, "On a balmy day at sunset Procol made a triumphant return to the UK with strong performances from their new album the magnificent *A Salty Dog.*"

A Salty Dog received its Canadian festival debut at the Toronto Festival on June 22 where Procol shared billing alongside The Band, Chuck Berry, Steppenwolf and Blood Sweat & Tears in front of an audience of 50,000.

Promoter Bill Graham booked Procol Harum to headline over The Byrds at his Fillmore East Theatre in New York on June 27 and 28. The reviews following these shows were some of the best that Procol Harum ever received. Going from strength to strength, Procol went on to share top billing with their blues heroes Muddy Waters and John Lee Hooker; headlining over the mighty MC5, Iggy & the Stooges, and Bob Seger at Michigan's largest ever music festival Saugatuck on July 5.

Another 'first' occurred the following day when Procol's first live collaboration with an orchestra took place at the annual Stratford Festival in Ontario, Canada. Although pop groups like The Bee Gees had previously played concerts with orchestral backing, this was the first occasion that a serious rock band had been invited to perform live in concert with an orchestra at a prestigious event.

Gary Brooker: "It came about for two reasons. Firstly, there was the pure fact that 'A Salty Dog' had a string arrangement which was not pop, it was more classical. Secondly, there was the song that Matthew did, 'The Wreck Of The Hesperus'. It was more or less decided that 'In Held 'Twas In I' would also be an ideal thing to play too, with an orchestra. I did the orchestration ... The Stratford Festival was a very interesting festival. There was a lot of Shakespeare done there. There was also music going on there as well. In fact the choir that we had was not an official choir. Sunday was a day off, you see, and all the actors and actresses were our choir. They were in fact standing on the imaginary

Romeo And Juliet balcony over a stage. The set was still there and they were all up there on the balcony giving it some real shtick these actors, but they could *really* sing!"

Kellogs: "The orchestra played on a few selected numbers: 'In Held 'Twas In I' and 'A Salty Dog'. It was in the round and the band played at the bottom in a pit with the audience all around us. In those days bands didn't carry sound systems around. We unusually had a sound system probably because we had these strings, and probably because it was a test gig; something innovative that had *never* been done before; a rock band and orchestra playing live together. This was the first gig of its kind; pioneering. Deep Purple also did something similar, but that was later."*

Gary Brooker: "The Stratford Festival Orchestra was especially made up for the festival featuring the best musicians in Canada who were always booked for this very important annual arts event. I loved it. I mean at the end of 'In Held 'Twas In I' I was almost in tears. To hear this suddenly played live and with a great choir belting it out, and it rose to a tremendous crescendo. I thought it was bloody marvellous. And to play 'A Salty Dog' with a big orchestra was just fantastic, a great experience.

"Rob Trower hated it, because we had to play *very* quietly. It didn't bother me because I'm a piano player so just don't mic it so much, don't turn it up so much. The feel is still there for me. Same for the organ. It was difficult for drums, but BJ loved it. And it was very difficult for guitar, but Rob I think had trouble getting the sound that he was used to, whilst at the same time being quiet. Rob does like to be ever so loud..."

Kellogs: "I'd been up for four days straight. I'd probably driven there from Detroit. So I was very tired. Suddenly at a crucial moment in the show there was no live vocal coming out. So I went into this pit, testing every lead, cable, and canon plug to find out where the problem was, right in the middle of the show. By a process of elimination *nothing* worked!

---

* Deep Purple performed their 'Concerto For Group And Orchestra', written by organist Jon Lord and performed by the London Philharmonic Orchestra conducted by Malcolm Arnold, at the Royal Albert Hall on September 24, 1969.

I took my woolly hat off and threw it on the ground in frustration, and I got a round of applause from the audience. The problem was resolved when Ronnie Lyons, our tour manager and sometimes sound mixer, suddenly remembered to turn up the vocalist's sound pot [on the mixer desk]. I still have the woolly hat!"

Throughout August the band continued to appear at all the major American music festivals which were now seen as the ultimate revenue-generating exercise for promoters. On August 1 the band played at the Atlantic City Pop Festival in front of 110,000, sharing the bill with Janis Joplin, Creedence Clearwater Revival, The Byrds, and B B King, among others. The following day Procol Harum played The Singer Bowl Music Festival in Flushing Meadows in Queens, New York, with The Moody Blues, NRBQ, and billtoppers Steppenwolf.

Procol were also invited to perform at the Woodstock Festival held the weekend of August 15-17. Had they accepted the offer, Procol would have appeared on the final evening of Sunday, August 17 shortly before Crosby, Stills, Nash & Young. As time would show, Woodstock turned out to be the most famous rock festival of them all and the associated soundtrack is still the largest-selling music festival soundtrack ever. The feature film (edited by a team that included Martin Scorsese) grossed millions of dollars internationally and the DVD continues to recoup revenue from around the globe. So why did the band elect not to appear?

Gary Brooker: "We'd played at most major American festivals from 1968 onwards. Just about all of them."

Keith Reid: "We were on some really long three month American tour and just towards the end of it, I think the Woodstock thing came up ..."

Gary Brooker: "... and Robin Trower's wife, Andrea, was expecting a baby."

Keith Reid: "There was no way we could continue the tour and go and play Woodstock."

Gary Brooker: "Every artist who was on there got tremendous exposure, and became legendary, even when, in some cases, they didn't especially deserve it ..."

Robin Trower: "I often wondered what would have happened if we'd played Woodstock. Had Procol done it and been in the film, I think they would've been a much bigger band, and much more successful... I think the rest of my life would've been completely different!"

Gary Brooker: "Anyway, the trouble was, the baby ended up two weeks late!"

When the band came off the road things came to a head with Matthew Fisher vis-a-vis future Procol tours and his continued role in the band.

Gary Brooker: "I started to recognise a recurrent scenario with Matthew. As soon as he went out on the road, he didn't like it very much. He didn't like being away from home. He didn't like being in a hotel room. He didn't like travelling and flying. There was no aspect to it that he liked. And *even* if he *had* enjoyed it, or even if he did enjoy playing organ on stage for a couple of hours every night, that wasn't enough for him, you know, to make the day worth it. And he moaned about this *all* the time. I mean this went on for a couple of years! What Matthew really wanted to do was to be a producer or an engineer and to work in a studio, and get to know more about *that* side of things."

Eventually the decision was made that Fisher would stay on and work for Procol in his capacity as producer for the band's next album. The organist was not the only band member whose role was being re-evaluated.

Gary Brooker: "We wondered where could Procol Harum go now? And the decision was made that we needed somebody that was a bit more lively and musical on the bass. I don't know why Dave Knights got the brunt end of that. He was a nice bass player, and he had an interesting style, particularly when you listen back to him now. I know when Dave Bronze (Procol's bass player from 1991-1993) listened to a track to get exactly the feel that Dave Knights got – there was a bit more to it than meets the eye."

Following his departure from Procol, via Robin Trower, Knights got in touch with Southend-On-Sea musician Mickey Jupp who was then living in Bath and the pair hatched plans for a new band called Legend. At the request of Knights, Trower produced the single 'Georgia

George' B/W 'July' released by Bell Records in October 1969. Fisher played bass and Wilson drummed on the record.* Knights got Legend a three album deal on Vertigo Records from 1969 to 1971 with Tony Visconti producing. "If it hadn't have been for David Knights," Jupp acknowledges, "Legend would never have existed."

"Dave Knights wasn't just a simple bass plodder," says Brooker. "He was in some kind of strange McCartney school that's sort of different in some way. But I used to have to tell him a lot of things to play. It was different in those days. There were a lot of different bass notes used with chords – not the ones the bass player would usually play. It would be something different, which made it sound different. I remember I always had to explain the arrangement. So I think we probably thought that we needed different blood down at the bottom end there, in order to progress, to move on."

It was Robin Trower who took the lead in planning the next phase of Procol's career, suggesting the recruitment of old Southend school chum and former Paramounts bass player Chris Copping, who had just completed a post graduate degree in chemistry. "The idea at that point," says Copping, "was to bring some more R&B back into the band's overall sound. The plan was to revert back to being a four-piece as we had been in The Paramounts."

"It was a very strange decision to become a four-piece," says Brooker. "I kind of went along with it. It was probably something we talked about with Robin. We weren't getting rid of the five instrument idea. We were now getting it out of four people instead. This meant that we had to use different combinations. Either we didn't have an organ, and Chris Copping played the bass, which he could do, or we didn't use guitar and Rob played the bass. When we needed all five instruments Chris Copping had to play with his left hand on the bass keyboard, similar to the method that Ray Manzarek employed with The Doors whom we'd both seen and supported in America ... So we had these

---

* Also around this time, BJ Wilson guested on the track 'Hurt Somebody' from Leon Russell's Denny Cordell-produced début album.

three ways of playing things. And it would depend on the song, which combination we used. Where Rob played nothing on 'A Salty Dog' – never had – he played the bass on it, and we had piano, organ and drums."

With this new approach in mind, Procol cancelled all of their scheduled autumn gigs in order to rehearse and work up new material for the band's next album. A country cottage provided the setting throughout the winter of late 1969 and early 1970.

During this sabbatical Procol were asked to appear on *Disco 2* the BBC's forerunner to *The Old Grey Whistle Test*. With the new look four-piece still considerably under-rehearsed, Gary Brooker called upon former bandmates Matthew Fisher and Dave Knights, who joined Brooker, Wilson and Trower to videotape the TV show in early November. 'Repent Walpurgis' and 'Conquistador' were recorded at BBC TV Centre for transmission on January 17, 1970. This proved to be the final performance with the old line-up.

Ironically, the 'new' four man version of Procol featuring 'new man' Chris Copping then flew to Germany to record a TV special with Dusty Springfield which was transmitted by WDR on December 15. Procol were seen miming and debuting a new Robin Trower song called 'Whisky Train' from a newly pre-recorded backing track. This indicated the shape of things to come.

Copping's actual 'live debut' with Procol Harum took place in London on December 21, supporting The Rolling Stones on two 'Midnight Court' shows at the Lyceum Ballroom off the Strand. The Stones had just returned from their first major American tour in three years which culminated in the notorious Altamont debacle; and the Lyceum gigs were a testament to their rejuvenated love for the stage.

Chris Copping: "It was our first gig with a four-piece on stage, apart from Keith Reid's brief appearance to play the Hammond organ on 'Piggy Pig Pig'. It was also the first time we had to play musical chairs; 'Shine On Brightly' was me on keyboard bass (on top of the Hammond); 'Still There'll Be More' was me on bass, no organ; 'A Salty Dog' and 'A Whiter Shade Of Pale' was Robin on bass, no guitar, etc. We started with 'Pale', but the Hammond had not been switched on correctly, resulting in a low droning note when the definitive phrase should have opened the whole show!"

Jeff Dexter, who was the evening's MC, recalls Procol "being on fine form".

Kellogs: "I remember on that particular night, Keith Reid played the Hammond organ. And I'm pretty sure that this was the only time he ever did so live."

The Paramounts circa 1964; left to right: Robin Trower, BJ Wilson, Gary Brooker and Diz Derrick.

Guy Stevens—DJ, impresario, supplier of songs for The Paramounts, and creator of Procol Harum's name—was also the man who coined the phrase 'A Whiter Shade Of Pale'. GERED MANKOWITZ/REDFERNS

A Paramounts gig poster from The Tavern Club, Dereham from May 1966. COURTESY OF NICK SANDS

The Paramounts' EMI Parlophone Records' press photo from early 1964; left to right: Robin Trower, Gary Brooker, BJ Wilson and Diz Derrick. COURTESY OF HENRY SCOTT-IRVINE

Drummer Bill Eyden, who played on Procol's debut single 'A Whiter Shade Of Pale' because new drummer Bobby Harrison had only *just* been hired and was unready.

Pirate radio ship Radio London, the first station to air 'A Whiter Shade Of Pale'. MIRRORPIX

Procol Harum in London, May 1967; left to right: Bobby Harrison, Matthew Fisher, Gary Brooker, Dave Knights and Ray Royer.
COURTESY OF FLY RECORDS

Sunday
4th June 1967
TWO PERFORMANCES
in order of appearance

SAVILLE
THEATRE
nd Perf. 8-30
JUNE 4

STALLS
£1/-/-

025

To be Retained

DENNY LAINE
ITH HIS ELECTRIC STRING BAND
PROCOL HARUM
THE CHIFFONS

intermission

JIMI HENDRIX EXPERIENCE
FOR YOU

Apollo and the nine Muses :   Clio — history
                                      Euterpe — flute play
(Caption to outside cover)   Thalio — comedy
                                      Melpomene — tragedy
                                      Terpsichore — dance
                                      Erator — love poetry
                                      Polymnia — mimic art
                                      Urania — astronomy
                                      Calliope — epic poetry

A flyer promoting Procol Harum's support slot for Jimi Hendrix at London's Saville Theatre, June 1967. COURTESY OF NICK SANDS

Gary Brooker (at the piano), Keith Reid (seated) and Dave Knights (playing bass) at Advision Studios for the re-recording of Procol Harum's debut album in the summer of 1967. ROGER BAMBER/DAILY MAIL/REX FEATURES

Procol Harum arrive at London's Heathrow Airport after their first American tour in November 1967; left to right: BJ Wilson, Dave Knights, Matthew Fisher, Robin Trower and Gary Brooker (behind Robin). HOWARD/EVENING NEWS/REX FEATURES

Gary Brooker in 1967. HARRY GOODWIN/REX FEATURES

EMI Regal Zonophone's *Procol Harum* album press launch at EMI Records HQ in Manchester Square, London, January 1968; left to right: band manager Tony Secunda, an unknown EMI executive, Dave Knights, Gary Brooker and BJ Wilson. COURTESY OF FLY RECORDS

Camden Fringe Free Festival on Parliament Hill Fields, Hampstead, in the summer of 1969: Dave Knights (bass), John 'Kellogs' Kalinowski (behind cymbals), Matthew Fisher (Hammond organ) and Robin Trower (guitar). TONY JONES, COURTESY OF KENNY WHITE

A Salty Dog (1969), Procol Harum's third album, is widely regarded as their finest work. The iconic artwork, by Dickinson, Keith Reid's girlfriend, is based on a Players Navy Cut cigarette packet. COURTESY OF FLY RECORDS AND SALVO RECORDS

BJ Wilson with his wife Sue backstage at the Camden Fringe Free Festival on Parliament Hill Fields, 1969. TONY JONES. COURTESY OF KENNY WHITE

Gary Brooker, sporting a bowler hat, sharing a joke with members of The Creation and friends in Geneva in 1969. ERICH BACHMANN COURTESY OF KENNY WHITE

Keith Reid in 1967. HARRY GOODWIN/REX FEATURES

Chapter 5

Back Home

1970

*"This was the biggest band I'd ever worked with!
I was suddenly working as a producer and flying solo in my own right!"*
Chris Thomas

In the winter of 1969 and 1970 Matthew Fisher became Procol's producer of the forthcoming *Home* album, alongside engineer Ken Scott, for recording sessions at Trident Studios, but things didn't work out even though it was essentially the same production team that had made *A Salty Dog*. Fisher felt like he 'was no longer one of the gang' and noticed that his role had been demoted to that of fixer-cum-roadie. "Whenever they needed a Hammond organ they'd ask to borrow mine," he says, "and I'd have to drive all the way down to their country cottage with this damned thing in the back of the van. Then one of their roadies managed to lose the Hammond. I mean how can you *lose* a Hammond? They're huge and weigh a ton! So I thought sod this for a game of coconuts, and quit!"

According to Chris Copping, five songs were laid down at this session: 'Piggy Pig Pig', 'Nothing That I Didn't Know', 'Whisky Train', 'Dead Man's Dream' and 'Your Own Choice', but the recordings were officially scrapped and both Scott and Fisher parted company with Procol. Fisher went off to set up his own demo studio in Kingston, Surrey, whilst Scott went on to work on George Harrison's *All Things Must Pass*, which also featured Gary Brooker. Meanwhile, during early 1970, Procol picked up the pieces and went back to rehearse more new material in the country cottage rented by BJ Wilson.

Kellogs: "I have fond memories of Malt Mayes cottage in Horsham, Sussex. We had a barn in which the band could rehearse and "get their shit together", as we used to say in those days. There was a really old traditional pub nearby with a big log fire. All the band's wives came to visit on various occasions. A then girlfriend of mine, whom I had met in San Francisco, flew in to stay with me."

Chris Copping: "We stayed at Malt Mayes and I remember it snowed a lot. My brother Robin filmed a documentary about the band, which was later shown on Australian TV. It was called *The Procol Harum*."*

Nevertheless, at the beginning of 1970 Procol Harum's mood was upbeat. Keith Reid and Gary Brooker had just signed up with a new management company called Chrysalis, headed by Chris Wright and Terry Ellis whose right hand man, Doug D'Arcy, became Procol's fourth manager.

Determined to take care of ongoing business, Brooker and Reid formed a new music publishing company called Blue Beard Music to represent new Brooker-Reid songs, with both Brooker and Reid becoming 'equal shareholders' and 'co-exective directors' in this partnership. The agreed split would be 50/50 on any future song revenue. Meanwhile, the pair also set up a production company (and management company) called Strongman Productions, with both Brooker and Reid again as co-executive directors in order to protect their continuing mutual interests.

---

* The soundtrack of this revealing documentary featured four of the five songs produced by Matthew Fisher at the Trident sessions with Procol miming along to the tracks.

Former Paramounts producer Ron Richards suggested Abbey Road alumnus Chris Thomas might be suitable as a new producer for the group. So it was in this positive climate that Procol Harum went about making their fourth album, entitled *Home*.

Chris Thomas: "I was working at George Martin's newly formed AIR Studios. Hollies producer Ron Richards introduced me to Gary Brooker at AIR one day. The pair suggested that I might like to produce [Procol's] forthcoming album *Home*. I was really just a new boy to these things and I jumped at the chance to produce a name band!"

Procol were subsequently booked into EMI Studios at Abbey Road in the early spring of 1970. Having worked under the tutelage of George Martin on the Beatles' 'White Album' sessions, Thomas proved to be a brilliant choice, helping to capture Procol at their most magnificent. Even at this point, thanks to the Malt Mayes rehearsals, the band were already tight and would often warm up at the sessions with dynamic covers of rock'n'roll classics such as 'High School Confidential', 'Matchbox', and 'Down The Line'. This helped to fire them up with a completely re-invented vigour when tackling the new songs.

'Whisky Train', the album's opener, which also happened to be the very first track Thomas ever recorded with Procol, was laid down with a minimum of fuss as Thomas light-heartedly recalls: "At that time they were talking about having had problems with a guy who was managing them in the States. I naturally felt very sorry for them... Afterwards, Robin Trower [the song's composer] came into the control room, and asked me if I could turn the guitar up? I think he thought I was being a bit stroppy 'cos I said, 'No!' Robin said to me, 'Whaddya mean, no?' I said, 'Well it's on two-track!' He said, 'Whaddya mean?' I said, 'We've recorded it. It's live. We've recorded it onto stereo'. Robin went, 'What? Why aren't you recording in eight-track?' I said, 'Well you told me that you were skint and I just tried to save you some money. And that's it'. And that *was* it! It's the track you hear on the album. The *very* first take ...

"So I was *very* nervous and conscious of wanting to save Procol loads of money. Anyway I got severely chastised by Procol who all collectively stated, 'We will be doing the album in eight track *not* two track'. So eight-track was the order of the day!"

The percussion work on 'Whisky Train' is trademark BJ Wilson, in particular his use of cymbals, hi hat and cowbell. Around this time, The Who's Keith Moon became an admirer and friend of BJ Wilson and although to become friends with Moon was a chancy business health-wise The Who's drummer was not one to bestow praise loosely. Al Kooper, musical Zelig and a former collaborator of Bob Dylan, recently covered 'Whisky Train' with considerable aplomb.

'Dead Man's Dream' was erroneously revealed by Reid in Robin Copping's 1970 *Procol Harum* documentary as having been inspired by *Midnight Cowboy* although none of the words actually pay reference to that Oscar winning movie. "It was not inspired by *Midnight Cowboy*," Reid now says, laughing. "Edgar Allan Poe would be *more* likely!" Seen from the perspective of a deceased person 'Dead Man's Dream' was considered to be so 'disturbing' that John Peel's peers banned it from airplay after it was recorded for a BBC Radio 1 *Top Gear-In Concert* special.

'*I'll blacken your Christmas and piss on your door,*' wrote Reid in 'Still There'll Be More', an uptempo rocker composed by Brooker. Reid later explained on Texas Radio's *The Big Beat* that the song was, "supposed to be a venomous outpouring at someone by really telling somebody off!" An existing early outtake of the song begins with the band in high spirits. Buzzers keep ringing, possibly the night bell at Abbey Road Studios? The band can be heard mimicking Terry Jones' cackling 'old mother' character from *Monty Python's Flying Circus* (which had recently begun on the BBC) with outbursts of "allo!" being shouted out by various band members. Brooker is heard to say, "The producer is losing his temper". To which Trower replies, "The bass player is losing his hair!" This is met by peals of laughter all round.*

'Nothing That I Didn't Know' is an acoustic lament with superb vocalising from Brooker who is unusually accompanied by his own

---

* When the author played this tape to Chris Thomas over three decades later, he smiled fondly when recollecting those heady sessions.

accordion playing. Wilson's precise metronomic drumming drives the piece providing a dark and intense beauty as a counterpoint to this delicate ballad.

'About To Die' is a Trower/Reid composition with a curious theology by Reid. The original lyrics occasionally differ to those which Brooker actually sings on the track – a habit of Bob Dylan's with many of his early published compositions. Along with several other *Home* songs, it soon established itself in the band's set list.

Chris Copping: "As we were taping 'About To Die', Paul McCartney was recording his first album in a neighbouring studio at Abbey Road. I remember hearing the mix of McCartney's 'Maybe I'm Amazed' and being pretty *amazed* by it at the time. I believe he had his guitar through a fairly beaten up Leslie speaker. Robin put his Gibson guitar through the very same speaker [not literally] the next day when we recorded 'About To Die'. And it came out sounding just right!"

'Barnyard Story' was the third song on the album to allude to mortality – '*I was living in a graveyard. Maybe death will be my cure*' – and was also the second song to be recorded on the first evening that Thomas worked with Procol. "The next song we recorded after 'Whisky Train' was 'Barnyard Story', which was a piano, vocal and organ piece only... At that point everybody else went home for the night, whilst Gary sat alone in the studio in the dark having decided to have a crack at doing 'Barnyard Stories'".

"Gary sang this line: '*I once stood on a lamp post*'. I said, 'What's that '*I stood on a lamp post*' line about then, Gary?' Keith Reid, who I thought had gone home, shouted out from somewhere in the dark, '*I stood on Olympus!*' Anyway, despite this faux pas, they allowed me back the next day."

'Piggy Pig Pig', featuring Copping on Hammond organ, went on to become a particular Procol favourite and still features in their set lists to this day.

Gary Brooker: "'Piggy Pig Pig' used diminished chords. I felt that these 'diminished chords' should be examined and used a bit more. Those classical things were in there a lot at the beginning with us. Mainly as little influences, not as smart-arsed quotes, and because I thought, 'Oh, they were good chords'. A couple of classical notes can often set you off on something, and you can take them in a different direction when used within a rock context."

"Those classical things" were an integral part of the widescreen concept for 'Whaling Stories', a song that Brooker would often introduce on stage as "the Procol Blues". It was a magnificent magnum opus; a surreal, nightmarish sea–shanty. "Let's have every verse different and not like a pop song," was Reid's maxim.

Asked if the lyric's first word is 'Pailing' or 'Paling' Reid cannot remember, but he refutes that the latter spelling was a nod back to 'A Whiter Shade Of Pale'.

Gary Brooker: "It wouldn't have been a reference to that song, no. In fact we stopped doing 'Pale' live at that point. We left 'A Whiter Shade Of Pale' out of our repertoire for almost three years. 'Whaling Stories' was a long piece to start with: 16 lines across four verses. And it had changes all the way through. In the end we decided to include a big choir of voices as we were not all that good at harmonies ourselves. So Chris Thomas rounded up the Ealing Technical College Choir, and they all came along to the studio session. They were pretty awful at first. So we sent out for some beer, but after that they sounded *even* worse. Anyway, we got it down eventually and it turned out well."

With 'Whaling Stories' the group entered into realms that were almost Wagnerian, not only in terms of the song's epic proportions, but also its gothic qualities. "It had so many complex chords," says Chris Copping. "It was like the effect of daylight on a vampire to a blues guitarist, but Robin Trower drove his bus straight through these gothic chord structures with such power and authority that it had to be right!"

Both musically and lyrically the song was simply groundbreaking. Rock music had never fully explored this territory before, and with both 'Whaling Stories' and 'Barnyard Story', Brooker and Reid unwittingly helped to give birth to that dubious beast, 'Progressive Rock'. 'Whaling Stories' had to be an influence on many exponents of the genre. Artists such as ELP, Yes and Queen all owe a vast debt to Procol Harum, and the example set by 'Whaling Stories'. Queen's Brian May has certainly gone on record citing Procol Harum as "an influence" while Rick

Wakeman is still an admirer. Of course these groups ultimately became far more successful and self-indulgent than Procol Harum.

'Your Own Choice' concludes with an uncredited chromatic harp solo provided by Harry Pitch, well-known to British audiences of the long-running BBC TV comedy series *Last Of The Summer Wine*, which features Pitch's playing on the theme tune.* '*There's too many poets and not enough rhyme...*' wrote Reid, gently mocking his own craft at the end of 'Your Own Choice', concluding what many consider to be one of Procol's finest albums.

There is an underlying theme of 'death' on *Home*, most notably in the songs 'Dead Man's Dream' and 'About To Die'. Reid furthered this gothic theme in the lyrics for 'Nothing That I Didn't Know' – "*Twenty-six, and now she's dead, I wish that I could have died instead*" – and 'Whaling Stories' – "*Those at peace shall see their wake*". In the light of this darkness, one could be excused for considering *Home* to be a gloomy album. In truth it's quite the contrary. More than anything it established the band's power and authority as musicians.

Rolling Stone's Gary Von Tersch noted in his review, "The most important switch in Harum's sound is due to the fact that guitarist Robin Trower has stepped up, and is truly playing a lead guitar."

Home was also a testament to Chris Thomas' prowess as a budding record producer. "This was the biggest band I'd ever worked with," he says. "I mean I'd never ever told anyone that I'd worked with The Beatles when I was working for George Martin [in 1968] ... And here I was suddenly working as a producer flying solo in my own right!"

The album was called *Home* simply because all four musicians had been in The Paramounts and, as Brooker described, "It felt like coming home." In the US the LP charted at a *Billboard* position of 34 and reached 49 in the UK – Procol Harum's highest-charting British album up until that point.

---

* Earlier in 1970 Harry Pitch provided harmonica on 'Groovin' With Mr Bloe', a surprise UK number two hit that May.

Procol Harum premiered virtually all of *Home* at London's Lyceum on June 5, a month before its UK release. In the US A&M issued the album in a gatefold sleeve, featuring artwork parodying the popular board game 'Snakes & Ladders' – once again designed by Reid's girlfriend Dickinson. The sleeve photos were taken by esteemed British fashion photographer David Bailey.

Over in the States, Procol were given a primetime slot on *The Smothers Brothers Summer Special* on July 1, confirming their higher profile in America with a live performance of 'A Salty Dog' which was shown nationally on ABC TV.

On Independence Day the band played to approximately 200,000 at the Atlanta Pop Festival sharing top billing with Captain Beefheart, The Allman Brothers and Jethro Tull. On the weekend of August 3–5 Procol headlined over upcoming star Leon Russell and Blodwyn Pig at San Francisco's Fillmore West and on August 14 and 15 at New York's Fillmore East over Country Joe McDonald. But some of the gigs booked earlier in the year by managers Bennett Glotzer and Ronnie Lyons left something to be desired, as Brooker revealed to *Record Mirror* when describing the band's experiences down South.

"In one town in Tennessee there were lots of rednecks and football players where everybody sported crew cuts and the sheriff had a pearl handled gun. Out of the blue they had these long haired ravers and they didn't like it at first. We discovered a local group who lived in a caravan and had a few blows [jam sessions] with them. The leaders were twins who had long blond hair and they worked in a local factory. They had short blond wigs which they had to put on whenever they went to work. The drummer and bass player were members of the National Guard and had crew cuts, and whenever they went on stage they put on long blond wigs.

"When we got to New Orleans we were booked into a place on the waterfront and the posters all read, 'Procol Harum – Tonight – Free Beer!' We were very surprised to find that very few groups had been to New Orleans and that people were still talking about The Beatles' appearance there, which was in 1963 or 1964. We've had reasonable success in America, not fantastic success, we're no Led Zeppelin, but we've had a good following and good receptions and people buy our albums. I think they'll still buy them in years to come, because they're not dated and we're not 'fave raves' of the moment, so we mean to go on for a long time!"

On paper at least Glotzer and Lyons had promised to be a dream team management wise (Bennett had managed Blood Sweat & Tears) but the two men fell out almost immediately. It's alleged that Procol felt that these actions potentially invalidated the contract between the band and the management which would lead to further out of court settlements, which increased an ever growing band debt scenario.

Tour manager Derek Sutton recalls, "There was a dispute in the States through 1970 to 1971 due to monies that were owed to previous management, which resulted in the last show of the 1970 American tour at New York's Fillmore East having Federal Marshals coming in and impounding all the box office receipts that were due to Procol Harum. You can imagine that – after a long American tour to be told that 'all of the money that was in the box office has been taken away' – that might well cause a bit of emotion. The Federal Marshals kept the money in the country until the dispute between the band and the manager was resolved. I remember BJ Wilson being in tears in the lawyer's office, because he couldn't understand why he and the band weren't getting paid for an American tour they'd all just worked very hard on. For people like BJ, Robin, and Chris the only money they got was from the tours. Whereas Keith and Gary got songwriting royalties, which were not funded by the tours!"

Despite the success of 'A Whiter Shade Of Pale', mounting debt coupled with loss-making gigs and expensive albums meant that Procol desperately needed sympathetic management. But things were improving in the hands of Chrysalis Artists, which was much more switched on than those who'd gone before. By May, Derek Sutton was handling the American side of the company.

Chrysalis Artists was also handling two major-league acts at this particular time, Ten Years After and Jethro Tull, with Chris Wright managing the former and Terry Ellis the latter. This meant that Procol needed someone in Europe *and* America. Doug D'Arcy looked after

93

the band in Europe while Derek Sutton looked after Procol's interests in North America.

Derek Sutton takes up the story: "The very first tour I did with Procol was in the spring of 1970. We played an American University on May 1 and [sixties radical] Abbie Hoffman and his crowd of 'Yippies' tried to take over the stage, which was in an outdoor amphitheatre. When we got backstage after the show they'd trashed our dressing room and had stolen one of Robin's guitars... In those days rock'n'roll was *not* the business that it is now [in 2012]."

On August 28 Procol performed to their biggest-ever audience, over half a million people, at the five-day Isle Of Wight Pop Festival on the same day as Tony Joe White, Taste (featuring Rory Gallagher), Family, Chicago, and a host of other name acts. *Record Mirror*'s Lon Goddard ran a piece dated September 19 featuring the headline: 'Procol Smoked Out On Isle', describing how "In the bitter chill of the night, with miserable audience conditions and the fatigue of many listeners, Procol could do no wrong."

Gary Brooker: "I thought our Isle Of Wight performance would have been nice for a sunny afternoon but we sat around for a very long time getting cold before the performance. The other thing that really bothered me was the great billows of smoke that kept blowing over from the camp fires directly onto the stage. Because of the conditions the fast numbers went over much better. The act was more or less planned up until the rock'n'roll numbers at the end. Those we do if the time is right!"

Procol's performance of 'A Salty Dog' was included on the 1971 CBS triple album *The First Great Rock Festivals Of The Seventies*, compiling various artists' performances from both the Atlanta and Isle Of Wight festivals. However it took until 2009 for more of the band's set in the form of 'Juicy John Pink' to emerge on a four-disc Procol compendium *All This & More*. Most mystifyingly, despite having been filmed by Murray Lerner for the duration of their set, none of the band's eight songs made it to the final cut of Lerner's Isle Of Wight documentary *Message To Love*, which belatedly appeared in 1997, despite the band turning in an excellent set. Reid remains perplexed. "I have no idea

94

why our songs were not included. I even went to see Murray Lerner in New York, and he showed me the footage. I'll have to look him up and ask him one day!"

Procol's next major festival appearance was scheduled for September 5 at the massive Love & Peace event held on the Isle of Fehmarn which would have seen Procol Harum share equal billing with Sly & The Family Stone, Canned Heat, Peter Green, Ginger Baker's Airforce and Ten Years After. However advance warning of heavy-handed policing at the hands of German biker gangs motivated Doug D'Arcy to withdraw both Procol Harum and Ten Years After from the event and neither band left their hotel until the gig was over. It was just as well as there was a near riot and the promoter's offices were burned to the ground; so much for the promise of 'Love & Peace'.

The headliner at the event was Jimi Hendrix who played through heavy rain to the miserable, unsettled throng. Ironically the day before the Isle of Fehmarn debacle Procol also played with Hendrix at the Berlin Super Concert at the Deutchlandhalle.

Robin Trower: "I remember we played on the bill directly after him in Berlin. Jimi's set was really great. We had heard it whilst standing in the wings. But people were booing and throwing bottles and cans at him. We came on and I threw the bottles and beer cans back at the audience. How could they do that to Jimi? Anyway, that day, after all those gigs throughout all those years, I finally got to stand on stage on the *very* same spot that Jimi had played live. A few days later [sic] he was dead. Really sad!"

Recalling the gig to *Melody Maker*'s Chris Welch, Brooker also watched Hendrix from the wings. "Jimi played magnificently and the audience just booed him! Trower went bloody wild. He was totally enthralled with Hendrix's playing, and was ready to punch out 6,000 Germans!"

Robin Trower: "I think it was above their heads, you know? I mean, I couldn't take in a lot of what he was doing. And I'm a musician and a guitarist. So you can imagine what it was like for them. Anyway, I was walking up and down outside the dressing room after he'd come off stage, and I was sort of saying, 'Should I go in?' Then I burst into his dressing room all of a sudden and said, 'I've gotta tell you that was the best thing I've *ever* seen,' which it was. And he said, 'Uh, thank you, but uh naw.' And I just went, 'Whoops, that's it,' and walked out again."

During the *Home* sessions Procol had performed old rock'n'roll standards purely as a warm-up exercise. With all four members having been in The Paramounts, albeit not simultaneously, Procol decided that it might be fun to go back to their musical roots and tape the proceedings for posterity.

In September 1970 Procol Harum booked Abbey Road studios and, fuelled with beverage, recorded an album's worth of material that was taped non-stop for 12 hours from 7pm until 7am. Chris Thomas produced and Blodwyn Pig's Jack Lancaster, a friend of BJ Wilson's, played sax on a couple of tracks for an album that later came to be known as *Ain't Nothin' To Get Excited About.* The sessions were credited not to Procol Harum, but to 'Liquorice John Death & The All Stars'.

When listening back to the tapes a decision was made to put the experiment on ice until a later date. So the masters were filed away in Abbey Road's vaults and forgotten about until the following year when Chris Thomas dug them out.

Chris Thomas: "Sometime during the construction of Air Studios in Oxford Circus they were giving the Neve desk in Studio One a trial before the studio area was completed. I took the 'Liquorice John' tapes in and mixed down about a dozen of my favourites, and took a seven and a half inch copy for myself. A few years later Roger Scott at Capital Radio heard of these tapes, and I lent them out for broadcast."

In 1976, Scott slipped a cassette of the recordings to his colleague Nicky Horne, who gave them their first public airing on his popular programme *Your Mother Wouldn't Like It* on November 22. In an *NME* report, Procol's then manager Nick Blackburn denied the Capital Radio broadcast was an exercise in gauging whether or not the 13 tracks deserved to be issued. "There was no intention of a commercial release," he insisted.

That year Procol Harum found themselves without a new studio album for the first time in nine years. In light of this, Blackburn approached Thomas to see if he could find the 'Liquorice John' tapes, but the multi-tracks had been mislaid in the vaults. Apart from a couple of letters to *NME* there was no groundswell of interest surrounding the Capital airing, and the project was once again shelved.

The recordings would have slotted well into the pre–punk rock climate. During 1976, Southend's Dr Feelgood had a UK chart-topping album with *Stupidity*, partly recorded at Southend's Kursaal ballroom.* The year before, John Lennon released his *Rock'n'Roll* covers album, and before that the soundtracks to *That'll Be The Day* and *American Graffiti* revived many great rock'n'roll standards.

"Were the tapes released to Capital Radio solely to dispel the myth that Procol were a spent force [by 1976]?" enquired *NME's* Tony Stewart? "They can play rock'n'roll better than the heavy rock groups. They've got a great feel for it," said Blackburn.

So who or what was Liquorice John Death? The answer lay appropriately in Southend-On-Sea. "Liquorice John wasn't a real person," says Gary Brooker "When we were The Paramounts we started with what was a very dated name. A friend who I went to school with at Westcliff High School, Dave Mundy, always thought that we should be called 'Liquorice John Death & The All Stars'.

Mundy had often suggested to Brooker that The Paramounts should have aliases like many famous jazz musicians. So Trower was to be called 'Humdrum Pete', Copping 'Chris The Man', Wilson 'Shaky Jake' and Brooker 'Liquorice John Death'.

"So I was meant to be Liquorice John Death raving away at my piano," adds Brooker. "He would have liked me to change my name, my hair and everything. We kind of called him Liquorice John when he died. The reason we called him Liquorice John Death was because *he* was really the wild man. He was a wild dresser and everything else. He was in actual fact what he couldn't be. He was what he wanted us to be..."

---

* Coincidentally The Paramounts had also recorded an unreleased cover of the Solomon Burke track 'Stupidity' at Abbey Road back in the early sixties.

Mundy thought that it would be fun if The Paramounts, aka Liquorice John Death & The All-Stars, recorded an album called *Ain't Nothing To Get Excited About* and even did a painting which was to be the cover. Sadly, Mundy suffered from mental health problems and was taken into an institution. He was occasionally given release for weekends and his old pals from The Paramounts would often take him to gigs throughout the early Procol days. Mundy even came to the band's debut gig at London's UFO Club where, as an antidote to colourful psychedelia, he arrived dressed in a large brown paper bag!

Gary Brooker: "[Dave] was always a big influence on us. He just had a lot of style and was off the wall. He didn't care what trends were. He made his own trends. *We* didn't do that that much ... 'A Whiter Shade Of Pale' was the most off the wall we ever were."

In 1970, while Procol were away on tour, Mundy was unable to contact any friends and, feeling downcast, he jumped from the top of a 15-storey tower block in Southend-On-Sea. Reid and Brooker later wrote a song in tribute, 'For Liquorice John', which featured on Procol's 1973 album *Grand Hotel*.

It took until the mid-nineties for the 'Liquorice John' experiment to finally reach fruition, as Brooker explains: "The masters finally reappeared when we got a box of tapes back from EMI-Chrysalis [in 1995] said to contain Procol Harum albums. It took a long time to go through all the boxes of multi-tracks... but the lost *Liquorice John* album had been filed in the wrong department. It had gone into the archives at EMI and could never be found, because it was logged under 'For Liquorice John' (from the *Grand Hotel* album) but it wasn't. It was the Liquorice John Death & The All Stars album!"

Mundy's belongings had been left to Robin Trower and among them was the original painting intended for the album's cover. This duly became the sleeve for *Ain't Nothin' To Get Excited About* when it was finally issued in 1997 – some 27 years later. Featuring standards such as Vince Taylor's 'Brand New Cadillac', Little Richard's 'Keep A Knockin'', Fats Domino's 'I'm Ready', and a song co-written by the band and Mundy called 'Well, I...' the album more than lived up to its legendary status.

Throughout September and October 1970, Chrysalis paired Procol up in support to the agency/label's biggest act Jethro Tull for a major tour spanning the UK and France, concluding at the Royal Albert Hall on October 13. In an online review Glaswegian writer George Lovell described a gig at Green's Playhouse (later the Apollo) on October 2.

"Most people, unlike me, had come to hear Jethro Tull. In retrospect, their act was eclipsed by the set served up by Procol Harum. I think it was the R'n'B/rock medley that did it, especially 'Great Balls Of Fire'. Brooker just let it rip and the house went wild, a natural Glaswegian condition. Even though 'A Whiter Shade Of Pale' restored a fitting, but fleeting, serenity to the evening, by the time Jethro Tull appeared the crowd were still 'Shakin' All Over' as well as calling out for more. There was simply nothing Ian Anderson and crew could conjure up to stop the punters thinking back to Procol Harum, or should I say, given the band's configuration that night, The Paramounts (aka Liquorice John Death & The All Stars)!"

Two weeks later Procol were back in the US performing at San Francisco's Fillmore West for four nights, headlining over Poco and Mungo Jerry. While the band were in America, George Harrison's epic triple album *All Things Must Pass* hit the shops. Among the impressive cast of musicians who played on the sessions, produced by Phil Spector at Abbey Road, was none other than Gary Brooker. Harrison had been impressed by Brooker's piano playing on *A Salty Dog* and quite possibly remembered him from when The Paramounts had appeared low on the bill on The Beatles' final UK tour in December 1965. It was the start of a lifelong friendship. (Brooker would later play a prominent role in the 'Concert For George' tribute at the Royal Albert Hall in 2002.)

In November 2003 Gary Brooker talked to Holland's *Beatles Unlimited* magazine about his memories of working on George Harrison's *All Things Must Pass* in 1970. "I played piano on 'My Sweet Lord' and 'Wah Wah'. It was an unbelievable wall-of-sound. There's a lot of people on that; guitarists, keyboards and a lot of people in the studio, and all going at once. We all crammed into the tiny control room, studio three, and Phil Spector said, 'Right... Play it!' And there was this incredible wall-of-sound. Badfinger were also there strumming away. I was there for just a day. In fact it might have just been an evening!"

At the close of 1970 Procol's future was looking optimistic, even though they would have to work extremely hard to pay off their existing debts. Keith Reid and Gary Brooker's next plan was to get Procol away from Straight Ahead Productions and its anachronistic label Regal Zonophone, but in doing so they would be in breach of their UK record contract, owing a fifth album to Regal Zonophone. The label, however, agreed to what is termed 'an override on future sales', which related to Procol's next *two* albums. Meaning that their old label would get a cut of the revenue. Zonophone released Procol from their contract thereby enabling them to seek out a new deal with another British label.

Not surprisingly, at the end of 1970 Procol entered into a new agreement with their management company's counterpart Chrysalis Records, which was distributed throughout the UK by Chris Blackwell's highly efficient Island Records.

Chapter 6

Broken Barricades &
Conquistador

1971

*"Broken Barricades with guitarist Robin Trower now emerging firmly
centred as never before with the magnificent 'Song For A Dreamer' – a
high point from my favourite album of the year."*

Bob Harris

In January 1971 a "music industry secret" finally leaked into the public
domain: "BJ Wilson – Procol Harum's secret weapon, had been
noticed by a VIP with keen ears," according to *Sounds*. When forming
The New Yardbirds in late 1968 Jimmy Page had considered BJ Wilson
for the vacant drum stool. The New Yardbirds, of course, soon changed
their name to Led Zeppelin and burst into global superstardom in 1969.

"I was definitely into Procol," Page confirmed three decades on. "I'd
assessed BJ Wilson's playing through their music. They were very cool.
They came in on a level that nobody else did; particularly with *A Salty
Dog*... it was so atmospheric. It drew you right in. Anyway, I remember

saying to Robert [Plant] that as far as a drummer is concerned I'd got a couple of ideas in mind, and one of them was BJ Wilson.... But Robert said, 'I have a really good drummer you should see.' And when I heard Bonzo [John Bonham] that was it!"

Page had witnessed Wilson's drumming in close-up during the 1968 sessions for Joe Cocker's *With A Little Help From My Friends.* "I've gotta tell you he was pretty tasty on those sessions. Just fantastic! He was *so* in tune with the vibe, and with the part he was playing; a *very* important part in the overall delivery!"

Loyal to Procol and to Brooker, and possibly having received wind that Bonham was the likely pick, Wilson turned down Page's offer. Meanwhile, Trower's increasing virtuosity was also being singled out as "a powerhouse lead guitarist" from influential American music journals such as *Rolling Stone, Crawdaddy* and *Raves Magazine* throughout 1969 and 1970.

Procol Harum had proved to be extremely popular in Italy in late 1967 and on their return to the country in early 1971 they were greeted with much publicity. However, this time Robin Trower was getting all the attention and, possibly due to his drinking, BJ Wilson's performances were met with criticism in both the press and from within the band itself. Instead of facing up to the truth, Wilson allowed things to get worse when Italian hospitality compounded matters.

According to Chris Copping, wherever Procol went hotel staff realised they were 'rock musicians' and any chance of a glass of mineral water or milk was almost impossible. Waiters always arrived with bottles of complimentary Chianti saying "milk Italian style", says Copping. Parties would also go on well into the early morning with both Copping and Wilson being chaperoned down country roads in speeding Maseratis amidst early morning fog, arriving back at their hotel just in time for breakfast and more "milk Italian style"!

On March 13, 1971 British music paper *Sounds* ran a report stating, "Rumours that Procol Harum were planning to split and that drummer BJ Wilson had joined The Grease Band were unconfirmed... A Chrysalis spokesman told *Sounds*, 'Maybe one of the members is discontented?'"

Sounds asked the drummer to set the record straight in an interview printed in its March 27 edition. "I can't see the day when the group will split up – we still have a long way to go," Wilson told Ray Telford, while adding rather cryptically, "When we came back from our last visit to Italy, we were very tired and everyone was a bit crazy, and I think things got a bit out of hand."[*]

In an *NME* interview with Ritchie Yorke (dated June 5) Brooker remarked, 'No matter how hard we work, we still only find time to make one album [per year]. In the past 18 months, we've only had one week's holiday. In 1970 we spent 12 weeks on the road in the States and 18 weeks in Europe. The rest was TV, interviews, and the like. *Broken Barricades* was recorded in a hurry. We came back from our last US tour [in February] and we only had about a week before we started the album."

Recorded across 35 separate 12-hour sessions at AIR Studios' brand new facility high above London's busy Oxford Circus *Broken Barricades* utilised the latest 16-track recording equipment. BJ Wilson's drumming was reproduced with crystal clarity by producer Chris Thomas who was now considered to be "the unofficial sixth member of the group", according to Doug D'Arcy.

Procol Harum's fifth album took just over four weeks to record between February and March 1971. Conceived amid the *en vogue* climate of hard rock bands such as Led Zeppelin, Deep Purple and Black Sabbath, *Broken Barricades* saw Procol moving away from their dual keyboard sound and into the realms of guitar-dominated rock.

The album opened with the heavily produced and scored 'Simple Sister' which Brooker described as "music from the 23rd century. Lyrically it's quite simple, and there's something very personal about it. It's probably just a quick summing up of a situation from somewhere."

Chris Copping: "'Simple Sister' was one of the first big scale productions from Chris Thomas. Gary did all the orchestration ... I'm not sure who conducted the players. It could have been George Martin

---

[*] When pressed for specifics about this particular Italian tour, Chris Copping had no recollection of any alleged musical or personal "differences".

as it was his studio, but whoever it was would probably have had some say in the players chosen. They probably had session "fixers". I think Gary, BJ and I fine-tuned the middle bit in the studio. Gary wrote those bass riffs that the piano also plays. It would have been just him, me, and BJ in that section. Then all that middle part was a bed for building the pianos and orchestration. Chris Thomas organised slowing down the tape machine for the piano build-up in the middle so that, at normal speed, it had a slightly mechanical sound. Then with Gary's orchestration, the whole thing reached a mighty climax.

"Robin did a solo on his Les Paul and then another on the Stratocaster, which he'd just started playing, and you can hear where the Stratocaster solo takes over... I just remember being blown away when I heard [the track]... The last note, together with the Hammond on 'Power Failure', was the only organ playing on the whole album."

Procol's former American tour manager Derek Sutton still thinks that 'Simple Sister' ranks as one of Procol's finest achievements. "It's one of their greatest. And that's entirely a Robin Trower riff. A truly *great* rock'n'roll riff."

Two years later, when Lou Reed was recording his seminal *Berlin,* the album's producer Bob Ezrin asked both Copping and Wilson to join him while he played piano on the track 'How Do You Think It Feels'.

"I wondered at the time why I was asked to get my bass out," said Copping, "and it was much later when the penny dropped: Bob would have been impressed by the 'Simple Sister' production sound so why not get in the same rhythm section? My part was certainly not on the finished version [of 'How Do You Think It Feels'], but we built up a track just the three of us. It was similar to the middle of 'Simple Sister' in its way. Lou Reed was not in the room, because Morgan Studios had a bar. But we met him and BJ asked Lou if he could buy him a drink? Lou warned BJ that he only drank triple scotches ..." The expensive round of drinks paid off as Wilson was asked to play on 'Lady Day' and 'The Kids' (on *Berlin*).

Having played (unused) Moog synthesizer on George Harrison's *All Things Must Pass,* Chris Thomas became the logical choice to oversee and contribute to the title track. "When it came to 'Broken Barricades'

Gary had written these arpeggios on the top," Thomas remembers. "I had an idea for actually using them and breaking the song down into its constituent parts and getting a sound around that arpeggio. As opposed to *Home* which was quite a live album where you can hear the piano, the Hammond organ, the blues guitar, etc; a traditional Procol album.

"I had an idea of taking the song 'Broken Barricades' into a whole new direction. It had also got to the point in my own career where I wanted to take stuff and see where we went with it. I mentioned this to Gary and he said, 'Let's do it. Let's go with it!' So I brought in a whole bunch of people so we could cut this thing. I got this guitarist in from Ealing; a tape operator from somewhere else and I got in a Moog synthesizer, which I programmed as well. So that was the start of me doing stuff. It was Gary's encouragement that allowed me to do that, and I am always forever grateful wherever I was allowed to do stuff of my own volition."

Gary Brooker: "Chris Thomas was very good as the Moog man. Then we let BJ Wilson play a drum solo over the end. The music plays on over it and we just changed the arpeggios. There were also some good Keith Reid words on 'Broken Barricades'. To me it was kind of an environmental comment about the planet and how it was going to kill itself... It perhaps wasn't, of course, but that's what I thought it was about!"

'Poor Mohammed', co-written by Trower-Reid, was the first track cut at the sessions and features Trower playing steel guitar as well as contributing vocals. At the time of the album's release, Reid lamented to *NME* that Trower refused to play the song on stage as "he reckons he can't sing and play at the same time".

'Memorial Drive', another Trower-Reid co-write, featured Brooker on electric piano. "Leaving out the bass in the verses made a good dynamic, as it did in The Rolling Stones' 'Honky Tonk Women'," reckons Copping. "Gary did a [Rhodes] piano solo over [the basic track], probably only using a right hand."

Procol recognised the strength of 'Memorial Drive' when it became the opener for their gigs during one of their American tours that year.

Wilson felt that 'Luskus Delph' should be "banned because of its inherent obscenity". When promoting *Broken Barricades* on Radio Luxembourg, Brooker coyly stated that 'Luskus' was a word made up by Keith Reid, "a cross between 'luscious' and something that people like to do in the evening". When introducing the song on stage that year he was even more forthright, "Keith tells me that Luskus is a cross between 'lust' and 'suck'." Delph is apparently "a cross between demon and elf".

"It's like a Viennese waltz," Brooker elaborated. "It's very gentle and very dated. Also it's very fragile. It might remind you a little of [Bach's] 'Sleepers' Awake' the way it falls right into your head."

It certainly had an influence on Francoise Hardy and Michel Berger's 'Message Personnel' (1973) which featured Procol-inspired orchestration by Michel Bernholc. The orchestration and the percussion on the play-out is a dead ringer for Brooker's scoring and Wilson's drumming on 'Luskus Delph'.

Recorded live in the studio, the lewd 'Playmate Of The Mouth' incorporates horns played New Orleans-style towards the fade. "'Playmate Of The Mouth' is one of the tracks that we have to cross out when we send our albums to our mothers, otherwise they'll write back saying, 'What's this filth? *That* Keith Reid, he's getting more perverted with *every* album'," said Wilson in 1971 to *Raves*.

"'Power Failure' is about touring on the road," said Brooker, "and what it's like when everything breaks down in the middle [of a gig]. The situation where the mains cut off and it's all left to BJ on drums to carry it through until the power is restored. This song is very much what it's like."

The track would later be covered acoustically by the virtuoso guitar player Leo Kottke on his *Chewin' Pine* album in 1975.

The closing track, 'Song For A Dreamer', attracted attention upon the album's release, designed as a way of paying respect to a recently departed legend. "We'd done that show in Berlin [September 1970] with Jimi Hendrix." said Robin Trower. "I think more or less from there, straight away, we went out to tour in the States. We were in San Francisco when we heard he'd died. Anyway, Keith and I decided we'd do a tribute to him. I played Keith something that I wrote, and he'd already got some words. So 'Song For A Dreamer' just gelled. It just came together and turned into a really special track.'"*

Broken Barricades succeeded in highlighting Procol's individual strengths as musicians; Brooker was in fine fettle vocally, Copping making up half of the dependable engine room completed by Wilson whose playing continued to amaze, while Trower's playing was now entering a new phase of expression.

Robin Trower: "I was always very happy the way *Broken Barricades* turned out. Everybody played *so* well on that album. BJ was at his peak creatively and technically. He was unique as a drummer. He was always looking to do something different. Most drummers would always relate a new song to something else that they've already heard, but not with him. Oh no! You'd play him a new song and he'd want to come up with something of his own. It was almost orchestral what he did a lot of the time...

"Gary's voice was almost like a musical instrument. Combine that unique voice with his songwriting and his playing and you have a very special package indeed!"

When released in June, *Broken Barricades* was met with a general critical thumbs-up in the USA. *"Broken Barricades* is one of the most enigmatic, puzzling albums to come down the track in a long time," wrote Mike Saunders and Melissa Mills in *Rolling Stone*, "simply because of the high quality of the albums preceding it." *Crawdaddy* praised: *"Broken Barricades* is Keith Reid writing searingly direct words; Gary Brooker providing appropriately powerhouse music, singing most soulfully, and pumping his piano with abandon; BJ Wilson and Chris Copping laying down a beat that by no exertion of the imagination could be termed inaccessible; and Robin Trower, one of the most respected guitarists in rock, writing the music for the album's obvious choice for a single 'Poor Mohammed', singing and playing some of the best guitar we'll hear this year."

---

* 'Song For A Dreamer' would be the final song played over the PA prior to Robin Trower hitting the stage for his shows from 1973 until 1977. When concert audiences heard the final notes, they knew that the Trower trio were about to appear.

The UK music paper *Sounds* futhered this assertion by pointing out that, "It's Robin Trower on guitar and drummer BJ Wilson who come across *most* strongly. Just listen to 'Memorial Drive' and 'Simple Sister'."

On April 12, Procol performed five songs off the album as part of a 12-song live set for WPLJ-FM New York from A&R Studios in Manhattan. Reaching an audience in excess of 50 million listeners, the concert was bootlegged not once, but twice under the dual guise of *Shine On Live* and *The Elusive Procol Harum. Broken Barricades* peaked at a *Billboard* chart position of 32 shortly thereafter.

The album reached 42 in the UK charts after DJ Bob Harris named *Broken Barricades* as his "album of the year" on his BBC Radio 1 series *Sounds Of The Seventies*.

With all the positive coverage surrounding *Broken Barricades*, not least the contribution made by Robin Trower, it might seem extraordinary that this was the point where Trower chose to quit Procol Harum for a solo career. However, their latest champion Bob Harris didn't seem that surprised, even if he kept his views to himself at the time. "With his guitar playing now firmly focused and centre stage the news that Robin Trower was about to quit Procol Harum [September 1971] was not at all surprising," said Harris some three decades later.*

"I always think about being in Procol Harum as like going to school and learning what the real thing was all about," said the guitarist later. "Playing in America and making albums... I always felt that it enabled me to go on and do what I did..."

Trower continued under the watchful eye of Chrysalis Records' Doug D'Arcy, firstly forming Jude, a short-lived four-piece consisting of himself on lead guitar, Frankie Miller (The Stoics) on acoustic guitar and vocals, Jimmy Dewar (Stone The Crows) on bass and vocals, and Clive Bunker (Jethro Tull) on drums. Dewar and Trower soon formed a strong alliance, paving the way for the beginning of Trower's solo career. A year later drummer Reggie Isadore joined forces with Trower and Dewar and international stardom beckoned.

---

* 'Whispering' Bob Harris would become a household name as the host of BBC TV's rock showcase *The Old Grey Whistle Test* from 1972 until 1977.

The impact of Trower's departure was mainly felt in the USA. It hit like a bomb. A&M Records were tremendously worried that Procol had lost their powerhouse guitar player and this was reflected in the American music press. American photo archives also provide a clue as to how important Trower was in the scheme of things. Nearly all of the photographs retained on file show Robin Trower and *not* Gary Brooker!

In September 1971 Procol rehired the Rolling Stones' rehearsal rooms in Bermondsey to audition a new guitar player. About 60 turned up. At the end of a sweltering hot day a tall young guitarist from Birmingham played an impressive blues number by BB King, cracked a few jokes, and suggested going to the nearby pub. Dave Ball (born March 30, 1950, in Handsworth in the West Midlands) had formerly played with the post-Move project Ace Kefford Stand and with Cozy Powell's Big Bertha. His suggestion was taken up and after a few drinks in the nearby Southwark pub he was hired.

Some weeks later, having heard that Ball had the right credentials to replace Trower, Matthew Fisher phoned up Keith Reid with a view to rejoining Procol. After a chaotic rehearsal that featured Chris Copping on bass, Fisher quickly changed his mind. As a consequence, Copping reverted to being the organist while Alan Cartwright, an old school mate of Wilson's (born October 10, 1945, Edmonton, London) whose last gig was with former Nice drummer Brian Davison's Every Which Way, was enlisted on bass. After having spent 18 months as a quartet, Procol reverted back to their original five-piece format.

On September 17, Procol undertook a prestigious concert on London's South Bank at the Queen Elizabeth Hall, but received mixed reviews. *Sounds'* Steve Peacock described Wilson's percussion work as being like that of "an octopus in a hot bath". The term stuck and later became a laudable tag to describe Wilson's playing in the wake of what was to be a momentous occasion.

Gary Brooker: "I think we'd probably been asked to do a certain number of gigs with orchestras after *A Salty Dog* and again after that first orchestral collaboration in Stratford, Ontario. So after that gig –

109

what with Matthew being a bit of a misery and Rob not liking playing with an orchestra because he had to play quietly – there wasn't really any internal support to do that kind of thing. So when the Edmonton Symphony Orchestra gig was offered we'd finally got the right line-up to do it. And we all thought, 'Hang on, it's only one concert, we might never get the chance of this again, let's bloody well record it!' We got the finances from our American label A&M and it squeaked through."

Keith Reid: "Robin Trower had left the band and I remember that A&M Records were very concerned about this. So we told them, 'We're gonna do this show with an orchestra and we're gonna record it...' I think they thought that we were mad! They were worried that we'd just lost our great guitarist, and we were saying, 'Oh don't worry about it... It'll all be fine ...' And funnily enough it was."

"There was more than a hint that Procol wanted to prove something with the concert and [their live] LP," wrote Jon Faulds in *Circus* magazine in December. "They felt that their viability as a force on the rock scene had been shaken." With Chrysalis' North American heavyweight tour manager-fixer Derek Sutton overseeing proceedings, things began to take shape very quickly.

According to *OOR Magazine's* Frans Steensma, "This was (to be) one of the first artistically successful unions between rock and classical music, but it was not the first such collaboration for the Edmonton Symphony Orchestra. A full year earlier, the ESO had presented a pair of concerts with the Canadian rock band Lighthouse. These concerts were so successful that the Board was amenable to doing more of that type of 'pop' concert."

The idea germinated in early 1971 when one Holger Pedersen suggested to Bob Hunka, the assistant general manager of the Edmonton Symphony Orchestra, that Procol Harum were a natural choice for an orchestral collaboration. Allied to this Ritchie Yorke, dean of Canadian rock critics, *Rolling Stone* contributor (and a big Procol Harum fan) heard about the ESO's history of collaborating with pop groups and made a separate approach to Hunka at a rock competition that April. Although Hunka didn't immediately act on the suggestion, on August 7, while Procol Harum were on a Canadian tour, a meeting was arranged between Hunka, Sutton and Brooker at the Edmonton Inn, where the idea for the concert crystallised and a date was set for November 18.

Procol's twelfth US and Canadian tour started in Atlanta, Georgia on November 5. Gary Brooker's wife, Franky, had copied out the orchestral scoring during the long flight from England and Hunka remembers, "The ink [on the contract] was still wet when they landed here in Edmonton."

Chris Thomas: "We had two engineers: Ray Thompson looked after the band and Wally Heider looked after the orchestra. Heider was very encouraging. I was pretty young and I sat there in this auditorium with all this complicated stuff going on. And he was a legend..."

Heider was the hottest engineer in North America at that time, having previously worked on Jimi Hendrix's album *Band Of Gypsies* and Van Morrison's *Tupelo Honey*. With a combination of the world's best mobile recording facilities in the shape of the brand new Heider 16-track mobile studio and the finest technicians in America, one would have expected the proceedings to have been plain sailing.

Chris Thomas: "At the rehearsals, it was very difficult to sync the orchestra and the band together. The percussion parts were already written. BJ was used to being pretty fast and loose in his drum fills, which were so idiosyncratic. And you couldn't really write a rock percussion part to place behind an orchestra, because it would sound like somebody kicking a pair of drum kits down the stairs."

According to Peter Greenberg in *Coast* (February 1972), "The orchestra read and talked musical symbols [whereas] Procol was used to 'sets and solos.'"

Brooker devised a simpler but unorthodox method. He had 13 symbols drawn on a sheet of paper in front of him on the piano. "I know what I'll do," he explained, "I just say 'man' eight times, 'dog' eight times, then 'bat', 'tree' and so on. It was certainly an awkward translation, but when conductor Lawrence Leonard suggested that the orchestra drop four bars from the coda of one of the songs, chances are Brooker dropped a 'bat' or a 'tree'."

Tensions were already running high due to an argument that took place at the conductor's house two days before the gig when the ESO's

Lawrence Leonard and Brooker fell out. "Discussing the concert, particularly the first half, which we (Procol) had not intended to partake in, ended in an argument between Lawrence and myself," Brooker noted in his diary, "causing him to say he didn't want to do the concert and me telling him he needn't bother. Chris Thomas acted as referee to the contest (the conclusion?) Lawrence was being childish."

The next glitch was later reported by *Circus* magazine's Jon Faulds: "Suddenly a storm in a tea cup brewed up between Procol and the orchestra's representative of the Musicians' Union. The Union representative at first demanded that the recording machine not be used until the actual concert, making it impossible for the engineers to set their sound level. Procol and the engineers made their point. The machines were turned on for rehearsal; but the Union man continued his harassment. He sat through rehearsal with a stopwatch and when time was up he pulled the orchestra off the stage in the middle of a song ('A Salty Dog'). Guitarist David Ball, however, eased the tension somewhat by striking up a first name friendship with ESO concert master Charles Dobias. The compact and sartorially perfect Dobias plus the lanky Ball made an incongruous pair, joking as they left the stage."

Coast magazine's Peter Greenberg set the scene: "In the empty, wood-panelled auditorium, there was a visible tension as the rehearsal became a race against the union clock and the nervous realisation that the concert, besides being the group's next album, would be the third such live concert recording ever to be made with a rock band and symphony orchestra, in addition to being the first gig ever done on 16-track.

"During the first run-through of 'Whaling Stories' neither the orchestra nor the Da Camera Singers were heard above the amplification of Dave Ball's guitar and BJ Wilson's drums. Pianist Gary Brooker begged, 'Can you get some more orchestra in the monitors – we can't hear them.' The monitors were turned up. Coordination was the next barrier. At first there was the physical handicap that the band was located in front of both orchestra and conductor. While organist Chris Copping and Brooker merely had to look up for their cues, drummer Wilson could not. And so, in the final moments of the last run-through, just when it seemed that they had thought of everything, they added a final funny touch: a truck-size rear-view mirror for BJ Wilson!"

At 7.30 pm, shortly before the ESO concert took place on November 18, Brooker wrote the following entry in his diary: "In about 30 minutes Derek Sutton will collect us to drive down to the Jubilee auditorium where a capacity audience of 3,000 is waiting with 52 musicians, 24 singers and a regiment of sound, recording, lighting, stage and special effects people. To say our one and a half days of recording (rehearsing) had gone smoothly would not be true, and so an excited nervousness is present instead of confidence. The previous experience of the group [at Stratford, Ontario] has shown us that symphony musicians tend to save their best until the performance. This is what we base our hopes on at this late hour.

"We found time to try our quadraphonic effects tapes this afternoon; that explosion should shake the foundations. Keith Reid tells me the seagulls (that will accompany the performance of 'A Salty Dog') sound like they're circling above your head when you're out there. The amplified choir should be coming from both the stage and the back of the theatre to surround the audience with their sound. They do know what they are doing and their enthusiasm has been contagious. We've left Chris Thomas and Wally Heider to take care of the recording, nobody is more capable. 'For what they are about to record, may the Lord be truly helpful.'

Tonight, the opportunity is there for us to play together with the instruments and voices we feel at home with and I know that we and everybody will be at our best."

The evening began with Chris Copping performing alone at his Hammond organ in a prelude to the main event. Both he and the ESO played a flawed version of Albinoni's *Adagio*. "The 'Abalone' was a shocking idea," said Copping recently. "I was sent out alone with this Canadian orchestra. I may have fluffed my lines, but not as badly as their lead violinist!

"Not until Procol launched into 'In Held 'Twas In I' did the orchestra and the band sound comfortable together," reported *Circus* magazine. "Layer upon layer of instruments in octaves piled upon one another, building the tension to a screaming climax. Doom–inspiring bass and guitar figures followed. Then a slight, stooping figure in wire-rimmed glasses and tweed coat [Keith Reid making his third concert appearance] apprehensively clutching a sheaf of papers, appeared by a microphone on the left hand side of the stage, and his voice thundered out softly over the sound of the instruments.

"The last tough step to triumph: The standing ovation stretches into minutes and Procol announced that they will re-perform several of the songs – as much for the benefit of the 16-track recorder as for the enthused audience, but the audience stays with them. They repeat 'Conquistador' (and 'Whaling Stories') the second attempt joyously refuting the uncertainty of the first and the program ends in open triumph."

Chris Thomas: "When we recorded the actual concert it was only an hour long. At the end of it I thought, 'We haven't got an album!' However, I knew that we had another hour and a half of available time to use the orchestra. So everybody came off stage. I'd managed to persuade Gary to get the band to go back on and do two songs again. When they came off stage after the encores, I said, 'And now the bad news. You've got to do the whole of 'In Held 'Twas In I' as well. All 20 minutes *again*.' BJ Wilson immediately went to the bar and said, 'I'm not doing any more.' I managed to bring him back. Gary then went and spoke to the audience and said, 'We're doing a job of work here!' And explained that they could stay if they wished, or they could go home. They remained in their seats and Procol did 'In Held 'Twas In I' again."[*3]

"A great choir and not a bad orchestra," was Derek Sutton's final verdict, "but hardly up to the calibre of the London Philharmonic, but definitely not a bad orchestra." Careful listening afterwards revealed the ESO drummer to be persistently out of time. It would prove necessary

---

* During the concert 'Shine On Brightly', 'Luskus Delph', 'Simple Sister' and 'Repent Walpurgis' were undertaken but did not make it to the final cut of the album, although the former three songs are now on the CD reissue as bonus tracks.

to mix him down and sometimes eliminate him completely during the final stages of the album's post production back in London.

Chris Thomas: "When we got back to England we were very lucky. If there were any mistakes, or the orchestra went out of sync with the band, we had another available take. Amazingly it worked. 'Conquistador', however, featured an overdub. It was the first song that we worked on when we went back to London. Dave Ball wanted to do his guitar solo again. Basically we had 16 tracks and they were all used up. So it meant wiping the live guitar solo and then Dave putting down a new solo in the studio. Even though we spent quite a long time on it, it wasn't actually as good as the previous one that we'd just wiped. So we threw away the key for the idea of overdubbing anything else. So nothing else was overdubbed. Everything else was done purely by editing between the two different performances: the main concert and the encores. When the multi-track went through the tape machine it looked like a zebra crossing (laughs) because there were so many edits. Yet it held together. We were kind of fortunate. Somebody up there was looking after us!"

Chris Copping: "When I heard the [2008] remastered *Edmonton* album *that* is the definitive version of 'Whaling Stories'. Sure it hasn't got Robin Trower, but Dave Ball was pretty good on these numbers: fairly straight blues playing which was his forte."

In the closing weeks of 1971 Procol taped concerts for French TV's *Pop Deux* on October 30, followed by a one-hour Christmas Eve special for the German TV series *Beat Workshop*. Still hot from their North American tour the band delivered their finest TV performance to date. An almost flawless live set saw highlights in the shape of 'Simple Sister', 'A Salty Dog' and 'Still There'll Be More'.

Chapter 7

Go Global Or Go Bust

1972

"I kept telling everybody to go out and buy the Edmonton album. It was such a happening album. The mixture of rock and classical music worked so well, unlike any album before or since. The new version of A Salty Dog *was really happening. It's even better than the original. And that takes some beating, I can tell you."*

Jimmy Page

At the beginning of 1972, three issues looked likely to undermine the potential success of *Procol Harum Live In Concert With The Edmonton Symphony Orchestra*: huge production costs, being eclipsed by other British groups and Procol's increasing debt issue.

Despite being a popular touring band Procol Harum had amassed considerable debts relating to out-of-court settlements with former managers and departing members, and they had been increasing steadily since 1967. As a working 'collective', the six Procol members were contractually bound to participate in paying off this unholy sum. By January 1972 the band debt scenario was significant enough to actually threaten Procol Harum's continued existence. A vast hike in ticket and album sales was a prerequisite or the band would simply cease to be.

With many established British acts hitting the road in 1972, Procol had serious competition from the likes of The Rolling Stones (their first US tour since Altamont), Led Zeppelin (always a guaranteed draw) and The Faces (now big stars). Add to this the emergent British singer-songwriter/glam-rock genre headed by Elton John and David Bowie, and the newly lucrative progressive acts in the shape of ELP, Jethro Tull and Yes, and Procol Harum had heavyweight homespun competition.

The group also had production costs to meet. To break even on their forthcoming album, the band would have to sell between 120,000 and 150,000 copies. Fortunately, 3,000 *ESO* ticket sales covered some of their bills, not least of which was $2,000 for Edmonton Holiday Inn plus transportation costs. However, in order to pay off the staggering bills demanded by Wally Heider Trucking, the ESO and the Jubilee Auditorium, the *ESO* album would have to sell more copies than *any* other Procol album to date.

Thankfully *Procol Harum In Concert With the Edmonton Symphony Orchestra & The Da Camera Singers* proved to be Procol Harum's most successful album ever when released in April.

In the run-up to its release, with the full weight of an almighty A&M and Chrysalis Records press campaign behind it, the record gleaned the attention of rock journalism's elite. The highly influential *Los Angeles Times'* critic Robert Hilburn described *Procol Harum Live In Concert* as belonging "on the shelf reserved for your most prized rock albums", adding, "It is certain to ignite a new wave of popularity for the group, which has enjoyed a loyal, but limited following in the days since its monster hit of 'A Whiter Shade of Pale'. Yes... an album to respect."

Melody Maker's Mark Plummer said that the album rated "along with Neil Young's *Harvest*... and Todd Rundgren's solo double... as one of the finest pieces of music to be released in 1972". He also singled out Dave Ball's "funky guitar work on 'The Grand Finale'" for considerable praise.

Rolling Stone's Richard Cromelin described Procol's orchestral collaboration as being, "among the most viscerally powerful and emotionally devastating music available", adding that Gary Brooker had "matured into one of rock's premiere vocalists".

The album also caught the attention and respect of Procol's peers. "I kept telling everybody to go out and buy the Edmonton album," Jimmy Page recalled. "It was such a happening album. The mixture of rock and classical music worked so well, unlike any album before or since. The new version of 'A Salty Dog' was really happening. It's even better than the original. And that takes some beating, I can tell you."

At the beginning of the summer *Live In Concert With The Edmonton Symphony Orchestra & The Da Camera Singers* reached number five in the American *Billboard* charts and went on to earn Procol Harum their first American gold disc. Despite all the good journalistic copy the album stalled at 48 in the British charts, being usurped by the 'doubleback' reissue of *A Salty Dog* and Procol's eponymous debut, which had been re-titled *A Whiter Shade Of Pale*. The Fly Records' repackage eventually reached number 27 and earned Procol Harum their first two gold albums in Britain.

More successful than the live LP in the UK was the track extracted from it, 'Conquistador', which became Procol Harum's first significant hit single since 'Homburg'. After a five year absence from the singles charts in both America and Britain, 'Conquistador' reached a UK 22 and a *Billboard* 16. This chart activity led to Procol visiting America no less than four times as well as venturing across mainland Europe, Scandinavia, and Japan through May 1971 and September 1972.

On a very tight schedule Dave Ball recollects leaving Scandinavia for London to quickly jump on a plane to New York only to discover that the band had missed their connecting flight to Ohio. Tour manager Derek Sutton had a contingency plan in place and Procol were whisked off to a nearby army base to take a Lear Jet to their final destination. "When we arrived," says Dave Ball, "the runway was illuminated by a sea of swirling red and blue lights. Due to the band's lateness, a fleet of interstate police cars were there waiting to escort us to a 10,000-seater stadium where an almost riotous crowd were impatiently stamping the floor to its very foundations."

Support acts on the American treks often featured future headline acts such as the Eagles, Mahavishnu Orchestra, Yes and King Crimson. In Germany Procol not only found themselves billed over Alice Cooper, but also his ubiquitous snake and hangman's noose.

In May Procol played three Japanese gigs with Chrysalis label mates Ten Years After. The first two shows took place at Tokyo's legendary Budokan, a sacred judo arena. The Beatles had been the first group to perform there in 1966 and more recently Led Zeppelin had rocked the venue to its very foundations in September 1971.

On their arrival in Japan Procol and TYA were led straight into a press conference. Each group sat on either end of a large table. "Is your music serious music?" Brooker and Reid were asked. The pair replied politely. Then a young female journalist asked Dave Ball, "Do you take drugs?" A worried BJ Wilson hastily waved at Ball, hoping he'd refrain from answering. The bemused guitarist replied, "Well I sometimes take an aspirin. Of course when I have a bad headache I might take a paracetamol, or a disprin, perhaps?" Ball then enquired why the question. She curtly replied, "Out of all the band members, you look like the one *most* likely to!"

To further incite matters, the local promoter had billed the gigs as "Ten Years After versus Procol Harum", a move not authorised by Chrysalis. Derek Sutton was understandably furious, especially when he spotted the huge onstage banner with 'Ten Years After' emblazoned across it.

"This led to some serious disagreements," Sutton recalled. "I couldn't explain enough to the Japanese promoter how a banner above Procol Harum saying 'Ten Years After' was wholly inappropriate. I then made the terrible mistake of shouting at the Japanese promoter, and in public, so it never got resolved. It was already very difficult having two very different kinds of bands on one stage in one night. On the first night the next surprise. Japanese audiences never applaud out of politeness. At the end of the concert they erupt. Up until that point the bands hadn't felt like they were getting across. The third and final problem was the fact that we'd signed a contract, which meant that we'd given the Japanese promoters the rights to *all* the merchandise!"

This 'agreement' had somehow unwittingly permitted the promoters to televise the final Osaka show, something that both bands and management were totally unaware of until the day before.

Dave Ball: "Procol Harum always enjoyed a drink, especially cocktails. We spotted this particular drink that had the word Amour on the label. Procol had a new song that we were trying out called 'Toujours L'Amour'. So that was it! We were going to make a brand new cocktail called Toujours L'amour. We tried out all these different combinations, drinking each one that we rejected. It was some kirsch, then some white rum, some vodka, some gin, some vermouth and a measure of lemonade and that special drink [Amour] that we had discovered earlier. When we finally came up with the right mixture we later celebrated by rolling some herbal cigarettes back in our hotel rooms."*

This occurred immediately *before* Procol's first Osaka show. Looking decidedly worse for wear the band took to the stage. Brooker introduced a new song called 'Bringing Home The Bacon'; played much slower than usual, it was met with muted applause. According to Ball, Brooker then proceeded to introduce another 'new' song, also called 'Bringing Home The Bacon'! As the opening bars were pounded out it all became too much for Sutton who rushed onstage to forcefully holler into Brooker's ear, thereby preventing a third and final rendition.

The next day both bands were to be televised across Japanese network television. Sutton followed them around for the whole day, making sure his 'no drinking' edict was adhered to. Making it to the Osaka stage stone cold sober Procol delivered a superb set. They even attempted 'Toujours L'Amour'. "Not wishing to tempt fate, we opted to drop 'Bringing Home The Bacon'," recalls Ball with a smile.

By the end of the summer, the heavy touring schedule had paid off, and according to Ball, "Keith and Gary celebrated their final payment of 'band debt' by sending their former manager a bottle of champagne and a box full of raspberries!"

The recording sessions for *Grand Hotel* began at London's AIR Studios in April 1972 with Chris Thomas producing once again. Thomas now

---

* A very brave thing to do in Japan.

confesses that whilst making Procol's seventh album, he was "also secretly moonlighting at Abbey Road studios co-producing Pink Floyd's *Dark Side Of The Moon."* Thomas was clearly gaining a solid reputation based upon his work with Procol Harum.

The key to Procol's new album would be its variance. "It will be intentionally very European in style," said Brooker in a Chrysalis press release. Meanwhile, another European artiste renowned for his 'variance' was David Bowie who shot to fame in Britain in 1972. When Bowie decided to augment his band the Spiders From Mars, he chose none other than Matthew Fisher!

"I played with David Bowie at London's Rainbow theatre on August 19 and 20," said Fisher. "I played a Steinway grand piano, but was behind a curtain so the audience couldn't see me. I seem to remember that on the second night Bowie did bring me out to take a bow at the end of the show."

"I was quite surprised to find out that David Bowie was a fan and admirer of Procol," says Gary Brooker. "I believe that one of the things that he liked about Procol Harum was its variety. David seemed to realise that in fact Procol had made everything from rock to opera, almost, and everything in between; including busking, skiffle, blues, and every sort of music that you could think of. And he is a bit like that. He can do one thing, and then another."

The 'Grand Hotel' concept was there from the outset and while the album was still being made, the sleeve's photo session was undertaken on July 4 at a villa on Pacific Palisades in Malibu. It was the same mansion that was used for the interiors of Roman Polanski's movie *Rosemary's Baby,* where the action was supposed to have taken place in New York's famous Dakota Building, and also *Sweet Sweet Rachel* starring Stefanie Powers. According to Dave Ball the *Grand Hotel* location is often erroneously cited as being the Grand Hotel by Lake Leman in Switzerland.*

---

* Indeed this error was later perpetuated by *Circus* magazine in May 1973 in a six-page Procol Harum feature that included a photograph of the vastly differing Grand Hotel by Lake Leman.

During the *Grand Hotel* sessions, tensions between Ball and Wilson came to a head over a joke Brooker made while light-heartedly mimicking Ray Charles on the piano. Ball laughed along, but Wilson was not amused and things suddenly erupted into a punch-up. Sometime later, Brooker asked Ball into the privacy of an AIR Studios production booth. "It's not working out," he told the stunned guitarist. At a band meeting Ball demanded to know "why" while the others sat in a brooding silence. "It's because of him, isn't it?" said Ball pointing at Wilson who refused to look him in the eye. Ball was on the money, but decided to leave Procol without any fuss. It was collectively agreed that the press announcement would state that "Dave Ball wanted to get back to playing the blues."

"Dave Ball was showing signs of unrest," Keith Reid told Cameron Crowe in a *Circus* magazine interview in May 1973. "He was uninspired in his musicianship, and his attitude. In his eyes he had just finished his stint with us."

Ball joined up with Long John Baldry shortly afterwards, before quitting Baldry's band to form Bedlam with his old mate, drummer Cozy Powell, who Ball had known since their days together in Big Bertha.

Chris Copping: "Dave was always good fun on tour. With his height he could do Pythonesque things like silly walks to liven up a boring airport. He also seemed to bring an element of luck to Procol Harum. When we were gambling in Reno, Dave kept winning and I for one followed his lead. Reno was so small time that they noticed and kept putting extra shots in our drinks, which we didn't spot until Franky Brooker 'poured' us home. Also, for the record, Dave was on our only American gold album [*Live In Concert With The ESO*]."

Ball's replacement was Mick Grabham, born January 22, 1948, in Sunderland. Known to the members of Procol from his days in Plastic Penny (who had a Top 10 hit with 'Everything I Am' in 1968), Grabham moved on to Cochise featuring pedal steel guitar legend BJ Cole before releasing a solo album in 1971 called *Mick The Lad*. Grabham thought so highly of Procol that he turned down the opportunity of joining former Free bassist Andy Fraser in a new venture. With Grabham's former

Plastic Penny bandmates Nigel Olsson and Dee Murray now backing Elton John both on disc and stage, he seemed like a good choice. His joining Procol Harum would see the band move into a more secure phase for the next four years.

Mick Grabham: "Doug D'Arcy from Chrysalis phoned me up [in September 1972] and asked me to come and have a play with Procol Harum. I remember auditioning and playing 'Shine On Brightly' and then attending a concert rehearsal at the Lyceum Theatre in the Strand and playing 'Bringing Home The Bacon'. And that's where I found out I'd got the gig, shortly before the Rainbow Concert with the RPO."

On July 29, *Sounds* announced that Procol Harum were to play the Rainbow Theatre in London with the Royal Philharmonic Orchestra and the London Chorale on September 22.* Following this Procol would do a short tour of German-speaking countries with Das Orchester Der Münchener Kammeroper and a boys choir called Der Toelzer Knabenchor taking in Vienna, Montreux, Zurich, Nuremburg, Stuttgart, Munich, and Frankfurt.

Grabham made his Procol stage debut at the Rainbow, road testing the title track to *Grand Hotel* and 'Toujours L'Amour' alongside the songs that featured on the ESO album. "The first gig I did with Procol Harum was frightening to say the very least," Grabham confirms. "I was concentrating on getting all the notes right, rather than really noticing the orchestral side of it. From my point of view their timing is different. That was the main thing that I noticed, but it seemed to work out."

"Very few guitarists, including Dave Ball, could have done what Mick Grabham did with 'Toujours L'Amour'," says Chris Copping. I mean the chords are Bb Db Eb Gb/Ab Db/Ab Ab G Bb C Eb Bb F D. Very complicated. However, with 'Whaling Stories', Mick's *Rainbow Concert* approach was more akin to negotiating the one-way systems in Cambridge!"

Returning to the stage to debut 'A Souvenir Of London' without the orchestra, Procol ended the concert on a high note. However,

---

* The concert was to be filmed by Sanford Leiberson, the producer of the movie *Performance*, although no film ever materialised.

Brooker later pointed out that the horn section had seemed uninterested throughout and were even spotted playing cards during the quiet sections of *Grand Hotel*.

"At the Rainbow we didn't have the equipment; the equipment that we used wasn't good enough," Keith Reid later complained to *Zig Zag's* Michael Wale. "It was ridiculous. We didn't have enough microphones; the equipment didn't work very well. We rigged up bits of scaffolding with all the microphones held up on bits of string. They were all swinging around. Not enough thought went into it. In fact, Gary was kind of designing the stage for them; ridiculous. We were at the office and we were trying to work out how many chairs we needed. We were all standing up with Chris [Thomas] saying, 'Well, if he's a fairly fat chap playing cello he's going to need about this much room...' Oh, it was just a farce. But eventually it worked out all right. Even though I don't think the sound was as good as it could have been, it was a really good concert. I felt good about it when it was all over."

His reservations were not shared by the British music press who adjudged the ambitious gig an overall success. "'Grand Hotel', a lovely piece of nostalgic tongue in cheek," wrote *Sounds'* Penny Valentine on September 30. "The crowd's response at the end of the set was one of the most intense I've ever seen at the Rainbow" added *Disc's* Andrew Tyler. 'If there's one band with class and elegance," James Johnson opined in *New Musical Express,* "it has to be Procol Harum."

Years later, the Rainbow gig made an unexpected reappearance in *Engleby*, a critically acclaimed novel written by English author Sebastian Faulks, first published by Random House in 2007. In a key scene, the central character Engleby recalls how he once "took a train to London from Reading to see Procol Harum when they premiered their new album, *Grand Hotel* with an orchestra and choir (at The Rainbow). It was good, but I wasn't sure Mick Grabham was up to it as Robin Trower's replacement on guitar, particularly on 'Whaling Stories', a song of which I need only to hear the opening note to find my stomach tense and my saliva fill with the re-experienced taste of Glyn Power's A-grade hashish. There's something essential in Trower's tone that Grabham didn't catch."

125

Conductor Eberhard Schoener had invited Procol Harum to mainland Europe in October to play shows in Switzerland, Germany, and Austria. This short stint enabled Procol to further debut songs from *Grand Hotel* as well as the popular *ESO* album.

Chris Copping: "I *think* the first gig on that tour was Vienna and I *think* there was a statue of one of the greats, probably Wolfgang Amadeus Mozart, but maybe Ludwig Van Beethoven? I believe we started by alternating between the orchestra doing pieces from Mozart's *Coronation Mass* and our songs unaccompanied. We joined together for the orchestrated songs. Hearing just the *Coronation Mass* performed by everyone at rehearsal, or soundcheck, hearing that sound with a professional orchestra with boy sopranos, in that hall, was a complete epiphany... It was a fantastic tour."

"At the German concerts there was a much better mix between the group and the orchestra," Reid informed Michael Wale. "The other major improvement was that we also had a choir, the Munich Boys' Choir, who were incredible. They were from the ages of about 8 to 16... It was quite funny to see them on stage singing like cherubs whilst round the back they were a real bunch of hooligans, throwing their music on the floor and punching each other. In fact I was standing around the side watching them one night and one of them was pinching the boy beside him. It really was like a choirboy's kind of thing, but they were great.

"It was funny the last night after the last show; we laid on a party for them. We said, 'We'll have champagne for the orchestra, but what can we give the kids? We'll get a load of the *Edmonton* albums and sign them all and give everybody an album.' So we had about 40 bottles of champagne and about 40 albums and we signed the albums and put them in a big heap ... Then the kids ran in and drank all the champagne. They got in earlier than the orchestra, and all the champagne was gone. They didn't want to know about the albums. They were great. It was really touching."

Chris Copping: "On the subject of drinking, I remember sneaking off to the Oktoberfest – as you do – and sliding down three litres of Hofbräu pre gig, but when the timpani player told me he had drunk five litres I didn't feel quite so guilty ... One interesting sideline: at that time the Monty Python team were there doing a German TV special. Some of us were invited up to Eberhard Schoener's country place where John Cleese and Eric Idle happened to be. Cleese seemed to be with a German woman who was no oil painting, but had big tits. He looked like a tall city businessman until these great lank limbs folded and unfolded; then the 'Silly Walks' sketch all fell into place. Eric Idle was telling us about the Olympic Games sketch that they'd done where they had a marathon for people with weak bladders and the 100 metres race for people with no sense of direction...[Apart from that] They just couldn't understand how we could actually manage to be on tour for more than a few days at a time ..."

Chapter 8

Grand Hotel

1973

"Now they had one very particular effect on my life. It was a song they did, which I expect some of you here will know, called 'Grand Hotel'. Whenever I'm writing I tend to have music on in the background, and on this particular occasion I had 'Grand Hotel' on the record player. This song always used to interest me because while Keith Reid's lyrics were all about this sort of beautiful hotel – the silver, the chandeliers, all those kind of things, but then suddenly in the middle of the song there was this huge orchestral climax that came out of nowhere and didn't seem to be about anything. I kept wondering what was this huge thing happening in the background? And I eventually thought … it sounds as if there ought to be some sort of floorshow going on. Something huge and extraordinary, like, well, like the end of the universe. And so that was where the idea for The Restaurant At The End Of The Universe *came from – from* Grand Hotel.*"*

Douglas Adams

Grand Hotel had originally been scheduled for an October 1972 release, but this was scrapped when Procol decided to re-record

90 percent of the album in order to replace Dave Ball's guitar parts. As a consequence, the album's issue date was put back until the early spring of 1973. Additionally Procol cancelled a raft of gigs in order to return to AIR studios in November 1972 to undertake the re-recordings. The band was also now out of contract with A&M Records in the USA and poised to embark on an exclusive international output deal with Chrysalis. It was with a certain amount of pride that Procol's press officer (and later Hollywood director of renown) Cameron Crowe announced, "The *Grand Hotel* sessions have moved swiftly and proficiently with the album being completely finished by January 26, 1973."

Meanwhile, Matthew Fisher's debut LP for RCA was filled with good Hammond organ playing and strong melodies. It received excellent reviews in 1973 with full-page spreads in both *Sounds* and *Raves*. *Journey's End* featured a re-recording of Fisher's 'Theme From Separation' (the 1967 Jack Bond movie) which featured orchestration by David Katz. Unfortunately, the album proved to be a commercial failure. More significant was Robin Trower's debut album, *Twice Removed From Yesterday,* produced by Matthew Fisher for Chrysalis, which indicated the promise of better things to come.

Grand Hotel, however, was something of a *tour de force* for Procol. But one constant question seemed to pre-occupy British music critics in particular, "Was it a *concept album*?" The cover showed the members in front of a fictitious Grand Hotel suggesting that it might be. On March 17 *Melody Maker* reviewer Richard Williams felt that the title track lived up to its subject. "Expanding on the mood of Van Dyke Parks created with 'Hung velvet overtaken me, Dim chandelier awaken me' in the Beach Boys' song 'Surf's Up', Keith Reid's lyrics speak of fine wine, rare meats, serenade and sarabande, Dover sole and Oeufs Mornay, Profiteroles and Peach Flambé, and around all this rich imagery Gary Brooker creates sad minuets and stately slow foxtrots, based on the rock rhythm, but amplified by a superb arrangement for orchestra and chorus. He has really learned how to use this medium, making a joke of the most avant-rockers who try to borrow from classical music, and 'Grand Hotel' stands with 'Whaling Stories' and 'A Salty Dog' as the group's finest achievements. They are, too, almost unique in that the more ambitious they get, the more they succeed."

"'Grand Hotel' reeks of nostalgia," wrote *Sounds'* Penny Valentine on March 10, "and of the Cannes seafront in the winter of 40 years ago; of paved ballrooms and maitre d's with smoothed down hair; of palm trees, vast mirrors, and cherubs smiling with plaster mouths – the music tinged with the kind of empty sadness that Gary Brooker writes so well. In fact it was this track that got the whole album underway to start with – Reid having come up with the name of the track before he did anything else!"

Keith Reid: "It's about the grand life that we don't lead very much of the time. It's more wishful thinking than reality. It's quite humorous in parts, and maybe that's what I intended it to be in the first place."

Gary Brooker: "The middle instrumental section on that was a throwback to what you might have heard in a Grand Hotel. This captured music which we had heard in Grand Hotels all round Europe. For us that stopped when they closed the Palace Hotel in Southend-on-Sea. It was the end of Palm Court orchestras. We used to see them. So the middle section with BJ Wilson playing 22 mandolins was really just a Venetian input to 'Grand Hotel'. Wilson used to play it like that onstage!"

Chris Thomas: "'Grand Hotel' was a case of how big can this go? Megalomania set in there! In the middle we got BJ Wilson to play 22 mandolins. Then we mixed them all down so we had this fluttering effect in the background. There was a choir that we tracked three times, and an orchestra. In actual fact one of the problems with this song was that we put down so much that we made copies of copies of copies and started to wear the tape out. So it never sounded as wonderful as I had wanted it to. It got more worn out at one end, so we put more stuff on top to try and compensate for it. Despite that it's a fabulous song… one of Gary's masterpieces."

Reid's lyrics display a black humour in the rocking 'Toujours L'Amour'. "The song means long live love," he confessed, "and it is an obvious quip about the song itself. The title is humorous because in the song the woman goes off leaving a chap who comes home to his empty flat to find a note she's left for him; she's taken the cat as well." Was the song self referential? "No," smiled Reid, "I've still got the cat!"

The ballad 'A Rum Tale' shows Reid further spoofing "love gone wrong". Copping provides some fine Hammond work on a song which features no guitar whatsoever. Reid told *Circus* magazine, "That's a real drinking song. Well not a drinking song as such, but a song from the bottom of a bottle! The music is actually quite romantic. It's sort of a South Sea island type of thing – very Caribbean."

'TV Caesar' made for an epic end to side one of *Grand Hotel*. The song, actually written in AIR studios when the band reconvened there in November, was inspired by American TV chat show hosts who came over as being far more perspicacious than their European counterparts. Reid recollected a time in 1972 when he turned down the chance to go to Disneyland with the rest of the band, preferring to kick back in his hotel room watching Johnny Carson and Dick Cavett. "When we come to America we avidly watch all the talk shows," he told *Hit Parader*'s Beryl Felice. "Johnny Carson, Dick Cavett, and David Frost... I remember when David Frost was very big about two years ago. Now he's not that popular any more, but when he was at his peak, Frost could have been – and maybe was – ruling the world. Just like Procol's 'TV Caesar' whose 'mighty mouse tops the pops in every house'."*

The actual moment that inspired Reid to pen this somewhat overlooked song came from a typical moment of disingenuous TV chat show banter, no doubt prompted by the producer's autocue, featuring Frost's trademark "Great to have you on the show", which he told *every* guest. "So that prompted me to think about these guys being the real rulers of America... as being TV Caesars," Reid continued telling *Hit Parader*. "The song is about that whole situation. It's about a TV Caesar who's got a 'mighty mouse' and gets the news in every house. Instead of the theory that we are watching him, it's really that they're watching

---

* Between 1969–1972, David Frost was at his primetime peak in America. Procol appeared on Frost's show in 1969 performing 'A Salty Dog'. In between camera rehearsals and live taping, a life-sized Madame Tussaud's-styled wax effigy of Frost was placed into a swivel chair as a stunt double or 'sit-down stand-in' for the man!

131

us whilst we're eating our TV dinners '... creeping into eyes and ears, finding out our secret fears'."

'A Souvenir Of London' was Gary Brooker's affectionate tribute to London's former cockney buskers. Having witnessed street musicians each day outside Oxford Circus's underground exit, situated next to AIR Studio's entrance, Brooker decided to do a kind of Don Partridge tribute. Reid came up with a set of cheeky, saucy lyrics. "I've said this before, but I always find it funny the way songwriting works," Reid said wryly. "I was just trying to do some writing, and I didn't know what to write about and I had a pencil, which said, 'A Souvenir Of London'. I thought to myself, 'hmm ... so what else could that be?' So I wrote a song about venereal disease!"

The recording itself was a lot of fun. "The guys all sat around in a semi-circle inside AIR studios," recalled Chris Thomas. "BJ had a big bass drum. There was a banjo, an accordion, acoustic guitar, and a mandolin. Gary then had an idea for a spoons solo. Nobody could actually play spoons. So our roadie Denny Brown, who was a London guy, had a go. In the end he couldn't do it properly so someone else [Dave Ball] joined in. Both of them played; one tapped out the rhythm, whilst the other guy played the offbeat. We cut it together and it does actually sound like *one* guy playing spoons."

'A Souvenir Of London' was the only cut to make it to the album with Ball's guitar and spoons performance intact. Mick Grabham was gracious enough to concede this point: "That's Dave Ball on guitar there – not me! I didn't play on that one," he said. Although Ball was uncredited on the original 1973 album release, the matter was later rectified with the 2009 CD reissue. This is possibly a moot point in retrospect because when it was originally issued as a Chrysalis single, 'A Souvenir Of London' received a blanket ban across the nation's airwaves.

"'Bringing Home The Bacon' was inspired by American hamburger joint menus," Reid told *Street Life's* Angus MacKinnon in May 1976. "It's about American menus we saw on all our visits there," added Brooker. "Tender juicy steaks, breast fed baby duckling, three day old honey-fed fresh thin-sliced delicious gourmet veal, wrapped in a heavenly blessing of crushed bread crumbs and egg yolks grilled to your personal delight on a bed of lettuce garnished with dill pickles. Keith got all that off actual American menus. I suppose you could say that 'Grand Hotel' is one end of touring and 'Bringing Home The Bacon' is the opposite end." Reid added recently, "It's really just a song about obesity in America."

In 1997 the author Douglas Adams said that "the song was almost certainly the inspiration (along with 'Grand Hotel') for *The Restaurant At The End Of The Universe"* – Adams' sequel to *The Hitchhiker's Guide To The Galaxy*.

The song is essentially a great Brooker–Reid rocker featuring stylish guitar licks from Grabham, classy organ work from Copping, and impeccable rhythm from Wilson. The track also features the debut of the Pahene Recorder Ensemble, which in truth is Procol humour, the name 'Pahene' being a euphemism for the recorder and flute work undertaken by Ball, Brooker, Wilson and Copping.

Chris Thomas: "I really don't know where the idea came from to use the recorders. We came in to re-record the song with the speeding up of the piano for melodramatic effect. When Mick Grabham joined and did it on the road, it worked better at a faster tempo. So after Dave Ball left we redid it in this faster tempo, but still using [the earlier tapes of] the Pahene recorders."

"One final point concerning 'Bringing Home The Bacon'," adds Chris Copping. "A part of the song that might have been 'borrowed' on another record is 'the Pahene Recorder Ensemble'. Listen to 'The Colour Of Spring' by Talk Talk. The last track ends with recorders. Tim Friese-Greene was a tape operator back in our day..."

'For Liquorice John', with its phased down piano and chromatic harp sounds, is dedicated to the late Dave Mundy, the friend of Brooker's who had inspired Procol's 'secret' rock'n'roll sessions recorded at Abbey Road studios back in 1970; later released in 1997 under the guise of *Ain't Nothing To Get Excited About* by Liquorice John Death & The All Stars.

Reid's lyrics nod in the direction of poet Stevie Smith's 'Not Waving, But Drowning'. It is without a shadow of a doubt Procol Harum's most overlooked song and one of their greatest. The song should have been a single and a hit to boot, being every bit as good as David Bowie's 'Rock'n'Roll Suicide' and as evocative and haunting as Elton John's 'Funeral For A Friend', issued on his *Goodbye Yellow Brick Road* album later in 1973. 'For Liquorice John' is also arguably the finest piece of Procol production work undertaken by Chris Thomas. The song features his trademark qualities as a producer; a wall of sound; layering of instruments; and a perfect integration of percussion within some of the most magnificent melodies ever written by Brooker.

Chris Thomas: "On 'For Liquorice John' I seem to remember having some very strange set-up with out-of-tune-pianos. I wanted the thing to sound like it was underwater [to create the effect of drowning] and I didn't do it by messing around in the control room. This was in the days before any boxes for digital post production trickery. A twelve-string guitar was played and then picked up through a Leslie. This was connected to an upright de-tuned piano with Gary playing the same riff in perfect time to the guitar part. The result was a very weird sound indeed, which just seemed to work!"

Chris Copping: "There are so many great production tricks on 'For Liquorice John' like the piano through a Leslie; a guitar amp mic'd close to an upright piano with the sustain pedal held down ..."

Gary Brooker: "... And drumming parts cascading around and all through it ... 'For Liquorice John' wasn't a happy song because it was about suicide. It had quite a bit of aggression about it and a lot of sweetness too along the way."

'Fires (Which Burnt Brightly)' is most European in tone and could well have featured in a French movie by Claude Lelouch. It features the voice of Christiane Legrand, lead singer with the Paris-based Swingle Singers – a lady with a magically resonant voice. As Andy Tyler described in *Disc* of March 17, 1973. "Her noo nah noo backings and scat solo near the middle are exactly right."

Gary Brooker: "The opening of 'Fires' is a little bit from Bach's 'Well Tempered Clavier'. I don't know which one though. I hadn't written anything which was Bach-like since 'A Whiter Shade Of Pale'. So I thought I'd have another go there. The Swingle Singers had probably always been a favourite from about 1966 – especially their Bach renditions. Christiane Legrand their lead singer, the sister of the film composer Michel Legrand, had such a sweet voice. We were at AIR Studios with Chris Thomas. We'd probably already recorded that song, but we thought that we needed somebody else doing that one. Suddenly Christiane Legrand was *there* like the next day or the day after!"

Chris Thomas: "She had listened to the song and had a few ideas. She flew in from Paris and when she arrived she said, 'If I could just go and have a large steak and a bottle of wine, then I will be ready for you!' We were all ready to go, but she went off and had lunch for about an hour and a half. But when she came back she sang this *fantastic* solo, straight away and in one take."

Gary Brooker: "She really got into it and then double tracked and quadruple tracked herself. I think *Les Parapluies De Cherbourg's* soundtrack by Michel Legrand must have stuck in my mind. Having thought I'd written a great tune, I suddenly realised there was a bit of unconscious plagiarism going on there... The French have always had strong melodies and Procol Harum-like strong melodies. They've got that romanticism and a bit of emotion in there ..."

Chris Thomas: "The keyboard on the track was in fact one of those Baldwin Electric harpsichords that had been left from a film soundtrack recording session. At AIR there would often be interesting instruments left lying around like pipe organs, harpsichords, etc. I'd always find out how long they were hired out for and then I'd 'borrow them' until they had to be taken away."

Keith Reid: "'Fires Which Burnt Brightly' is a sad song. It's me talking to somebody and saying the war we are waging, we are waging it, but it's already lost. The thing we were fighting for was finished a long time ago. It goes on to say 'malice and habit has now won the day', which means all that we are left with is the habit of fighting with each other ... 'the honours we fought for are lost in the fray' ... the thing that we were fighting for was lost in the fighting ..."

Gary Brooker: "When we were about to do 'Fires...' at a concert in Paris, unknown to us, Christiane Legrand was in the audience. She just got up and climbed onstage and sang 'Fires', which was one of those great, great moments!"

135

The concluding track on *Grand Hotel,* 'Robert's Box', is lyrically reminiscent of The Beatles' 'Doctor Robert' about a certain New York physician whose large bag of pharmaceutical goodies kept his clients permanently abuzz. The song's conclusion is also slightly reminiscent of 'The Grand Finale' from *Shine On Brightly's* 'In Held 'Twas In I'. Brooker's rumbling bassy vocal refrains and Thomas' full wall of sound help to give this track a distinct flavour, thereby providing the perfect ending to another truly great Procol album.

To match the ornate nature and European style of much of the music, the sleeve to *Grand Hotel* was something of an artistic masterstroke. The large glossy lyric booklet contained black and white illustrations by Spencer Zahn while the cover photographs, taken by Jeffrey Weisel, attracted the attention of upmarket Italian art magazine *2001* whose Renato Marengo wrote, "The move back to the antique, the decadent, and the *fin-de-siecle* in music coincides with that in the field of photography. Black and white on the outside, printed so as to substitute black with the browny-beigey colour characteristic of photographs from the early years of this century, a sepia effect caused by the poor fixing that the grandfathers of photography, pioneers of the lens, came up with...

"For interiors Jeffrey Weisel has used photo-colour, as it were intervening in the printing process: to get the black and white effect almost washed-out with a fake-restored feel for the gatefold. The inside of the sleeve re-proposes the same meanings, but much more explicitly, more transparently. It looks like the last gathering of survivors of a middle class society all but extinct. There's pride and desolation in the expression of the 'guests', and at the same time an atmosphere of waiting for who-knows-what eventuality, positive or catastrophic. The 'enchanted' scene reminds us of the expectation of 'nothingness' in the Alain Robbe Grillet/Alain Resnais film *Last Year In Marienbad*."

With one notable exception in the shape of *Rolling Stone's* Bud Scoppa who opined that *Grand Hotel* was "a collection of overblown production jobs that at their worst approach self-parody, and simpler, less grandiose tracks that suggest Procol Harum may yet find a way out of the corner they have worked themselves into", it seemed that the critics were again virtually unanimous in their praise for Procol's new epic. "There are nine tracks on *Grand Hotel*," wrote Procol champion Penny Valentine in *Sounds*, "covering a great maze of emotions from nostalgia to lost love, suicide, decay and desolation, and throughout there is no let-up in pitch. Procol have come up with music here that steadily assaults your nerve endings – without a moment to recover from the last attack, they move off into the next."

However, with very strong competition from the likes of Elton John (*Don't Shoot Me I'm Only The Piano Player*), Pink Floyd (*Dark Side Of The Moon*) and Led Zeppelin (*Houses of The Holy*) rock's heavyweights would once again fly in the face of Procol's serious creative efforts. As a consequence, when released in March 1973, *Grand Hotel* was not to be a Top 10 album in Britain nor America. Nevertheless, it reached a *Billboard* chart position of 21, remaining in the US charts for five months. Failing to chart in the UK it did go on to earn Procol a UK silver disc for 250,000 sales some three years later.

Procol's first major tour of Britain's municipal halls as a headline act finally took place during March 1973 when they were supported by the long-forgotten Hemlock. After this 12-date sweep Procol geared up to a serious assault on various territories across the globe, starting in America where, once again major names such as Dr John and up-and-coming folkies Steeleye Span and The Strawbs lined up in the support slot. With the might of Chrysalis now promoting them globally the release of *Grand Hotel* was a high profile event for Procol Harum. Images of the band wearing top hats and tails appeared on huge advertising hoardings along Hollywood Boulevard as well as inside record shop windows throughout that spring.

On August 24, Procol performed at the first ever Edinburgh Rock Festival as star attraction at the Empire Theatre in a week of high-profile rock gigs, which ran in tandem to the 1973 Edinburgh International Festival. A video of the show was shown throughout the festival at the Scottish Arts Council Galleries in Charlotte Square for the remainder of the 21-day duration.

'Procol Tour The World' stated a bold headline on *Sounds'* front page dated September 15. "Seven British dates are confirmed for November (taking in) the Royal Festival Hall in November as a part of a world tour which takes place in Britain, Australia, New Zealand, the States, France, Germany, Belgium and Scandanavia." By the time the paper hit newsstands in England, Procol were already touring Australia for the first time. There was considerable press interest in Procol upon their arrival down under and Brooker and Reid were both interviewed for ABC TV's music show *GTK*.

Meanwhile following on from the successfully staged Edmonton Symphony Orchestra event, offers continued to be tabled for Procol Harum to perform more shows with an orchestra and choir.

Derek Sutton: "We had received several offers; one from an up-and-coming conductor in upstate Buffalo. We tried hard to get that happening. It didn't happen. Then the Los Angeles Philharmonic Orchestra offer came along. The gig was originally going to be done inside the Dorothy Chandler Pavilion in L.A., but then we got the chance of playing the Hollywood Bowl instead. Orchestras plan a year in advance. So we first got a date for a rehearsal, then a budget that we could afford and tickets that we could also afford. Playing the Hollywood Bowl to 18,000 people outdoors meant looking for the right team to make it work!"

Doing an open air gig with a full orchestra and choir would be a challenge, especially when *The King Biscuit Flower Hour* had offered to broadcast the event on FM radio across the USA as a one hour American network special. In essence the sound would have to work both for the transmission and for the audience on the night.

The Hollywood Bowl was no stranger to rock'n'roll. The Beatles had played there in 1964 and 1965, Pink Floyd road tested *The Dark Side Of The Moon* (prior to its release) in 1972, and two weeks prior to Procol's show of September 21, Elton John debuted his new album *Goodbye Yellow Brick Road* on September 7 in a much hyped concert that would be documented by the British film director Bryan Forbes. As far as 'spectacle' went, the bar had already been raised by Procol's peers. So Brooker and chums had to match, if not better, the *ESO* album that they had previously made with the Edmonton Symphony Orchestra in November 1971. The pressure was clearly *on* for all concerned.

The Bowl had their own sound man in the shape of Frank Supak as three sound desks would be required for this particular gig. The lighting and stage design would be undertaken be the legendary Chip Monck who had designed the stage and lighting for Woodstock. Furthermore, Isaiah Jackson would conduct the orchestra and the Roger Wagner Chorale was to provide the vocal backing. As well as being their record producer, Chris Thomas was Procol's regular sound mixer on the road at this particular stage. The band also had an able sound engineer in the shape of David Pelletier who had done the sound for Pink Floyd's show at the Hollywood Bowl the year before.

Derek Sutton: "David Pelletier decided to do the show in mono for the L.A. audience. It was the best sound that I had ever heard at the Hollywood Bowl, and *that* was Pelletier's genius."

David Pelletier: "We had just come back from Australia and the one-sided sound system was a suggestion of Bruce Jackson, then Elvis' engineer and later of Springsteen fame. We had used this technique in New Zealand and Australia and it actually worked beautifully during the Hollywood Bowl rehearsals. All that bass coupling filled the Bowl effortlessly. Only those on the very far house left needed a little vocal fill and that was provided... When it came to showtime we set everything just as it was the night before. Everyone waited. When the lights went down out of the darkness came the sickening sound of one string player after another standing up and raising the microphones to where they were used to seeing them for a standard symphony recording. We knew right then and there that we were cooked."

Chris "The Grouts" Michie (tape operator): "If Chris Thomas and Dave Pelletier were using mainly condenser microphones on stage, they would be much more vulnerable to *feedback*..."

David Pelletier: "Physics dictates that a microphone trying to pick up a soft string sound amidst the din of a rock'n'roll band is going to pick up very little string and maximum band overspill. To compound matters, at the moment the concert started, the Hollywood Bowl union sound engineer arrived and dictated under no uncertain terms – to Chris

Thomas and me – that he was going to operate the sound board, that he would mix the orchestra and feed it directly to the mixers carrying the band sound. Well, you can imagine how it went. Poor Chris was trying to replicate his Edmonton success and I was leaning on the Bowl guy to lighten up and not reach for the sky with volume: 'skreech'. In the end, after a two-hour struggle, it ended with everyone blaming it on a 'one-sided sound system'."

Despite the technical issues Procol received several standing ovations during the two-hour concert. The band was on fire and Brooker's singing was quite superb. The first encore featured the band performing 'A Souvenir Of London' without the orchestra, and then 'TV Caesar' with full orchestra, which segued into 'Rule Britannia' while a giant inflatable Godzilla suddenly appeared from the pool in front of the stage prior to a spectacular firework show, which lit up Hollywood's autumn skies. Procol returned to the stage wearing top hats and tails and took their bows to a 10-minute standing ovation. A positive *Rolling Stone* review was marred by reports of the screeching 'feedback' throughout the concert but luckily it was not in evidence on the quadraphonic tape recordings made for the *King Biscuit Flower Hour* transmitted on October 28.

Following hard on the heels of the LA Philharmonic gig Chrysalis management booked a spot for Procol on Burt Sugarman's prestigious Saturday night American network TV showcase, *The Midnight Special,* hosted by cult US DJ Wolfman Jack. Palm Court chic was very much de rigueur in 1973 and the broadcast was planned as a live transmission from an art deco building in London's fashionable Kensington High Street. Formerly known as Derry & Toms by 1973 it had become Biba, London's hippest fashion store, with a top floor club and restaurant situated beneath the famous Kensington Roof Gardens. The club had started to hold live gigs and the following month it would infamously play host to the ultimate in glam rock'n'roll chic, The New York Dolls.

"We only did the show because we were told it was going to go out live ..." says Pelletier. In the event the show was taped 'as live' on October 15 for transmission across three differing American time zones on Saturday November 30. After a year of touring Procol were in great shape performing five songs – four from *Grand Hotel* and 'Conquistador'. Bryan Ferry was rumoured to be in the audience wearing his trademark white tuxedo and spats.

Gary Brooker: "By the end of 1973 we all said, 'Enough of this poncing around with the orchestras. Let's get back to rock,' which is in fact what we did do when we went back to AIR Studios in December to start recording *Exotic Birds & Fruit.*"

Keith Reid: "We always did that! Whenever we were successful with something we always then ran in the opposite direction!"

Chapter 9

Exotic Birds & Fruit

1974

"It's all meaty positive stuff with some fine drummery. There's a latent power too, something like a huge engine cruising."

John Peel

The winter of 1973/74 marked a grim time in Britain. A hellishly cold winter was made worse by the country sliding into economic crisis, the coal miners' strike and 'the three day week'. The shortened working week was imposed by the government due to a fuel crisis brought on by the seemingly never ending strike, which meant power cuts across the country nationally. These cuts were imposed at any given moment which resulted in schools and homes working by candlelight and hospitals having to crank emergency generators into gear during operations in Britain's first 'winter of discontent'.

The studio sessions for Procol's eighth album, *Exotic Birds & Fruit,* were seriously affected by this unfortunate period of British history. The band seriously contemplated flying to the US in order to conclude the recording, but that wouldn't have been very British, unless of course you were The Rolling Stones.

In April 1974 Keith Reid told Lance Loud in *Circus Raves*, "We really didn't think that we would be able to finish [the album]. We'd rushed into the studio in the beginning of December absolutely brimming with ideas and plans. It had been a long time since we had been in to record and it felt really good. We were going full steam ahead when suddenly this three-day work week burst like a bomb into our lives. It was distressing to say the least. We tried to work on, but there began to be more and more complications and suddenly we were faced with the serious possibility that we might not be able to finish the record at all."

With the strikers, politicians and executives seemingly having all reached stalemate, life in not so 'Great' Britain showed just how intransigent people could be. The Conservatives accused the miners of "holding the country to ransom" and the Labour party accused the Conservatives of trying to destroy the mining industry. The resonance of these events was reflected in some of Reid's newest songs.

"We started talking about moving everyone involved over to America and trying to finish it up there," Reid told Loud. "We still had quite a lot to do, and stopping to wait in the hope that the problem would be solved soon was too big a risk. We could have been totally ruined just sitting around waiting. Being away from home for so long, especially when you're recording, you must have a place to go at the end of a session to think and rest, and I felt that we wouldn't have been able to have that in the States. There were quite a lot of things involved and we just got tremendously bogged down trying to think it all out straight."

A studio generator had to be hauled into action in order to complete the album for its scheduled release in the spring of 1974. Produced by Chris Thomas, his fifth for Procol, some earlier recorded sections used tapes that had suddenly cranked to a halt when the power went down but even these parts were used to add certain 'effects' to the songs. When probed, a smiling Thomas would not say which songs nor where!

Added to the industrial unrest, there was a record industry view that, in times of economic recession, lavish gatefold album covers filled with elaborate 'extras' were no longer the order of the day. A paper shortage meant Procol would have to forsake their planned booklet, as per their previous album, and a proposed gatefold sleeve, too. Of course if Procol Harum had been a million selling artist like David Bowie and Elton John things might have been altogether different. Having taken Chrysalis' stance personally amid other underlying 'issues', Reid wrote a rather biting song aimed fairly and squarely at the owners of the company. With Chrysalis potentially more interested in raising its own profile and placing this stance above the concerns of its artists, 'Butterfly Boys' would cause something of a stir.

They tell us that we're savages
who haven't got a hope
We're burning in the furnaces,
we're choking at the smoke
They say we haven't got a choice,
refuse to recognise our voice,
Yet they enjoy commissions
from the proceeds of the joke

Those Butterfly Boys
at play with their toys
Stinging like bees
itching like fleas
Butterfly Boys
you got the toys
You got the breeze
we caught the freeze
Butterfly Boys give us a break
We got the groceries you got the cake

They tell us that we're savages
who cannot understand
We're sailing on a sinking ship,
we're swimming in the sand
They put their fingers in their ears,
refuse to recognise our fears
And fly off to Jamaica

This bitter diatribe was the first song to be recorded for the new album. "We had a very close relationship with the people that we worked with over at AIR Studios," said Brooker, "[engineer] John Punter and Chris Thomas. They said, 'Let's boogie', so we started off with this one. They really enjoyed making it."

There was less enjoyment when Chrysalis bosses, Chris Wright and Terry Ellis, realised that the 'Butterfly' in question was their Chrysalis logo and the 'boys' in question were themselves – the word 'Chrysalis' being a phonic elision of 'Chris' and 'Ellis'. As Brooker revealed, they were perturbed by this – not least presumably by the up-front connection with 'fly-boy', i.e. someone not to be trusted.

Gary Brooker: "This song could apply to any situation where someone's doing well and the others are getting the shit. It's definitely about Terry and Chris swanning it up, doing very well and running a multi-million pound record label. Procol Harum is the 'sinking ship' here. The label owners, who were also our managers, are the ones that 'get the cake'. We weren't exactly ripped off, not like in the past, but Reid had spotted an imbalance. They were very upset about the song, and wanted us to change the words and title to 'Government Boys'. We said, 'Bollocks!'"

"Is it on, Tommy?" enquires Brooker of Thomas at the front of the opening track, 'Nothing But The Truth', before the song bursts into life. Yes indeed it was!

Chris Thomas: "'Nothing But The Truth' is a really great rocking track combining the best elements of Procol. It's like them going back to their R&B roots with The Paramounts. It shows that they could really rock out."

"Elton John also liked ['Nothing But The Truth'] as a piano piece," Brooker reveals. "And I know that Jools Holland [later] spent many, many weeks working it all out and trying to play it!"

When extracted from the album as a 45 John Peel made it 'Single Of The Week' in his weekly *Sounds* newspaper column (dated April 6, 1974). "It's all meaty positive stuff with some fine drummery [*sic*]. There's a latent power too, something like a huge engine cruising. Often the impression of restrained power is more exciting than the vulgar demonstration of that power. Such is the case here. There is an orchestra on the strength too, but it never intrudes as the side builds with subtlety and energy. A fine single!"

'Nothing But The Truth' was among the tracks Procol recorded for Peel's BBC Radio 1 show on March 12. They would also go on to record a slot for Radio 1's *In Concert* series at Golders Green Hippodrome in North London some ten days later, introduced by *Old Grey Whistle Test* presenter Bob Harris. At this juncture one has to query, 'Why did Procol Harum never appear on this long running BBC TV series?' Partly as a result, 'Nothing But The Truth' failed to chart.

'Beyond The Pale' carries the album's momentum forward in the spirit of a German drinking song, with a driving rhythm provided by a combination of piano, acoustic guitar (played by Brooker), mandolin (played by Wilson) and banjo.

Chris Copping: "I hear can hear a banjo on the track and it would have been me playing it; a Clifford Essex. As [Chrysalis PR] Chris Briggs once remarked, the shift from bass to organ also enabled me to concentrate on being the worst banjo player in the world ... But, no bouzoukis!"

Chris Thomas: "A lot of people think its bouzoukis, but I think you'll find its acoustic guitar and piano double tracked and then a little change in the speed of the tape machine so that you get that out-of-tune element to it. So we tracked the piano and then we had a combination of one piano played straight and one piano played flat. Then we did the same things on an acoustic guitar and then mixed it all together thereby creating a completely different sound; and *that* part is what's running throughout the whole song. Whenever Gary first played me a song I'd like to find something in the part that he was playing and isolate it, then find a sound for it and plonk it back on the tape. This happened in the same way when we took arpeggios on the song 'Broken Barricades' and made something of them. If you like that's what I brought to a song as a producer, and that's how it used to work with Procol."

The song was evidently inspired by an old Nordic/Icelandic folk song, 'Who Will Search For Holy Grail?', Brooker claimed prior to performing 'Beyond The Pale' in 1974. Keith Reid: "It's a toasting song to all those in search of something that they will never find. They who continue to look for looking's sake!" And, as online writer Roland Clare rightly asserts, "Historically 'The Pale' was the area to which Catherine the Great restricted Russian Jews, but in Procol-lore it harks back to the band's initial monster hit 'A Whiter Shade Of Pale' which they still played as an encore."

'As Strong As Samson' is one of Reid's finest sets of lyrics. The political timelessness of the song belies its strength, residing with the best of Bob Dylan's work and worthy of a cover by the mighty Zim himself. If one imagines Dylan singing this instead of Brooker it could almost pass as an outtake from *Blood On The Tracks*. As John McFerrin's online review states, "The melody in the 'ain't no use in preachers preaching when they don't know what they're teaching' is one of the most perfect, shattering, totally cathartic hooks I've heard in my life, and that it gets repeated in different variations during the coda only makes me that much happier."

In a May 1976 interview with UK paper *Street Life* Reid told Angus MacKinnon, "'As Strong As Samson' is about the Arab-Israeli confrontation and the general state of things, politics and so on: as profound as you care to take it.' Some years later in a 1984 Danish radio interview he added, "I wrote that at the time around Watergate."

Two years later, when 'As Strong As Samson' merited a standalone release, *NME* writer Steve Clark made it his Single Of The Week (dated January 7, 1976): "The pedal steel [from special guest B.J. Cole] halfway through contrasts well against the stately keyboards of Gary Brooker and Chris Copping. And there's the acoustic guitar finger picking [from Mick Grabham] which appears with a marked clarity seconds into the record... A fine, fine record!"

"'The Idol' might not be able to quite live up to 'As Strong As Samson'", according to McFerrin, "but it's still an absolutely wonderful, gorgeous anthem about false Gods being exposed for the frauds they are, at least, that's what I'm guessing it's about, not to mention that the guitar solo in the extended ending is absolutely superb."

The song also displays Reid at his lyrical best: "Just another idol turned to clay". As he stated in 1974, "It's concerned with anybody who desires something or somebody enough to worship it. But then realise that it's not as magical as you first thought."

'The Idol' has a magnificent yet rather complicated chord structure. Gary Brooker told BBC Radio 1's *Rock Speak* in March 1974, "I must have played about 16 different piano parts, to create this wall of sound." In retrospect Thomas feels that it needed "quite a bit of pruning" and that it was somewhat overblown. Nick Logan, reviewing the album for the *NME* felt likewise, an unfortunate state of affairs as he was then editor of the hugely influential music weekly and his indifference towards Procol Harum would colour the paper's growing distaste for the band in the ensuing years.

With its haunting harmonies and some spellbinding, unique and almost avant-garde guitar from Grabham, 'The Thin End Of The Wedge' still sounds distinctly different and modern which probably explains why Robert Fripp is such an admirer of this particular Procol song. Upon hearing that Grabham had kindly played the whole of the song to the author, Brooker looked somewhat astounded, "That's the hardest song to play of all the Procol Harum songs I've *ever* written," he said.

Chris Thomas: "The thing here would be to hear the guitar part and say to Mick Grabham, 'Now could you do that on a bass guitar too, and then track it.' It could be painstaking. 'The Thin End Of the Wedge' is all quite orchestrated and arranged. This was all done in the studio, rather than going back to the old (*A Salty Dog)* days when they rehearsed things first. Mick Grabham is right in that there *is* some kind of George Harrison influence in the arpeggios. I used to love using arpeggios.

"There is a lot of tracking and overdubbing of the guitar on 'The Thin End Of The Wedge'. It's one of the themes we used a lot on that album. It's like in the old days of having a big band with lots of different instruments playing the same thing at the same time. So when I say 'orchestrated' we were basically doing that with one instrument, with an electric guitar. So there's four guitars all playing one bit, then a bridge, and another bit there with two guitars, then back to four .."

'Monsieur R Monde' is a reworking of an unissued Brooker/Reid song dating back to 1967.* In April 1974 *Music Scene* aptly described it as "All-stops-out rock'n'roll!"

In his online review of *Exotic Birds & Fruit* Roland Clare writes that 'Fresh Fruit' is "the album's novelty item, following in the sporadic tradition of 'A Souvenir Of London', 'Boredom', 'Mabel' and so on. Ostensibly a paean to healthy eating – and as such an antidote to the tales of excess that pervade the preceding album – it is nonetheless also shot through with playful sexual imagery, which the voluptuous quasi-Caribbean presentation is presumably intended to enhance."

Another example of Procol humour at work, the 'phantom whistler' on the track must have had endless reserves of 'puff'. So who was it? Whistling Jack Smith or Kaiser Bill's Batman?

Chris Copping: "It wasn't me, sir! I can't whistle! I'll bet BJ was one of the whistlers. I think Gary may have done the marimbas. BJ would've certainly barked."

Roland Clare: "At a literal level, the song has claims to being the title track of the album, whose cover painting by Jakob Bogdani (1670–1724) was originally entitled merely *Birds And Fruit*. However the picture does not show juice, seeds and so forth, nor any expectant dogs or victims of disease, so we can scarcely claim that Keith Reid's song has grown out of the image. More likely the painting was selected on its own merits, a decision perhaps clinched by the part-overlap with a song in preparation."

Reid provided confirmation. "We named [the album] after the painting because we liked it and we hated the idea of naming any more albums after one of the cuts on it."

Doug D'Arcy thinks that Chris Wright had seen the painting in a London art gallery and bought it, but cannot be certain. Wright then suggested using it as a potential cover for the album to Brooker.

---

* The original *Shine On Brightly* outtake version, from October 20, 1967, first surfaced as 'Monsieur Armand' on the Cube Records compilation series *Rock Roots* in the summer of 1976, some two years after *Exotic Birds & Fruit* was issued.

149

The reflective 'New Lamps For Old' draws the album to a close, highlighting Wilson's prowess as a great percussionist, particularly at the song's end.

Chris Copping: "I think 'New Lamps For Old' was the last song we recorded, the end of the evening as it were. I seem to remember that it was done in the small studio at AIR. It seemed a magical evening. From memory Gary played a Rhodes Piano through a Leslie [amp]. And I believe the ending was my idea. I still regard *Exotic Birds & Fruit* as the best Procol Harum album ..."

A leftover from the sessions, 'Drunk Again' was relegated to the B-side of 'Nothing But The Truth'. The Eddie Cochran-styled guitar riff helped the song to rock along, but it's not a strong cut; hence its flipside status.

When released in April, the album received mixed reviews. "Best forget any notions you may have had that Procol are somehow lagging behind..." Ray Telford advised in *Sounds*. "Procol Harum are very much alive and kicking." *Stereo Review*'s Steve Simels praised the musicianship, "As usual, BJ Wilson's drumming continues to defy belief, Brooker's singing is marvellous, and the band overall is very strong. Another plus is the production by Chris Thomas, which is simply splendid; perhaps the best the band has ever been afforded!"

However, the hugely influential *Rolling Stone* hit a negative note when Alan Niester wrote, "*Exotic Birds & Fruit* is another slab of false majesty for which this band has become noted: elephantine, grandiose production, pretentious [and] empty lyrics."

The album failed to chart in the UK and reached a dismal 86 in *Billboard* over in the US. "The record company in their wisdom blamed the producer for not setting the charts alight," says Copping.

In 1982 Chris Thomas related the following to John Tobler for his book *The Record Producers*: "I was taking over a little too much, and I was running out of ideas, because on *Exotic Birds & Fruit* I didn't find the songs were really inspiring me very much. I was almost having to manipulate ideas, like "What can I think of for this one?" In fact, at one point I was sitting there looking completely vague and the band were stuck, because they were starting to wind down a bit, and Keith Reid said, 'Why don't you do a Chris Thomas production on it?' I think he meant to tart it up a bit, in the way that I had come up with some really crazy ideas for some of their songs."

"We did *Exotic Birds & Fruit* at AIR and I think we were getting sick of the place and sick of each other," Brooker admitted in 1992. "I think if *Exotic Birds & Fruit* has got any faults, and it has got faults, one of the things was the production. I think it could have been a little cleaner. I think on *Grand Hotel* we had a nice clean production. If we'd had that cleanness then it would have been a better album for it. I think production-wise or playing-wise it was getting a bit muddy. It was definitely time to say goodbye to everybody [at AIR Studios]."

Some of the album's alleged muddiness can be put down to problems at the mastering stage. These defects which were in evidence on the original 1974 vinyl pressing of the album were not overseen or checked by Thomas who by then had moved on to other projects. It took until 1995 for the deficiencies to be redressed when Castle Records' CD reissue of *Exotic Birds & Fruit* greatly benefited from excellent digital re-mastering overseen by Dan Kincaid at Master Cutting Rooms in New York. With further improvements made with the 2004 Friday Music edition, the album was finally available in the crystal clear, full wall-of-sound as Thomas had originally intended.

"I think the mistake we made with *Exotic Birds & Fruit* was that we tended to go about making it in the way that we had been recording for a while," Thomas reflected in 2004. "You get into a certain way of working and it's hard to break out of it ... What Procol were trying to do was break new ground and do new stuff as against the pop mainstream of the day."

Meanwhile, former Procol organist Matthew Fisher's production of Robin Trower's second solo album, *Bridge Of Sighs,* reached number three in *Billboard*, thereby overshadowing his former bandmates in the process. Chrysalis labelmate Trower had become Britain's latest 'guitar hero' and was on his way to becoming a superstar.

"Trower has been widely criticised for his influence," said King Crimson's Robert Fripp on November 19, 1996. "This has never bothered me. I toured America in 1974 with Ten Years After top of the bill, King Crimson second, and Robin Trower bottom. The chart positions were the opposite: TYA in the *Billboard* 160s, Crimson in the 60s and Trower climbing remorselessly through the Top 20. Nearly every night I went out to listen to him. This was a man who hung himself on the details: the quality of sound, nuances of each inflection and tearing bend, and abandonment to the feel of the moment. He saved my life. Later, in England, he gave me guitar lessons."

As Procol's *Exotic Birds & Fruit* hit the racks – albeit virtually unnoticed – the band were on tour in America throughout April and May before making a concentrated assault on mainland Europe, which is where they decided to concentrate their activities in years to come. This made sense as Procol were now big sellers in Scandinavia and Germany in particular. Despite having no television exposure in the UK, several major overseas engagements were lined up for the band starting with Dick Clark's *Wide World In Concert*, performing 'As Strong As Samson', 'Beyond The Pale', 'Simple Sister' and 'Nothing But The Truth', live from London's Rainbow, which was videotaped on June 4 and aired July 5 across the American ABC TV network.*

Flying to Norway for the RagnaRock open air festival in Holmenkollen on June 16, NRK TV transmitted 'Homburg', 'The Devil Came From Kansas', and 'A Salty Dog'. Procol also went on to make in-studio appearances for Danish, Swedish, German, and Dutch TV, where they performed 'Beyond The Pale' on the popular music series *TopPop* when the single became a minor Dutch hit.

On home territory, Procol played a mid afternoon set, recorded for Capital Radio, at the annual Crystal Palace Bowl event in South London on Saturday, July 27 with Leo Sayer and Rick Wakeman topping the bill. In his *NME* report Pete Erskine described Procol's set as being, "Incredibly moving. There's a kind of majestic quality to what they do!" Alastair Wright in *The Croydon Advertiser* added, "Procol Harum – a tremendous band grossly underrated in this country. In their first London concert for more than a year, they shattered the summertime

---

* According to Procol's sound man David Pelletier the show's genial host Jim Stafford and producer Dick Clark both helped to double up as band roadies after the show.

blues with a forceful rhythmic set that had the fans on their feet chanting for more."

Procol also filled the mid-afternoon slot at the annual Reading Festival on Saturday, August 24. *NME*'s Steve Clarke and Pete Erskine found Procol to be the best act in a roster that included Thin Lizzy and Traffic. "From the opening bars of 'Shine On Brightly' it was crystal clear that the Procols were the best musicians to take the stage so far that day, as their set progressed, the best band too. They met the demand for an encore with what they announced as "a song from the sixties". Everybody thought it was going to be 'A Whiter Shade Of Pale', but instead it was The Beatles' 'Eight Days A Week' and somehow lacking the buoyancy of the original. Then it was straight into 'A Whiter Shade Of Pale' with everybody standing on their feet. The day's only magic moment...."

Chapter 10

Procol's Ninth

1975

"Chrysalis Records contacted Jerry Leiber and I to do Procol Harum's new album Procol's Ninth. *We had a pretty good-sized hit with Procol Harum's single 'Pandora's Box'. We created the arrangements in the studios with marimbas and bass marimbas, and so forth ..."*

Mike Stoller

With Chrysalis Records, Procol Harum and producer Chris Thomas all in agreement that a fresh direction was needed production wise, Procol turned full circle with an unexpected return to their roots. Gary Brooker, in particular, was an eager bloodhound when picking up the scent that led him directly to rock'n'roll's wiliest pair of producer-songwriter foxes. Jerry Leiber and Mike Stoller were looking to work with another British band, having produced Stealers Wheel's debut album in 1972, which yielded the million-selling 'Stuck In The Middle With You', when Chrysalis made the approach.

Beginning in the mid-fifties with Elvis Presley, Leiber and Stoller wrote songs such as 'Hound Dog', 'Baby I Don't Care' and 'Jailhouse

Rock', among others. They went on to write 'Kansas City' for Fats Domino before revitalising the careers of The Drifters and then The Coasters for whom they wrote 24 *Billboard* hits alone. Their songs from this period included 'Charlie Brown', 'Searchin', 'Yakety Yak', and 'Poison Ivy' – covered in 1963 by a certain R&B group from Southend called The Paramounts – along with 'Stand By Me' (written with Ben E. King) as well as 'On Broadway' (written with Barry Mann and Cynthia Weil). By 1969, when penning the unorthodox 'Is That All There Is?' for Peggy Lee, they had already had 14 US number one hit singles.

Chris Copping: "When we first gigged as The Paramounts, Leiber and Stoller were like the gods, like Wotan or something from Wagner – another planet. We didn't ever dream that our paths would actually meet… We first met Mike and Jerry down at Gary's barn." [The studio next to Brooker's house in Dunsfold, Surrey]

Chrysalis booked Procol into The Who's Ramport Studio facility at 115 Thessaly Road in Battersea, South London, where along with engineer John Jansen, Leiber and Stoller set about producing *Procol's Ninth*.

Gary Brooker: "When we got to the studios it turned out that Leiber and Stoller wanted Procol to do an album of Leiber and Stoller songs. And I don't mean 'Baby I Don't Care', 'I Keep Forgettin'' and 'Stand By Me', I mean stuff they had written in fact for Peggy Lee, but which Peggy had rejected for her 1975 Leiber-Stoller covers album, *Mirrors*. And modern songs, stuff they had written a week before that they were trying to find a market for."

Chris Copping: "They played us small selections of unrecorded songs, one of which was called 'Big Shot' with Mike on piano and Jerry singing, which I think Peggy Lee had rejected."

Mick Grabham: "They also had this song called 'Tango' about some sailor home on shore leave with all kinds of pseudo surrealistic lyrics. It sounded like they were trying to sound like Procol Harum. But nobody was interested in it, none of us."

Gary Brooker: "It wasn't as if they were written for us or would have suited us. It was like, 'Hey do some of ours!' Every time they said that we'd play them one of our new ones. They would then play us one of theirs and we'd *then* play one of their old ones like 'Baby I Don't Care'. Mike Stoller said, 'That's the best fucking version I've ever heard of that, Gary!' We'd actually never played that one before but I knew it."

The standout tracks on *Procol's Ninth* were the openers to each side. With 'Pandora's Box', Leiber/Stoller beautifully reinvented a rejected 1967 outtake from Procol Harum's first album with such melodic vigour, using marimbas – an instrument so familiar from the Latin-tinged classics of The Drifters – that they ended up creating something of a pop masterpiece. "As soon as they heard that song they knew it was a hit and they just zeroed in on it and concentrated on that one," says Keith Reid. "They sure had an ear for a hit, because it turned out to be a hit!"

Gary Brooker: "Leiber and Stoller did a fantastic mix on that actually. Everything that's on that was on it all the time in the recording. They just reduced it a lot ... it starts off with almost just an acoustic guitar and a little bit of rhythm going on. And it just kind of builds from there..."

In his liner notes for the 2009 reissue of *Procol's Ninth* Roland Clare astutely points out that, "devotees of Procol's five-piece sound wondered why the new producers had ceded the stand-out instrumental break to an anonymous New York session flautist (maybe recalling the catchy woodwinds in Nina Rossi's 'Untrue Unfaithful' hit from 1965, a melodic cousin of the Procol tune?) but Leiber/Stoller's hitman ears were vindicated."

The track was as good as anything ever recorded by Procol and deserved to be the hit it was, becoming a UK Top 20 hit in September. Almost equal in strength was the sole Leiber-Stoller cover version on the album.

Chris Copping: "Jerry and Mike were legends so we definitely wanted to do one of their numbers as a tribute. And we had our way by doing 'I Keep Forgettin''."

While in The Paramounts, Brooker had seen Chuck Jackson perform 'I Keep Forgettin'' on *Ready Steady Go!* back in 1965 and remembered being "blown away" by the experience adding, "It was life changing!"

With its perfect combination of tight guitar licks, punchy brass, metronomic rhythms and spine tingling blue-eyed soul vocals, 'I Keep Forgettin'' should really have been the candidate for single honours to follow 'Pandora's Box' and potentially claim another hit. Instead Chrysalis issued Procol's worst *ever* song in the shape of 'The Final Thrust', having trusted the consensus of two utterly misguided music journalists, namely *Sounds'* Angus MacKinnon, who numbered 'The Final Thrust' among the album's three "most resilient tracks", and *NME's* Tony Stewart who called it "my own favourite". Making only one TV appearance on ITV's *Supersonic* the single sank without trace.

A laboured Chrysalis press release described 'Fool's Gold' as "multi-tiered with light R&B chord gliding on the one hand, and dark atmospheric chugging on the other, provided by the patented ascending basso piano/guitar tandem" and 'Taking The Time' as "clever wordplay about a man tired of lazing around, reflecting the man's slothful ways. A very different number for the band, it includes Big Band muted brass, and even a twenties clarinet run."

Mick Grabham: "Their [Leiber and Stoller's] songs were more about rhythms and the placing of instruments. I mean the usage of brass [on 'Fool's Gold' and 'Taking The Time']. Who did they think we were? Chicago?!"

In his *Rolling Stone* review, Bud Scoppa agreed that "the only obvious error is Leiber/Stoller's usage of overdubbed horns for coloration in places where Chris Copping's organ would have been more contextually apt."

Keith Reid borrowed the title for 'The Unquiet Zone' from a TV documentary about World War I. Brooker's vocals imbue the song's morbid subject with added gravitas on lines such as 'an awful waste of guts and gore'. It could have been an effective mood setter for Sam Peckinpah's 1977 movie *Cross Of Iron* where similar themes are explored with plenty of 'guts and gore' for added measure.

In early 1974 Grabham turned Brooker on to one of America's finest contemporary bands, Little Feat, who had supported Procol on an American tour. By coincidence, their drummer Richie Hayward had roadied for Procol on a US tour some years before. Later in '74, while on the road, Brooker wrote a new song, 'The Poet', whose title was changed to 'Without A Doubt'. The original arrangement was partly inspired by the particular bass lines displayed throughout Little Feat's music.

Gary Brooker: "A few months before we came to do 'Without A Doubt', [Lou Reed and Alice Cooper producer] Bob Ezrin was in fact going to produce us. We had a demo of this song 'The Poet', which I had recorded myself and there was a different approach entirely on *that* version. 'The Poet' had a really different groove to 'Without A Doubt'. It was a Little Feat song. I mean I don't know whether 'The Poet' would sound like a Little Feat song *now,* but it was directly and absolutely attributable to that, having spent time with them. This is how they do things, you know, with a cool groove that stumbles around – that's the way I wrote it. But I don't think it turned out like that. By the time it ended up on *Procol's Ninth* it ended up as a rather brash song."

Lyrically the album appeared to display the politics of disillusionment and possibly even provided the listener with an open admission of Reid's writer's block. In April 1977 Paul Kendall, the UK editor of *Zig Zag,* asked Reid if he found it difficult to come up with the goods. 'Without A Doubt?' Reid replied with a smile. "*That* song and 'Typewriter Torment' were intended to be humorous... I think people took them a bit too seriously and I thought I was getting paranoid about it all, where I was commenting on it in a humorous matter – I thought."

Typewriter torment, dreadful disease
Caught it the first day I touched the keys
You wear down your fingers and churn out your pap
It eats up your life like a dose of the clap
Typewriter torment it tortures me still
If only my doctor could see that I'm ill

Typewriter fever it harries me still
If only my doctor would give me a pill
Typewriter fever gives birth to a flood
It sweeps through your body and curdles your blood

You curse and discourse but you're damned for all time
The moment your fingers give birth to a rhyme
Typewriter fever it harries me still
If only my doctor would give me a pill

Typewriter fever I'm worn to a stub
I've dumped my Thesaurus and pulled out the plug
I'm rending my ribbon and bending my spool
Don't bother rewinding: I'm done with it all
But why can't my doctor just say that I'm ill?
Typewriter fever is paying his bill.

Having recorded an unreleased Scottish piper's 'lament' back in 1968 as a lighthearted tribute to one of their early roadies named 'McGregor', Procol attempted a similar experiment. Unfortunately it was a plodding dirge that would provide further fuel for Procol's detractors.

Gary Brooker: "'The Piper's Tune' ... was a different sort of song. Folky Procol if you like. It was a sequel to 'McGregor', which was also a Scottish tune. 'The Piper's Tune' to its credit made good use of a Lowrey organ in place of actual bagpipes."

An album of different moods and textures, with hindsight it's not surprising that *Procol's Ninth* should end on an unexpected note with an unusual choice of cover version. Grabham spoke to British fanzine *Deja Vu* in the autumn of 1977 about this controversial inclusion. "We'd just done ['Eight Days A Week'] live as a laugh a couple of times as an encore. We did it in the studio just for a laugh, too, and it ended up on the album. Big mistake! But there you go, so what? It's not like re-writing the facts of life or anything. We were just making a record and I've heard worse things by successful people."

Chris Copping: "'So Far Behind' should have been done instead of 'Eight Days A Week', but we didn't record it!"*

---

* 'So Far Behind' was finally recorded and included on Procol's *The Well's On Fire* in 2003.

Gary Brooker: 'I have no idea how The Beatles' 'Eight Days A Week' ended up on a Procol Harum album to this very day. I mean we played it. It's me singing it. I think we've always tried to maintain some sort of dignity, but if we'd had a hit with *that* I think I would have to become an insurance salesman or maybe even a monk. Talk about losing objectivity. It had gone out of the window by then."

If prepared to overlook four duff songs *Procol's Ninth* is in fact an album of reinvigoration. Gone was the layering and multi-track overdubs so redolent of the Chris Thomas period. In its place was a new consistent clarity to the recordings, which was hitherto unheard of on a Procol Harum release since the glory days of *A Salty Dog* six years earlier.

"Procol breathe again!" Angus MacKinnon gushed in his *Sounds* review. "Grabham's playing is throughout painstaking and concise, breaks thoughtfully constructed and chord work as accurate as Atomic Time, while Copping has opted for an evocatively metallic organ tone, rather akin to Irmin Schmidt on Can's *Future Days*, which lends substantial support to Brooker's interpretation of Keith Reid's reliably pessimistic lyrics ... Yes, *Procol's Ninth* signals reinvigoration for Procol Harum; you'd do best to savour it."

Such a review indicates how certain critics at the time were prepared to overlook the album's more obvious deficiencies. *Creem's* Ken Barnes described side two, which contained the weakest material as being "as strong a musical block as anything in the group's past five years". *Crawdaddy* even appeared to consider 'The Piper's Tune' to be one of the finest cuts. "The bagpipe-under-toned organ stops and BJ Wilson's ace Scottish marching-Al Jackson-sharp-highlight-funk-drumming makes the tune a minor masterpiece in the Grand Procol Style."

However, other critics were less forthcoming. *Melody Maker's* Allan Jones' review header, 'Insipid Shade Of Pale', said it all, opening with this glorious gambit, "No grace in action here sailor. Procol Harum sound like a tired and disillusioned band all right [sic]. Closer perhaps than they've ever been to curling up and dying on your doorstep...

And anyway, when Brooker starts coming on with his "let's play music while Europe falls" arrangements ['The Final Thrust'] one simply can't be bothered to investigate this possibility any further!"

"I expect *Procol's Ninth* ended up with some compromises and a lack of direction," Brooker concedes. "You can see that *that* is not the right way to make an album when you have got *that* sort of relationship going on [with the producers]; it's not heading towards anything. And frankly some of *our* songs on that album should never have got that far. They weren't of a good enough quality. If I had doubts about a particular song I would want an opinion. But at this particular point, for some reason, if I had a doubt about a song Mick Grabham would say, 'that's great' and I would believe him! Something like 'The Final Thrust' should never have got recorded. I don't think that that's a very good song at all."

Grabham now agrees. "'The Final Thrust?' We shouldn't have done it. Not very good at all!"

Chris Copping: "'The Final Thrust' is awful and the Scottish song ['The Piper's Tune'] is not much better. Leiber and Stoller didn't do anything *wrong* on that album. Writing and producing things like a string line on a Drifters track ... I mean Phil Spector was a guitarist on some of their sessions. They were legends – rock'n'roll royalty ... Anyway we got to meet them and work with them and got photographed with Ben E King into the bargain. Things like that – and having an autograph from Eusebio at a gig in Lisbon – seem to make your life worthwhile!"

On August 6, Procol Harum returned to the BBC's *Top Of The Pops* studio for the first time since 1968 to plug 'Pandora's Box'. As the song moved into the Top 20 Procol undertook a second taped appearance on September 4 for transmission the following day which was repeated September 18. Procol then flew to Holland to televise *TopPop,* the Dutch *TOTP* equivalent on September 19, where the single also became a hit. Released that same month, the variable quality of *Procol's Ninth* affected its chart placing, reaching number 41 in the UK and 52 in American *Billboard*.

Procol bounced back but Trower once again kicked them into touch with his third solo album, *For Earth Below,* produced by Fisher for Chrysalis, which reached a *Billboard* number 10. Now a huge concert draw in both Britain and America, Procol's former guitar player had front page stories and double page spreads in every single music paper. Some journalists even declared that he was 'the natural successor to Jimi Hendrix'.

Nevertheless, Procol seemed to be in good spirit and were regarded as something of a hot live act throughout 1975 with tours of Scandinavia, Europe and North America where they played shows with the Sensational Alex Harvey Band, Fleetwood Mac, Little Feat, and Rick Wakeman. It proved they were still a hot ticket despite massive competition from the likes of Led Zeppelin, The Rolling Stones, The Who, and Elton John – who tried to poach Mick Grabham as a band replacement for his guitarist Davey Johnstone.

In March Procol topped the bill at London's Rainbow Theatre in a special Farewell Concert for the venue, which in fact re-opened a year later. A rather tongue-in-cheek version of 'Grand Hotel' along with Procol backing 'Scotland's foremost poet' (and labelmate) Frankie Miller on his version of Allen Toussaint's 'Brickyard Blues' were two of the highlights from their live sets appearing on the Chrysalis live release *Over The Rainbow.*

On August 10 the band performed at the London Palladium. Taking the view that such a prestigious West End venue was the appropriate place to showcase *Procol's Ninth*, Brooker chose to perform not *one* but *two* sets! Then the jitters set in as Chris Charlesworth astutely pointed out in his *Melody Maker* review of August 16. "It could well have been two bands performing at the London Palladium on Sunday. The first was a shambling, incohesive bunch whose dull plodding attitude resulted in a number of fans walking out, while the second was a revitalised unit grasping for a victory they ultimately won... It became apparent that the audience, a large percentage of whom were tourists, were there only to listen to the group's older material. 'A Salty Dog' went down a bomb and deservedly so. [Former Bonzo Dog Doo Dah Band singer] Viv Stanshall compered the show and joined in on a hesitant, but enthusiastic tambourine whenever convenient. It was a welcome sign that Procol are not taking themselves quite so seriously these days."

Flying to France to headline the Orange Festival on August 16 over Ginger Baker, Tangerine Dream, The Pretty Things, and the unannounced, but newly emerging Dr Feelgood, also from Southend, Procol actually 'stole the show' according to French TV's *Pop Deux*.

At the end of the month Procol Harum were invited as special guests of the President of Mexico to perform at three large venues: one in Guadalajara on August 28 and two in Mexico City at the Auditorio Nacional on August 30 and 31. The President had been, according to Brooker, "something of a fan of the song 'Conquistador' and this was his rather belated invite to his country".

Jorge Ruben Ledesma Aguilar who attended the Guadalajara gig remembers paying 30 pesos (about two dollars in US money at the time) admission. "The concert was very important because at that time rock concerts in Mexico were *not* permitted at all!' The gigs in Mexico City were a huge deal and thousands were unable to get in to the shows, resulting in a near riot outside the venue and Mexican police bringing in water cannon to control the distressed crowds. Both nights were televised for network TV transmission on Mexico's Channel 13."

Gary Brooker: "I remember some people got shot outside. There was sporadic gunfire inside I think. Or was it people letting off firecrackers? A woman had a baby delivered and they sprayed water on the audience inside because it was so hot. And the Mexican police sprayed water cannon on those outside who couldn't get in because they were rioting!"

Chris Copping: "I don't remember the gigs apart from some water cannons spraying the crowds... I recall nice chilli sauces that weren't too devastating and going for a stroll in a leafy suburb of Mexico City on a Sunday and finding a slightly English bar. But my best memory of Mexico is that Derek Sutton would be with us on a tour if it was icy cold and (Chrysalis MD) Chris Wright tended to join us in benign Florida weather. So we phoned Chris and said the weather was gorgeous in Mexico City whereas it was *actually* dismal and raining. I spent my 30th birthday there consuming things ending in 'agne or 'aine...

"The tickets back home were a mess and Barry Sinclair, our tour manager, had to go back into town for some bean counting. Air France was not helpful, but BOAC said, 'All you need is a credit card and we can re-write the tickets and you can get your money back with the old ones.' I was the only one with an American Express card – my father-in-law had scored a free case of wine introducing me as a member – so I produced the plastic and we flew to Montreal to connect with a flight to London. This flight was jam packed with screaming kids and we asked if there was any room at the sharp end. Remember there was no business class then, just 'cattle' and 'first'. The hostess who looked and sounded like Juliet Mills said, 'First is pretty empty and an upgrade £90.' We just had to show our passports and we would be billed later. I didn't get billed, but I think some folk did... It was the most beautiful flight with proper crockery, cutlery, and different wines for each course. I had a lovely sleep and woke as fresh as a daisy at Heathrow. I don't think Alan Cartwright slept at all. It seemed as if he had continued availing himself of the refreshments as he was walking down the concourse in London saying 'Si, Senor' to everyone he encountered... Meanwhile, some months later, I discovered that American Express forgot to bill me... Shh!"

One secretive Procol Harum activity that took place in 1975 was the recording of a version of Strauss' 'The Blue Danube' with former producer Chris Thomas while still under contract to Leiber and Stoller for another album. *In Strauss Und Bogen*, recorded in April and May in Wieden, Landstrasse, Ottakring, Austria, and London's Apple Studios, had a limited issue in Austria only. Procol recorded the waltz in two differing versions of six and nine minutes, opting for the shorter version for the album. Copping hated his performance, then and now, while the others seemed satisfied at the time.

As Brooker noted in 2004 via the liner notes to the *Exotic Birds & Fruit* reissue, "In spring 1975 we were on tour in Europe when we had a call from the City Fathers of Vienna asking if we could record 'The Blue Danube' for a special release celebrating 150 years since the birth of Johann Strauss II. Feeling rather honoured, we all said, 'yes' and rushed out to buy a tape of it and were shocked to find out that it wasn't the short 'little ditty' we all know, but a long and complicated piece with close to a dozen tunes going on! Nevertheless, we learnt it, and, under the watchful eye of Chris Thomas at Apple Studios, duly and with great respect, did what only Procol could do."

Chapter 11

From East To West

1976

"Our producer-engineers Ron and Howie Albert said, 'Well you know you can take dog shit and you can cover it with chocolate. But when you bite into it, what have you got? Dog shit!'"

Gary Brooker

1976 proved to be a transitional year in rock. Over the next 18 months, the kind of music typified by Procol Harum would be overtaken by a tidal wave of young, aggressive upstarts. Having been among the cutting edge almost a decade earlier, Procol were to find themselves marginalised and, for a time, even forgotten as the music business underwent major changes thanks to the burgeoning movement of iconoclastic British and American artists radically altering how the business operated.

But punk and the New Wave were still to come. The year started in usual fashion with a staple 'meat and potatoes' diet of traditional British rock in the form of Status Quo, Bad Company, Thin Lizzy and Nazareth sharing the stage with headliners Procol Harum and Barclay James Harvest at the Great British Music Festival held between December 31,

1975 and January 2, 1976 at London's Olympia, a cavernous exhibition hall. Procol had rather cunningly chosen to relinquish the headline spot, knowing that the show was bound to overrun and that most of the audience would naturally leave midway through the final set in order to catch the last train home. Their assumption was correct and BJH played to a rapidly emptying hall.

With a rather compromised audio feed, Procol's set was recorded by Capital Radio for inclusion in Nicky Horne's regular *Your Mother Wouldn't Like It* evening slot. Online reviewer Richard Solley wrote of the gig: "Procol came out into this barn and turned the sound down. It was obvious they were there to rock. [The band] decided to play it straight by steaming in to 'Butterfly Boys' and 'Bringing Home The Bacon'. Not performing in front of a 'home' audience, as it were, and it seemed to work. 'Hernando's Hideaway' punctuated 'Grand Hotel'. 'Conquistador', 'The Devil Came From Kansas', and 'I Keep Forgetting' kept up the pace. The audience even swayed to 'The Blue Danube' ... brave move that was. 'Simple Sister' closed the set as I recall. An encore ensued: 'I Can't Help Myself' steamrollered into 'Nothing But The Truth'... 'Santa Claus Is Coming To Town' got everyone in party mood before 'A Whiter Shade Of Pale'. Heh! I don't remember it with three verses."

Behind the scenes things were changing for Procol. Reid and Brooker's jointly owned company, Strongman Productions, which controlled much of Procol's business affairs, had a new partner called Nick Blackburn who became Procol's new manager.

At the band's philanthropic request, one of Blackburn's first management tasks was to set up a tour of Eastern Europe. In 1976 this was something of a challenge, given that the Iron Curtain still separated Eastern communist dictatorships from Western democracies. Furthermore, the restrictive practices that existed in those times meant that Eastern European countries were directly answerable to the former USSR, and the Kremlin, through the dictats of the federation then known as the Warsaw Pact.

On January 24 Procol flew to Austria to play Vienna – the gateway to the Eastern Bloc, as it was then known. Procol naturally performed 'The Blue Danube' before waltzing off to the former Yugoslavia.

While other major groups such as The Animals, The Hollies and The Rolling Stones had toured behind the Iron Curtain in the sixties, Procol were the first British rock group to mount an extensive tour of Poland since The Rolling Stones some 11 years earlier. "Slade beat us to it," says Brooker. "I think they played Warsaw a couple of years before we did."

"We thought that we'd like to go and play that way," Brooker told *Street Life*'s Angus MacKinnon in May 1976, "not *necessarily* Poland, but we saw our name in the charts there about four years ago and mentioned the possibility to various people. We nearly went over in 1974, but negotiations broke down. I think that on this occasion it stemmed from an approach on their part: an exercise in cultural exchange, that sort of thing. It was all very different from what you might expect. We heard stories about the dockers' strikes and food riots of 1971, people killed, disappearing without a trace, a thousand people shot here and there. In all seriousness, that period does seem to have been rather unpleasant."

In 1976 Polish citizens still suffered under the brutal ruling hand of the Soviet Union. Rock was until this point seen as utterly bourgeois; a decadent form of western entertainment. The Rolling Stones' visit in 1967 had conspired to further this assertion. However, Procol were deemed to be a 'serious' band and 'Pandora's Box' had been issued in anticipation of *Procol's Ninth* – the first British rock album to be officially pressed up in Poland, according to the spin doctors in Chrysalis Records' press department. Reid told Angus MacKinnon, "the problem being that they need to keep foreign currency, and are only allowed to pay a much lower rate of royalties than in Britain or America." "Ten thousand pounds or 50 crates of cut glass!" Brooker elaborated.

When the band flew into Warsaw from Yugoslavia the temperature was 20 below zero and the musicians, dressed in thin jeans and leather jackets, felt as though they were freezing to death. They were greeted by one of the biggest press conferences ever seen in an Eastern Bloc country and all shows – 11 concerts in eight days, sometimes two a day

– were sold out. Procol played venues filled to capacity with audiences of 3,000 to 10,000 queuing patiently in the cold streets to see and hear this new brand of English 'Progressive Rock'. Surprisingly they seemed to know all of the lyrics.

"Understandably," said Reid, "they had no conception of all the amount of equipment a group needs on stage. But the road crew were very helpful and tried as hard as they could to do everything properly. We were lucky that it didn't snow, otherwise the roads would have been impassable, though it was somewhat cold..." "Cold?" Brooker jumped in, "it was sunny at about 30 below. No problems there!"

Chris Copping: "It was quite an experience. We were in a Mercedes van only just big enough to get us all in. The windows were iced up on the inside, but 'the Commander' [Gary Brooker] with impeccable timing produced a bottle of Glenfiddich."

"Personally I thought it was going to be a bit wild," Brooker told MacKinnon, "but in Poland they obviously listened to a lot of music and enjoyed it as well. Wherever you went there were bands playing – and most proficiently."

Chris Copping: "First gig was Krakow – huge culture there – we were very welcome. They didn't exactly have rock concerts every week – it was a fine gig. Then we went to an ancient building, which may have been the old university where there was a 'trad' band playing. We then moved on to another room where a slightly Weather Report fusion band were playing. I hate to say it, but we got on and jammed – somehow some vodka got spilt into a Fender amp. I don't think it was me, but maybe it was? A couple of these guys had waited ages to get decent 'gear'. One of our road crew had scored some hash in Yugoslavia so that was taken care of and a pound note could persuade any bar to stay open. The other thing was Eddie Butler of the road crew kept a vast tea urn going, which went down very well during soundchecks. He also had the means to heat vast quantities of baked beans with Polish sausages."

It hadn't snowed in Poland, but it was white-out in East Germany, although this wasn't as cold as the Cold War dictatorship that was then running Romania in 1976.

Chris Copping, "As for Bucharest, we had no idea what a monster Ceausescu was. We were staying at a supposedly good hotel, which was sort of OK and in the evening we strolled past the Government area to go to a slightly more decent hotel for the very silly cabaret. Once again a member of the crew happened to have a large lump of black hash stuck inside his sock. Happy days! I remember the government was also the promoter so you would have to be fairly obnoxious to be challenged."

Gary Brooker: "As soon as somebody said you can now play places like Yugoslavia, East Germany, Poland, and Romania, I thought, 'Of course we've got to go.' We were then told, "They've got no money!" I immediately said, 'Well that's not the people's fault, is it? Let's go over!' And a very rewarding experience it was, too. To see the smiles on people's faces – such happiness. Hearing some music without getting their ears boxed. It made it all worthwhile really!"

Whilst Procol were away touring Eastern Europe manager Nick Blackburn was quick to plug Procol's first 'gap year' since 1967, and 1976 ultimately proved to be a year without a new Procol Harum album. As a consequence [and as stated earlier in Chapter 5] Blackburn sneak previewed Procol Harum's unissued 1970 live rock'n'roll covers album *Aint Nothing To Get Excited About* by Liquorice John Death & the All Stars as an 'on air debut' on Nicky Horne's Capital Radio show *Your Mother Wouldn't Like It*. It received some positive press from Tony Stewart in *NME* before it was returned to the vaults, remaining unissued for another 20 years.

Having played a one-hour special for the German TV network WDR as part of the series *Rockpalast* back in January, Procol were persuaded to appear on something similar in the UK via a Saturday morning series called *The Geordie Scene*. Taped for Tyne Tees TV at Granada's studios in Manchester for ITV network transmission on March 20, Procol hadn't quite realised what type of show they'd been booked on to. The producer had clearly hijacked an audience of Bay City Rollers fans all decked out in tartan baggy pants with scarves tied to their arms. Geared to react to almost anything the teenybopper audience appeared oblivious to lyrics about "guts and gore" ('The Unquiet Zone') as well

170

as a song based on an LSD trip ('Shine On Brightly'). Innocent days indeed!

Three days prior to the ITV show Procol played a gig at Bournemouth's Winter Gardens that was taped for American audiences of the network radio series *The King Biscuit Flower Hour*. (This particular gig was part of a newly launched series of radio specials entitled *British Biscuit*.) Procol were clearly on fire and as a consequence, the show soon surfaced as a notorious vinyl bootleg called *Five And Dime* and later appeared as a CD, *The Eleventh Hour*.

For the first leg of the band's 1976 UK tour they were supported by Brooker's old Southend chum and former Bonzo Dog Doo-Dah Band frontman Vivian Stanshall. Procol members would join him nightly to sing 'Man's Browns', among other amusing ditties, prior to their own headline slot.

Gary Brooker: "After the success of *Procol's Ninth* in France the band undertook a 12 city sell-out tour, the first extensive trip there since the success of *Grand Hotel* in 1973. In order to give ourselves a challenge and something a little different to do, after the repertoire of the previous few months of concerts, we worked up a combo arrangement of Venetian composer Tomaso Albinoni's (1671–1750) 'Adagio For Organ & Strings In G Minor'. We were intrigued by the legend that the original manuscript had been lost to fire and that the version we know today had been reconstructed from just the bass and viola lines in the 20th century."

According to researcher Erik Mortensen's 2003 online account, "Albinoni cannot be held responsible for the beautiful piece written for strings and organ. Neither Procol, nor Brian Auger who recorded the 'Adagio' with his Oblivion Express in 1970, have noted that the 'Adagio' was really composed by Italian researcher Remo Giazotto in 1945.

"Albinoni's 'Adagio' is based on a surviving fragment of manuscript discovered in the Dresden State Library after the Second World War by Giazotto – a Milanese musicologist who was, at that time, completing his biography of Albinoni and his listing of Albinoni's music." However, as Brooker correctly asserts, "Only the bass line and six bars of melody had survived, possibly from the slow movement of a Trio Sonata."

Mortensen adds: "To Giazotto the now-popular 'Adagio' suggested a piece that would be played in church, so he added an organ. It is perhaps ironic that Albinoni's rediscovery by the wider public in our own times was largely based on this ever-popular piece which Albinoni would only barely recognise." J.S. Bach was influenced by Albinoni's ideas and one can hear the bass line (excluding the minor key) passing from 'Adagio' through 'Air On A 'G' String' to 'A Whiter Shade Of Pale'.

The 'Adagio' received enough of a favourable reaction on the French tour to the extent that the local division of Chrysalis Records asked the band if they would consider properly recording it for domestic single release in France only. Back in England the band booked a soundstage at Shepperton Film Studios, hired a mobile 24-track truck, manned by Chris Thomas, and recorded the piece, apparently in a single take using the large space to create the ambience. According to online reviewer Roland Clare: "Alan Cartwright used an acoustic Spanish style bass, and while the organ and piano handle the main theme and harmonies, it is left to Mick Grabham to pursue the cadenza. B.J. Wilson meanwhile comes up with surely the most inspired and unique part that only he could have played, assuring his place as one of the finest and most tasteful drummers of the era."

'Adagio Di Albinoni' was backed with a new version of 'The Blue Danube', re-recorded live at Bournemouth Winter Gardens and (allegedly) produced by Muff Winwood.* This particular coupling passed almost unnoticed as did the UK issue of 'As Strong As Samson'/'The Unquiet Zone' – although *NME*'s Steve Clarke did make it his 'Single Of The Week' on February 7.

Constant touring can test a band's internal dynamic and a situation had arisen between Alan Cartwright and Mick Grabham which manifested itself on stage. Cartwright played his bass with a plectrum and seemed to be the butt of many a joke. Somehow the band chemistry, which had worked so well for the past four years, was clearly in jeopardy. As

---

* These two tracks were not available outside of France, but did eventually reappear on a German Repertoire CD entitled *Procol's Singles Collection*.

Brooker would later remark in 1992, "The needling between Mick and Alan came to such a point that one of them *had* to go!" On July 5, 1976 a Chrysalis press release announced the departure of Cartwright, who quit the music business shortly thereafter, and Copping, the band's bassist and keyboard player before Cartwright joined, would now move back to bass, allowing a new keyboard player, Pete Solley (born October 19, 1948 in Hampstead, London), into the group.

Solley, whose pedigree extended back to the sixties and stints with Chris Farlowe's Thunderbirds, Los Bravos, Arthur Brown, Terry Reid, and later with his own bands Paladin, Snafu and Fox, was brought in to help modernise Procol's sound.

Chris Copping: "Pete's Farfisa organ was the one that Sly Stone used, and through a Leslie amplifier, it didn't sound too bad. It was better for modern sounds; the slalom pedal for instance. Pete also had a Multiman synthesizer, which did brass and harpsichord and he was pretty nifty with an ARP Odyssey, which could sound crap in the wrong hands, but not his. His keyboard sound gave us a kick up the seventies."

"With the Hammond organ now officially banished, Procol were becoming distinctly different," says Copping. Meanwhile, Procol wanted to get out of their contract with Leiber & Stoller. Thanks to some deft manoeuvring from Blackburn, they managed to break their commitment for another album. Luckily, Jerry Leiber and Mike Stoller found Elkie Brooks as the next recipient of their services (and songs) and the matter was amicably resolved.

Gary Brooker: "We now had a new plan. It didn't work out with Leiber and Stoller so we were not going to do another album with them. So the latest plan? We'll go to America and in fact we'll produce ourselves. We hired two engineers, Ron and Howie Albert in Criteria Studios in Miami, which was a 'happening' place. All the good sounds were coming out of there. The *new* Bee Gees had made 'Jive Talkin'' there; Clapton, The Eagles and Aretha had all recorded there, as had many others... Procol's always been willing to take on board influences from what's going on."

Having previously recorded all of their albums in England, leaving Britain to make an album would be a new departure for the band, so a foreign studio seemed just the ticket. With financial backing from both Chrysalis in London and Procol's new American distributors Warners, what could possibly go wrong?

As Britain's economic woes continued to fester and the new street movement punk gained momentum, Procol, along with Blackburn and their respective wives, flew off on October 20 to the Florida sunshine and the luxurious confines of Ocean Boulevard near to where Eric Clapton had stayed in 1974 when making his *461 Ocean Boulevard.*

Having spent the best part of a year on the road Procol had been far too preoccupied with touring and as a consequence they were unprepared for their tenth album. Reid had some words ready but Brooker had very few finished songs.

Mick Grabham: "Gary ended up writing music each night in his room. He seemed to be writing songs *every single night* which had *never* happened in all the time I'd been in Procol Harum that I was aware of."

Tour manager Barry Sinclair's memory tallies with Grabham's: "Gary was writing songs the whole time he was there. He hadn't really got around to writing the music before he left England."

Chris Copping: "We *had* started rehearsing *some* songs at Gary's house – definitely 'Strangers In Space', 'Skating On Thin Ice', 'Something Magic' and I think Gary helped Mick Grabham with a demo 'Mark Of The Claw' to play to us others ..."

Gary Brooker: "When we got to Florida we had our 16 songs, which we played in the studio to these two engineer brothers so that they could hear what we'd come to do. It takes a long time to play 16 songs – the best part of an evening. So afterwards we all went back to the control room and they just shrugged and said, "Well what is that you want us to do guys?""

Keith Reid: "We said, 'We want you to engineer and help us co-produce these new songs!'"

Gary Brooker: "They said, 'Well, you know, you can take dog shit and you can cover it with chocolate. But when you bite into it, what have you got? Dog shit!" It didn't go very far from there. I mean we still made this album, but we should have taken time out to rethink things.

But we were booked into the studio, so we ended up doing about five or six songs."

Keith Reid: "The sessions clearly weren't working. So in desperation we had this idea of a song that I'd written called 'The Worm & The Tree', which was this little fairy story that I'd come up with that should have remained in my bottom drawer."

'The Worm & The Tree' was pushed forward by Blackburn who felt that Procol should have a follow-up to 1968's 'In Held 'Twas In I'. Earlier, in 1975, Brooker had made a significant contribution to the concept album *Peter & The Wolf* of which 'The Worm' could potentially be deemed to be a cousin so there may have been some kind of rationale to this.

Nick Blackburn did just that, his parting shot being, "Looks like a platinum album, guys!"

Back in Blighty the British music press was going through a major transition thanks to punk. *NME* in particular rang the changes when editor-in-chief Nick Logan brought in two young verbal assassins, Tony Parsons and Julie Burchill, to critically assault most of the music and the artists that had existed prior to 1975. Locked away in the Florida sunshine in a studio next to the Eagles, who were recording *Hotel California,* Procol Harum remained blissfully unaware of what was around the corner. They also remained 'blissfully unaware' that the Eagles were recording next door, but that's another story...

Chapter 12

Something Magic Or Something Awful?

1977

"Looking back... Something Magic came out when punk was taking over. Disco ruled; and Procol came out with this new album that had a recitation that was 20 minutes long...Anything that was longer than three minutes in 1977 was dead in the water."

Gary Brooker

'Lost At Sea,' wrote Dave Fudger in his *Sounds* review of Procol's performance of *Something Magic* at London's Hammersmith Odeon on February 26, 1977. This was furthered by the album's artwork which consisted of a painting showing Procol Harum sat on the deck of an empty ship that was 'lost at sea' at sunset. Unfortunate imagery or an apt allusion? In 2004 Keith Reid started to laugh in response to this.

The right hand corner of the sleeve showed an upside down goldfish bowl featuring a pregnant goldfish looking startled. When abbreviated *Something Magic's* 'The Worm And The Tree' spells 'TWATT'.

176

According to Wikipedia 'it is commonly thought that a "twat" is a noun to describe *a* pregnant goldfish'. There is of course another meaning.

Was 'The Worm And The Tree' aimed at a former manager perhaps? Was that person the 'Twat' or the 'Worm' in the tree? And was the 'dying' old 'tree' Procol Harum? Reid wasn't saying a word, but fits of laughter indicated that the nail had been firmly hammered.

Released in March 1977, the results of the Florida escapade, *Something Magic* were met with a critical mauling. *Sounds'* Dave Fudger contributed one of the less abrasive appraisals: "I've been dreading writing this review. I've had a cassette of the album for a couple of weeks and I've been playing it as much as possible – background music as intent-upon-getting-into music as just plain listening music, but I'm very disappointed.

"[However] there's one real beaut of a song on side one, 'The Mark Of The Claw', which features some classic Harum touches. Dominated by a grand and slightly sinister Mick Grabham guitar phrase it proceeds to show everybody off at their best. New man Pete Solley makes the most of the slightly macabre setting of the hard edged guitar line, Gary Brooker's piano grand and the mini-apocalypses from the best British rock drummer on the planet to throw in a haunting synthesizer line. The lyrics are Keith Reid at his claustrophobic, hypnotic, and obsessive best, over a Brooker melody line and chord change that stretches straightforward statements into mystery. The closing sequence has the Grabham guitar riff punctuated by key sounds from a murder – footsteps, a door opening and closing, a distant scream, and finally a door slamming – after a few plays I found myself impatient for that bit. It's almost worth buying the album for that track alone. Sadly the rest of the album is tame by comparison."

'The Mark Of The Claw' was the first and only song that Grabham wrote for Procol Harum, despite having composed most of his solo album *Mick The Lad* (1972) and with B J Cole for Cochise prior to that. These days Grabham is fairly modest about his only undertaking for Procol. "It's *just* a song," he says with a shrug. "I mean it aint 'A Salty Dog'. It's OK ..."

As had been the case with the previous two Procol albums an old reject was dusted down in the form of 'Wizard Man' as a possible follow-up to the success of 'Pandora's Box'. Originally the song wasn't going to be included because it didn't really fit in with the album's other tracks. But, according to Grabham, "record companies being what they are, said, 'You've got to put that out as a single!' It suited me because I thought that it would have been a hit. As it was, I was totally wrong, but Warners in the States wanted it on the album, putting forward their point that if the single is on the album and the single is a hit, then that helps to sell the album. That's the reason 'Wizard Man' went on".

Uptempo and filled with some great Farfisa organ from Solley, 'Wizard Man' became a crowd pleaser at Procol gigs throughout 1977 but unfortunately failed to chart anywhere.

Similarly, 'Skating On Thin Ice' would be Chris Copping's one and only contribution to a Procol Harum album. "Gary suggested that I score 'Skating On Thin Ice' recommending a Swiss type woodwind thing in the bridge," says Copping. "Pete Solley suggested the string line in the following verse – he was very helpful and briefly sketched some notes, which worked out well – full marks to him." In retrospect Copping wishes that he'd avoided the various distractions on offer to a successful seventies rock band. "Sorry Gary for not having got off my arse earlier in life, if only to assist in the orchestration."

Reviewing the album in *Beat*, one P.D. wrote, "'Skating On Thin Ice' is the best track on Side 1 with some truly admirable sound effects on synthesizer and phased snare drum. It is also the best orchestrated of all the songs – congratulations to bassist Chris Copping here," while Patrick Humphries, writing for the normally unforgiving *NME*, considered 'Skating On Thin Ice' to be the album's "piece de resistance... with a melody which reminded me of a music box tune. Choir and orchestra blend beautifully behind Brooker's voice and piano as he sings Reid's doomy, Tarot inspired lyrics, while BJ Wilson's cymbals and Pete Solley's synthesizers swish away in good atmospheric vein".

The ersatz Hollywood B-movie glitz of 'Something Magic', also not scored by Brooker but farmed out by the Alberts to Miami arranger Mike Lewis, was released as a single in the Netherlands in the wake of the disco boom but failed to dent the charts there (the song also appeared as the B-side of 'Wizard Man' in the USA).

'Strangers In Space', the last track on the first side, is actually the best on the album. In an online review John McFerrin noted, "'Strangers In Space' is sad, but also has the added effect of conveying a real feeling of floating in the middle of space, knowing you're not going to find anybody ever again, all the while feeling somewhat numb emotion-wise and yet also quite depressed about where circumstances had led them."

Brooker/Reid's pure blues–soul crossover fared even better live. As Joe Roman rightly stated in the *Atlanta Gazette*, "Keith Reid was surely speaking of his band when he wrote [it].'"

Strangers in space
Passing through time
Travellers in haste
Partners in crime
Trace of a feeling
Trace of regret
Hard to remember
Hard to forget
Something uncovered
Something unsaid
Strangely repeated
Long ago dead
Hard to remember
Hard to forget

Strangers in space
Travellers in time
Passing in haste
Partners in crime
Trace of a feeling
Trace of regret
Hard to remember

Hard to forget
Fruits of discovery
Some distant form
Something repeated
Something reborn
Trace of a feeling
Trace of regret
Hard to remember
Hard to forget

With regard to the first side of *Something Magic* McFerrin summed up, "In terms of pure musical worth, these songs may not amount to much in the Procol Harum catalogue, yet within their context, they're quite powerful – they're like reading the diary entries of somebody who knows he/she is going to die within a very short time, and spends time lamenting over time lost and opportunities wasted."

And then there was 'The Worm And The Tree', the wooden three-piece suite furnishing all of side two. "Fans will see 'The Worm And The Tree', a long musical allegory along the lines of 'In Held 'Twas In I', as the highlight of the album," wrote *Rolling Stone's* Alan Niester. "Its theme is either the classic one of good triumphing over evil or a disguised comment on America's government, depending on how you read it. Like its predecessor, 'The Worm' manages to touch numerous musical bases, mostly orchestral and funereal, although guitarist Mick Grabham does manage to slip in a few good riffs early on."

The *Rolling Stone* review was as good as it got. The general consensus on the lengthy piece was negative – a view not improved with time; music journalist Patrick Humphries recently described the lyrics as "bargain basement Zen" while John McFerrin's online review simply dismissed it as "awful".

Certainly the band members were less then enthused with 'The Worm And The Tree'. Gary Brooker: "Very soon after [the album's release] I wish I'd sung the damned thing instead of speaking it. You know it was always intended that [the actor] James Mason was going to speak it anyway. I can't *stand* the sound of my own voice talking!"

180

BJ Wilson at his drum kit and Dave Knights with his back to the camera, photographed prior to a 1969 Procol Harum concert at the Constitution Hall in Washington DC. WILLIAM HATFIELD

Dave Knights at the Fillmore West, San Francisco, 1968.
RON SANCHEZ

The poster for Procol Harum, Santana and Salloom Sinclair at the Fillmore West, San Francisco, 1968.

Robin Trower at the Fillmore West, 1968. RON SANCHEZ

Robin Trower and Matthew Fisher (top) and Gary Brooker, Dave Knights, and BJ Wilson (below) at the San Francisco Pop Festival, 1968.
RON SANCHEZ

Gary Brooker (top left), Robin Trower (top right) and Matthew Fisher (below) at Washington DC, 1969. WILLIAM HATFIELD

Keith Reid (top left and right) backstage at the Constitution Hall, Washington DC, in 1969 and 1971. Below: BJ Wilson relaxes in his hotel room after the 1971 Washington gig. WILLIAM HATFIELD

Keith Reid, BJ Wilson, Dave Knights and Gary Brooker chat after a sound check in Washington in 1969. Robin Trower and Matthew Fisher prefer to sit. WILLIAM HATFIELD

Backstage at the Constitution Hall, Washington DC in 1969; left to right: Dave Knights, Robin Trower, BJ Wilson, Keith Reid, Matthew Fisher and Gary Brooker at the piano. WILLIAM HATFIELD

Procol Harum on stage rehearsing 'The Devil Came From Kansas' in Washington, 1969; from left: Gary Brooker, BJ Wilson, Matthew Fisher on rhythm guitar, Robin Trower and Dave Knights. WILLIAM HATFIELD

Procol Harum's *Home* album photo sessions in 1970; left to right: BJ Wilson, Gary Brooker, Chris Copping, Robin Trower and Keith Reid (foreground). COURTESY OF FLY RECORDS

Gary Brooker and Keith Reid—'the creative force behind Procol Harum'—at the *Broken Barricades* photo session, 1971

Many online intellectual morticians of 'magic' have imbued this simple fairy tale with much meaning. Similarly online revisionist musicologists have deconstructed the chord patterns to shed new insight into this much derided musical magnum opus. Was 'The Worm And The Tree' a political allegory? Was it about one of Procol's many former managers? "It's certainly about worms," says Reid. He was less enigmatic when questioned about the song's origins by *NME's* Tony Stewart at the time of the album's release. "It's about how the press nearly caused the band to break up. That was three years ago ..."

Sounding severely under-produced and badly mixed (on the original vinyl pressing)* the producers clearly held no love for 'The Worm And The Tree' either.

Gary Brooker: "Originally we didn't really plan to do 'The Worm'. Perhaps on the second morning of being there we played it to the Alberts. Nobody really knew it and it was very much improvised on the spot ... Upon the conclusion of this 'demonstration' the Alberts said, 'Listen, guys, we could be spending time on our yacht. We don't *need* to be here!' I mean we really should have packed up and gone home then..."

Chris Copping: "My final words on Ronnie and Howie Albert? *Something Magic* was not entirely their fault, but their attitude could've been better. At one time Mick (Grabham) wanted an edit on one of his solos, but they didn't get it at all. Luckily Steve Stills was passing by and he kind of translated Mick's wishes to them. I always thought Manassas' first album sounded good – I think Ronnie engineered that (for Steven Stills). The Alberts, however, were *not* producers. They got our signals recorded accurately and recorded the orchestral players well. But they couldn't mix cake... But then we weren't really producers either...."

In an April 1977 edition of *Zigzag* John Peel's radio producer John Walters provided an amusing photo strip showing three pictures along with bubble captions. Picture 1 showed Walters talking to singer/songwriter Andrew Gold. The bubble coming out of Walters' mouth

---

* In 2009, 32 years after first being issued, a special edition CD version of *Something Magic*, fully remixed and remastered by Gary Brooker, actually sounded good at last!

said, "I've seen the future of rock'n'roll and it's *not* you old chap!" Picture 2 showed Keith Reid smiling wryly, the caption bubble said, "Is it me?" Picture 3 showed Mick Jones of The Clash: the bubble said, "Nah... it's me, innit!"

Around the same time Peel played the title track from Procol Harum's *Something Magic* on his midweek show. Ripping the record off halfway through, Peel complained, "More like 'Something Awful' but this isn't – The Buzzcocks and 'Orgasm Addict'." The record kicked off at a hundred miles an hour, completely knocking Procol into touch. The writing was clearly on the wall and in the press, too. Punk rock and 'the new wave' had arrived to blow away the old guard. And it duly did, albeit briefly...

However, Procol's remaining champions still found life in the old Salty Dogs. Reviewing a February 11 gig at Edinburgh University's Refectory for *NME,* Ian Cranna commented, "[The best part of the set] came from their treasure chest of oldies – 'Conquistador', 'Beyond The Pale', 'Grand Hotel' (complete with Palm Court section), 'Pandora's Box', 'Unquiet Zone' (including multi-rhythmed drum solo) and 'A Salty Dog'. The encores were firstly the new single 'Wizard Man', and (an unreleased) hoedown, 'This Old Dog', and secondly a string of rock'n'roll oldies as the audience refused to let them go – 'Roll Over Beethoven', 'Long Tall Sally', 'Jailhouse Rock' and 'Old Black Joe'. And you thought Procol Harum were pedestrian...

"The only possible way to stop was to dust off 'A Whiter Shade Of Pale' again. But here's one for the Believe It Or Not Dept: Gary Brooker actually got the words wrong after the number of times he must have sung that song... Now for the new member – on keyboards, Pete Solley, a name that will bring a smile to those who remember that ace original Terry Reid trio. This man is an astute acquisition. He slotted right in, and his excellent synthesizer work is a fine foil to Brooker and Mick Grabham. Talking of Grabham, he must be the most underrated guitarist this side of the Zambezi – and probably the other side as well. Definitely one of the most powerful, but tasteful axe men on the boards... I have certainly heard them play better, but at no stage could they be said to be poor, and it was vastly enjoyable. The band evidently enjoyed it too – they played for 2 and 1/4 hours!"

"Audiences were always great for Procol," Pete Solley stated three decades on. "No one went to a Procol Harum concert unless they actually wanted to be there. It wasn't a voguish, hip thing to do. People went because they really dug the band. I do think that they were one of the top five live bands *ever* in rock music. I don't think their records *ever* did them justice. But on a good night a *phenomenal* electricity used to happen!"

On March 12, Procol Harum were transmitted live simultaneously over BBC 2 and Radio 1 in the groundbreaking new series *Sight & Sound In Concert* from the BBC TV Theatre on Shepherd's Bush Green (now the Shepherd's Bush Empire). This TV event was groundbreaking in the sense that standard mono TV sound could be turned down and polished FM stereo radio could be turned up to replace the inferior audio. While the Beeb had tried a similar one-off experiment with The Rolling Stones back in 1964, in the days long before NICAM and digital stereo, this was another first for Procol.

Gary Brooker: "It was very interesting that show because it was shortly before we packed it in. About three months. What I can see in that old *Sight & Sound In Concert* was that we were almost playing with our old standards, we were throwing them away. I mean 'Grand Hotel' (complete with segue into 'Hernando's Hideway') had almost become vaudeville. Some songs were too fast and we weren't really getting into them. The *only* ones we did get into that came across best were the new songs like 'Strangers In Space' and 'Skating On Thin Ice'. They were much better performances. It was two different bands. Pete Solley really added something to those two. He really made them come to life!"

Shortly after this broadcast Chris Copping collapsed before a gig. "He couldn't take the pace," was BJ Wilson's flippant explanation to *Circus* magazine's Richard Hogan. In 1992 Brooker said, "I think the beer got to him. He was never without a quart tankard of beer... He really needed to take a little rest for a while, which is what he did."

"In retrospect I wish I hadn't propped up the bar quite so much and spent so much time enjoying myself. Instead I just I wish I'd helped out

Gary with some scoring or arranging. He took on so much back then. He wrote the songs; played them, sang them, arranged them, toured them. He did it all... It's incredible looking back on it," said Copping

Copping took an enforced rest before joining Frankie Miller (managed by Reid) for a late summer tour of America. Meanwhile, Dee Murray (aka David Murray Oates born April 3, 1946 in Southgate, London) Grabham's old mate from The Plastic Penny and a former member of Elton John's band from 1970 until 1974, joined Procol Harum on bass, replacing Copping for the American leg of the *Something Magic* tour. Six of the dates would see Procol relegated into the support slot beneath a band they had once headlined over in 1972, namely Supertramp. Six other dates saw Procol share the billing with Foghat alongside a couple of shows with their old mates Little Feat. Procol headlined in California and in New York where they had a strong and loyal following. An unreleased mixing board recording of two shows at San Francisco's Old Waldorf Theatre on April 8 and 9 displays Procol Harum on absolutely blistering form. The addition of Murray (who lived in Los Angeles) seemed to push the other musicians back to their very best. By the time the band reached New York's Palladium Theatre for their final live concert on May 15 they were on form and on fire!

Richard Hogan wrote in *Circus*: "The tenth anniversary show is the climax of a hectic tour which began in Europe last January. 'New York's always been good for us', added Gary Brooker on the fittingness of celebrating Procol's Tenth here at the Palladium. When the announcement came, the crowd erupted ecstatically, the promoter set a candlelit cake out on stage, and Procol soared giddily through five encores plus its May 1967 evergreen 'A Whiter Shade Of Pale'."

Procol Harum ended their career in the same unassuming fashion as it had begun ten years previously. The split was never announced but an early clue came in the shape of a press release to the *NME* dated June 11, which, in the wake of punk rock, went largely unnoticed. "Guitarist Mick Grabham has left Procol Harum after five years with the band. He came into the line-up in 1972, filling the spot vacated a few months before by Robin Trower [sic] but now he has decided he wants the freedom to choose his own work. He is currently in the studio with the Sutherland Brothers & Quiver, taking over temporarily from Tim Renwick while the band prepares to record their new album. And when that is finished, says Grabham, he may form his own group."

Grabham told *NME*: "I have been generally dissatisfied with my role in Procol Harum for some months. I didn't think that what musical ability I may have was being used to best advantage. It was during our last American tour that I finally decided to leave, and I quit when we returned to Britain recently." The paper added, "Grabham insists that the other Harum members fully accepted his reasons for going, and that the split was amicable. But it has left the band in a state of flux, and they are apparently still considering how best to cope."

"We had a tenth anniversary dinner in New York," Pete Solley told Ronald Smith for *Shine On*. "I think everyone knew that was pretty well it. When we got back to England I talked to Gary on the phone, then I drove down to his house in Surrey and we talked for an hour. I think that was about it. There was no big meeting. It petered out; it was not a big finale. It just whimpered out. Gary was tired; he'd been doing it a long time. He carried a lot of the load. Every night he was the guy that was singing. He was the guy that was writing the songs. He was the guy who was doing an awful lot; a lot more than BJ, or Mick Grabham or Chris Copping or me. I think he was just tired of doing it all. I know for me it wasn't a big 'Oh, my God!' I just went on from there. I went on and became a jingle writer, got into production; all kinds of things happened. So for me everything worked out well. It was just a great experience for me and a *marvellous* chapter in my life....

"I always asked Keith [about his lyrics] and I still do... I even spoke to him on the phone last week and I said, 'What the fuck were you talking about, Keith?' He said, 'Well it made sense when I wrote it ...' [Reid's stock answer usually stated with a wry smile.] The songs have imagery, more than anything. It's not a question of making sense. They are like a tone poem. That's how I look at it."

Procol Harum got together one final time on October 18 for a show held at the Wembley Conference Centre, London to mark the Queen's Silver Jubilee. 'A Whiter Shade Of Pale' was named joint winner (along with Queen's 'Bohemian Rhapsody') as 'Best British Pop Single 1952–1977' at the British Record Industry's Britannia Awards, which later spawned the annual award ceremony run by the British Phonographic Institute under the banner of the Brit Awards. With a line-up of Brooker, Wilson, Chris Copping playing Hammond organ, Alan Cartwright on bass and Tim Renwick (formerly of Sutherland Brothers & Quiver) on guitar, Procol performed 'A Whiter Shade Of Pale' live.

As Dutch music journalist and Procol Harum historian Frans Steensma attests, "This was remarkable as Renwick was part of Procol for the first time. Alan Cartwright had left Procol in June 1976 and Chris Copping had joined Frankie Miller's Full House (managed by Keith Reid) in April 1977. It's also interesting to note that it was the last time BJ played with Procol. At the same show Julie Covington performed Alice Cooper's 'Only Women Bleed' backed by Procol – the first time Gary Brooker and B J Wilson had played behind a female singer since The Paramounts backed Sandie Shaw for five months in 1965."

The show, hosted by Michael Aspel, was broadcast two nights later by Thames Television. Aspel asked Brooker if he knew what the lyrics of 'A Whiter Shade Of Pale' actually meant. "Well, I'll sing them," he replied, "and perhaps we'll find out..." And with that Procol Harum performed 'A Whiter Shade Of Pale' for the final time...

Chapter 13

A Solo Shade Of Brooker
1977–1990

"I think Gary Brooker could sing anything and it gives me goose pimples every time he sings. With a voice like I am just amazed that he isn't the biggest star in world. He certainly deserves to be …!"

Sir Alan Parker in 1997

In the latter half of 1977 punk rock and New Wave continued to flourish. Independent record label Stiff had sprung up the previous year featuring a roster of oddballs and eccentrics who were too old to be punk rockers, but who still appreciated the new wave's energising ethos. When Brooker and Reid's management company Strongman Productions sought a deal for Mickey Jupp, Dave Robinson quickly signed him to Stiff Records. Jupp had been a longstanding chum of Brooker's since the early sixties. Deemed to be a sympathetic choice as producer of the 1978 *Juppanese* album, Brooker elected to produce side one only, leaving Nick Lowe to produce side two. When the Jupp-written and Brooker-produced 'Down At The Doctors' didn't make the final cut, the song was suggested as a possible single for fellow Southenders Dr Feelgood who scored a minor hit with it in 1978.

Having no previous connection with the Feelgoods, apart from a shared Essex background, Brooker was apparently put forward as a potential producer. However, in 1979 vocalist Lee Brilleaux angrily retorted, "[Brooker] tried to tell us how to make our records. We weren't 'avin' none of it!" This hitherto untold story remains shrouded in mystery. The Feelgoods' original drummer 'The Big Figure' has no recollection of this whatsoever, according to fellow Southend musician Will Birch.

Possibly feeling a little miffed at having been moved sideways, Brooker spent the rest of 1978 'guesting' for his peers. He had already turned up on Frankie Miller's 1977 album *Fullhouse* providing piano and arrangements for Miller's covers of John Lennon's 'Jealous Guy' and Victor Young's 'Love Letters'. The Hollies' *531-7704* album featured a Brooker/Reid song, 'Harlequin'. At this juncture The Hollies were still being produced by Brooker's former Paramounts producer Ron Richards and according to some accounts Brooker very nearly joined them during one of singer Allan Clarke's sabbaticals.

On October 3, 1978 Brooker was among the 'Rockestra', an array of British musicians, including members of Pink Floyd, The Who and Led Zeppelin, handpicked by Paul McCartney to play on two tracks at Abbey Road Studios where former Procol producer Chris Thomas was co-producing Wings' *Back To The Egg* album. A year later, on December 29, a version of the Rockestra (featuring Brooker) closed a 'Rock For Kampuchea' charity concert at London's Hammersmith Odeon.

According to Gary Brooker he received a phone call from Mick Jagger late one evening in 1978 asking him to become the touring piano player with The Rolling Stones. With the assembled Rolling Stones all on speaker phone shouting, "Come on Gary", how could Gary Brooker turn them down? Flattered by the compliment Brooker actually declined the opportunity of joining the Stones as their new piano player some days later.

188

It took until January 6, 1979 for *Melody Maker* and *NME* to officially announce that Procol Harum had "split up" two years after the fact. When Dutch music journalist Frans Steensma asked Brooker what he had been doing after Procol's split, next to fishing and resting after 10 tough years, Brooker revealed he'd been writing songs with Tim Renwick of Sutherland Brothers & Quiver which eventually lead to a solo venture, *No More Fear Of Flying*.

Apart from the title track by Reid and Brooker, and four cover versions, the album's lyrics were written by former King Crimson and ELP writer Pete Sinfield although the sole Renwick/Brooker/Sinfield collaboration, 'Give Me Something To Remember You By', ended up being the finest original cut on the album.

"I want to try new things musically, and on the words side, this time I'm going for easily identifiable lyrics," Brooker said in a 1979 Chrysalis press release, adding, "It makes a difference when you are singing about a woman as opposed to a typewriter." In an immediate retort *NME's* Harry George commented, "Fair enough, but what does he [Brooker] do next? Ropes in Pete Sinfield, that's what! Nothing like jumping out of the dictionary and into the thesaurus!"

The Gary Brooker Band comprised Tim Renwick on guitar, Bruce Lynch on bass, and Dave Mattacks (formerly of Fairport Convention) on drums, with backing vocals provided by Stephanie De Sykes. Looking for an old school producer Brooker hit the jackpot with George Martin. "I'd known George for years," he explained. "I first met him when The Paramounts signed with Parlophone. There were four producers back then: George Martin, Ron Richards, Peter Sullivan and John Burgess. Burgess was doing Manfred Mann, Sullivan was doing Tom Jones, George had The Beatles and Cilla Black, and Ron was doing all right with The Hollies and The Paramounts."

In his production role, Martin chose two of the covers, namely Matthew L. Moore/Tom Kosta's 'Savannah' and Murray Head's 'Say It Aint So Joe', while Brooker had a pair of Mickey Jupp songs lined up in the form of 'Pilot' and 'Switchboard Susan'. In a May 1979 edition of BBC TV's nightly current affairs programme *Newsnight* Robin Denselow made a special report on *No More Fear Of Flying* and Brooker appeared in the studio singing the lead-off single 'Savannah', but with little radio play and no *Top Of The Pops* coverage it flopped.

Despite having been covered by other artists – most recently Roger Daltrey in 1977 – the follow-up 'Say It Aint So Joe' was voted as 'Single Of The Week' in *NME* by Julie Burchill, who proceeded to pay Brooker a backhanded compliment by stating, "The song not the singer." The record nudged into the UK charts briefly, while 'No More Fear Of Flying' became a Top 20 hit single in Holland. "The song's words were written by Keith Reid about the break-up of Procol," Brooker explained. "The way I see it it's about the fact that I can embark on playing on my own in freedom."

Possibly more than slightly disappointed, Brooker showcased a few of the album's songs at The Parrot in Forest Green, Surrey, the pub that he'd bought in 1976. All-star gatherings featuring a coterie of Surrey rock stars were not unusual in The Parrot and late night gigs with lock-ins were very much the order of the day in an establishment that rarely called "Time gentlemen, please!"

Gary Brooker: "I organised a few blues gigs with Eric Clapton. There was no rehearsal, so what I did was I played all the songs that I'd known from The Paramounts days – the sort of stuff that was played around the clubs in the early sixties. What fun we had! The first time we ever did that we started at 9 p.m. and at 4 a.m. I said, "Thank you and good night". Eric was saying, "Thank god, I thought we were never going to stop playing. We've been playing for seven hours." And we had! And we must have played every song that we'd ever liked. Everybody was well into this – both the band and the audience. It was quite a big band and had some good people in it like Andy Fairweather-Low with Dave Mattacks on drums and Curved Air's Darryl Way on violin. We did this a couple of times and Eric said "Do you wanna come out on the road?"

Gary Brooker had been an old friend of Clapton's from early Yardbirds days. In the mid-seventies Brooker started playing at the Parrot pub two or three times a week and Clapton would regularly jam with him. Shortly afterwards Clapton put together a band consisting of Brooker (Hammond organ), Chris Stainton (piano), Albert Lee (guitar), Dave Markee (bass) and Henry Spinetti (drums).

Following on from a large world tour Clapton's band were on particularly fine form. The set featured numerous Clapton standards, blues classics as well as new songs co-written by Clapton with Brooker – some of which ended up on Clapton's 1981 album *Another Ticket*. The highlight of the set was a new Brooker song, 'Home Lovin'', that was meant to appear on the great 'lost' Clapton album *Turn Up Down*. Brooker played Hammond organ throughout the shows and often handled lead vocals, too. Reaching Edinburgh in the summer of 1980, at The George Hotel in the city's famous George Street, the band enjoyed a late lunch while answering a few press questions. "Why is Gary Brooker playing the Hammond organ and not the piano (played by Chris Stainton) each night?" a callow lad enquired. A slightly startled Clapton replied, "Because Gary Brooker played the Hammond organ on 'A Whiter Shade Of Pale'." Those gathered around Eric were too polite to point out that Brooker had in fact played piano on 'Pale' and that Matthew Fisher had been the organist. From that point onwards Brooker and Stainton would both be credited as "keyboard players".

During his time in Clapton's band Brooker became 'Surrey Fly Fishing Champion' and taught Eric the pastime near his home in Surrey. "I used to look at Gary with amusement, with his little bag with some flies in it and a rod and reel…" Clapton recalled in his 2007 autobiography. (19)

In 1982 Brooker's second solo album, *Lead Me To The Water*, issued on Phonogram, featured the single 'The Angler'. Brooker produced the album and wrote all the lyrics for the first time, including 'Home Lovin'' the highlight of the 1980 live show. Guest musicians included Eric Clapton's entire band with special guests George Harrison, Tim Renwick, Phil Collins and hot engineer Tom Dowd, among a host of other names. However, with Brooker utilising Clapton's band – possibly for a good reason in the light of the aborted *Turn Up Down* album – things started to unravel.

Eric Clapton: "In the beginning I was happy playing with these guys. We were doing it for fun and companionship and the love of music… But Roger [Forrester – Clapton's manager] wasn't too sure, and neither was Tom [Dowd] who was producing again, and to be fair to them, after two weeks of this, we'd hardly completed one track…Also, Gary

Brooker and I had become very close, and as a result he was having a lot of input into the way the band worked, which for whatever reason, was not popular with management and production.

"After a couple of weeks, Tom Dowd came to me and laid it on the line that nothing was going to happen with this new album unless we had a radical change of musicians. He recommended that I fire the current band, with the exception of Albert Lee ... That night I had dinner with the band members and told them, 'I'm very sorry, but I've got bad news. This just isn't working, and it's been suggested to me that I try something else. So I'm asking you all to go home, and I'll let any of you know if I want you to come back and play on tour.' A stunned silence fell over us when I told them. Sacking the band was a huge thing for me to do and very painful. For Henry Spinetti and Gary Brooker, the wounds took a long time to mend ..." (19). To add insult to injury Clapton's tepid post-rehab album *Money And Cigarettes* (1983) saw Brooker being replaced by former Procol Harum keyboard player Pete Solley on Hammond B3. (Having produced The Romantics' 'What I Like About You' – a *Billboard* 12 in 1980 – Solley also regularly worked as a producer.)

In what was to be the only live concert to showcase his solo output, Brooker's 'SS Band' appeared on German TV's *Rockpalast* live from the Markthalle, Hamburg on February 18, 1983. Despite suffering from a bad cold Brooker put in a fine performance with old mate Tim Renwick guesting again on guitar.

Work commenced on Brooker's third album in 1984. Procol fans had good reason to be excited when leaked reports from the session indicated that a quasi-Procol reunion was in the pipeline with Matthew Fisher, BJ Wilson, and words from Keith Reid. The album was being co-produced and co-composed by Brooker and Fisher with the pair also both playing keyboards together in their first collaboration for 16 years.

Since leaving Procol Harum in 1969, Fisher had successfully produced a clutch of albums throughout the seventies for Robin Trower, James Dewar and Tir Na Nog among others as well as a series of his own solo albums.

Matthew Fisher: "Gary contacted me with regard to making a solo album. He'd just released *Lead Me To The Water* and it hadn't been very well received. Gary was a much more comfortable person to be around at that time. The album was a long, slow process and took over a year to complete. He'd already written 'Missing Person' and 'Count Me Out' with Gavin Sutherland, and the music of 'Mr Blue Day' (lyrics later supplied by Iain Sutherland). The rest of the material was written at various writing sessions down at the barn by Gary's home in Dunsfold."

The Sutherland collaboration came about through Nick Blackburn who, by 1985, had managed Brooker and Sutherland for the best part of 10 years as a partner in Brooker-Reid's company Strongman Productions. Reid, who had continued to provide lyrics for people such as Robin Trower with *Victims Of The Fury,* supplied the lyrics to five of the 11 songs on *Echoes In The Night.* Brooker penned two sets of his own lyrics, including the insipid 'Two Fools In Love'.

If Fisher felt at ease in Brooker's company, the feeling appeared to be mutual. "He's a very nice guy – and talented," Brooker said of Fisher at the time, "very easy to work with. It was great because you could work out an idea and he would go away and put it down on tape, which took the pressure off me for a bit!"

Matthew Fisher: "We started work in 1984 at RAK Studios near Regent's Park. Henry Spinetti was on drums and we originally had Alan Spenner on bass, but that didn't work out too well. Nick Blackburn suggested we try a young bass player who had done some work with Robin Trower; his name was Dave Bronze. The tracks we worked on were 'Saw The Fire', 'Trick Of The Night', 'Two Fools In Love' and a pseudo-Motown number called 'Old Time Girl' that got dumped. A couple of months later we did a few tracks down at Jacob's studios (in Farnham, Surrey) with John Giblin on bass and a rather uninspiring drummer whose name I can't recall (Matt Lettley). The songs were 'Echoes In The Night', 'Missing Person', 'Count Me Out' and a version of 'Mr Blue Day' that ended up on the cutting room floor.

"A couple of memories from RAK. Keith Reid got really annoyed at the harmony vocals on 'Two Fools In Love'. For some reason he really didn't like them, but couldn't explain why. Gary and I were rather perplexed, especially since it wasn't even one of *his* songs. The second was that when Keith announced he'd found a can of lager in the fridge in the kitchen, Gary started singing 'Saw The Fire' as 'Found a lager. Found a lager in the fridge...'

"The rest of the recording was for the most part done at Strawberry South in Dorking, with Dave Bronze on bass and BJ Wilson on drums. Exceptions to this were a few overdub sessions at my studio the Old Barn (in Croydon) which included the guitar (from Eric Clapton) on 'Echoes In The Night' and the vocals on 'Ghost Train' and 'Saw The Fire', and a session at Decca Studio 4 recording the London Gospel Choir. After hearing the new basic track of 'Mr Blue Day', Nick Blackburn remarked, 'I can hear the strings now!'"

Gary Brooker: "Thousands got spent making 'Mr Blue Day' at Abbey Road with an entire orchestra in Studio One. Phonogram put a lot of advice and effort into that album. And yes we were making songs in batches of three or four for approval and 'where shall we go next?'"

Almost two years in the making *Echoes In The Night* was finally mixed at Audio International Studios in London. However when issued in 1985, the album quickly disappeared. Considering the time and expense involved and not only featuring Procol Harum's original organist, drummer, and lyricist, but also contributions from high profile guest guitarists in the shape of Eric Clapton, Rory Gallagher, Tim Renwick and Phil Palmer, this seemed an odd state of affairs.

According to Brooker, he was a victim of record company politics. Back in 1982 former Chrysalis press officer Chris Briggs became head of A&R at Mercury-Phonogram and signed Brooker to Phonogram. "We'd just finished making *Echoes In The Night* and suddenly Chris Briggs leaves the company as does [Managing Director] Bill Shepherd who had been my mentor. And on the day the album is due to be released the *worst* thing that you can be is a Chris Briggs signing. And it just totally disappeared. They buried it the moment it came out. They hardly released it. I don't ever remember it being advertised."

Like so many others of his generation who had fallen out of fashion, Brooker found the going rough when confronted by the new policy of unit-shifting record companies. After *Echoes In The Night* Phonogram declined to renew its option. Brooker was suddenly out of contract. At this point Strongman Productions ended as a management company with Nick Blackburn departing the company, and Keith Reid relocating to New York.

In 1986 Dutch singer Lori Spee invited Gary Brooker to Holland to duet on 'Two Fools In Love' from *Echoes In The Night.* The duet was issued as a Dutch only release through Philips and became a minor hit. TV appearances followed, but it signalled a career low point, as Brooker is the first to admit.

"Back home in Surrey," says Brooker, "I decided to stop making music and went and made a fishing video. I had a fishing shop, fished in as many places as I could, and even went abroad with the England team. In 1987 I became Fly Fishing Champion of Europe. I won the European Open. Luckily I did realise that this was not going to lead anywhere and Franky, my wife, said, "I married a musician not an angler. And I thought, "You're right!"

"So in 1987 I formed the band No Stiletto Shoes, which came about from those Parrot Pub days, and Eric Clapton. So that tradition carried on and we always played for charity. I sold the pub and the fishing shop, and we moved the venue to Dunsfold Village Hall. Eric Clapton would often come and play with us. In the end the band consisted of guitarist Andy Fairweather-Low, drummer Henry Spinetti, bassist Boz Burrell and saxophonist Frank Mead. We played a lot of gigs and came to London and did the 100 Club and the Half Moon in Putney. We always promoted our own gigs."

The charity gigs grew and grew. In 1990 Dave Gilmour of Pink Floyd joined for a gig at Alexandra Palace, and by this time they had two drummers, Phil Collins and Jody Linscott on extra percussion. "We added a five piece brass section and Mike Rutherford of Genesis came in in on guitar with Howard Jones on keyboards. Sam Brown, Vicki Brown and Carol Kenyon were on backing vocals. [It was a] big band," adds Brooker.

With tickets at between £60 and £100 the concerts raised money under the banner of the Red Balloon Ball for the British Lung Foundation. Venues would be outdoors in the summer, at Wintershall, Surrey, and indoors in winter at the Natural History Museum where the likes of Chrissie Hynde, Mark Knopfler, Gary Moore, Chris Rea and Stevie Winwood would join in along with Jools Holland and his Big Band.

During this period Brooker also played piano in Bill Wyman's rhythm'n'blues band, Willie & The Poorboys, which also featured Andy Fairweather-Low and Frank Mead from Brooker's band No Stiletto Shoes. Brooker's mind, however, was full of *other* ideas...

Gary Brooker: "Over the years German conductor-orchestra leader Eberhard Schoener's been in the habit of putting on orchestral extravaganzas that mix classical music and rock music. And I've done many things like that in Germany that were all televised. When *Lead Me To The Water* came out in 1982 I got invited to Munich to play with the Symphony Orchestra and choir. For this particular concert I'd already orchestrated 'Home Lovin'', 'The Angler', 'The Cycle' and 'The Symphony For The Hard Of Hearing'."

Schoener, with whom Gary Brooker had maintained contact since Procol's German orchestral tour of 1973, asked Brooker to tour again as a part of more Rock Meets Classics tours of Germany, Austria, and Switzerland. Brooker's 'Echoes In The Night', 'The Long Goodbye' and 'Ghost Train', in particular, were all epics in the true Procol Harum tradition that would lend themselves to orchestral interpretation, along with old some Procol classics.

Gary Brooker: "So when Rock Meets Classics invited me back to Germany we added quite a few songs off *Echoes In The Night*, along with some Procol material. And it all worked out very well.

"I think that, coupled with the fact that we'd moved into the era of the home fax machine, got me thinking... Suddenly I was getting faxes [in the era before email] asking me, 'When are you going to reform Procol?' And, 'Hey Gary, how come you *never* reformed Procol?' And I thought hmmm... well if we were to reform Procol, it would *have* to be with BJ Wilson..."

Chapter 14

The Return Of The
Prodigal Strangers

1991

*"B J Wilson? There was nobody to touch him. He almost orchestrated with
his drumming – with his uniqueness on the kit. And that's what he had.
He was very special indeed. There was nobody in the world that could drum
like B J Wilson. And that's simply it."*

Jimmy Page

BJ Wilson started the eighties with Joe Cocker whose band he had
joined in 1978 after electing not to tour with Frankie Miller.
Unfortunately, while still a brilliant musician, his excesses had not been
curbed since Procol's demise. While on the Japanese leg of Joe Cocker's
1981 world tour, Wilson is said to have held the band record for saki
consumed: "34 small china jugs," according to Cocker's former head
roadie. It may be an amusing anecdote, but in truth "34" would kill
anyone – even a seasoned alcoholic.

Two years on and Wilson's drinking began to interfere with his
drumming. Suddenly the situation took on a more serious tone. Cocker

admits, "The band spotted it long before. If we were due to meet at 7.30 in the hotel lobby, he'd be there at 6.30 and he'd chase down about four doubles...

"When he was on target he was a magnificent drummer – ballads, there was no one to touch him – but he just got into this *crafty* drinking... always behind closed doors. On stage he'd been dragging time and it got to the point where the band said, 'Hey Joe, something's got to go. Either us or him.' So it was like five against one. I was trying to pretend it wasn't happening..."

Cocker, never averse to a drop himself, realised the situation was untenable. After four and a half years in the band, Wilson had simply got out of control. Tales of his eccentricities became legion within Cocker circles and remained so long after his being fired from the band in 1983. Stories about him falling asleep on an aircraft and accidentally setting his hair alight with a lit cigarette and waking to the smell of burning hair, only to mutter, "I'll have to change my socks!"

"We were incorrigible drinking partners," Cocker related. "We were in this famous hotel in Holland, on the beach down Rotterdam way. We're sat in the bar and I said to BJ, 'I'm going to put my head down a bit, ready for tonight.' So he said, 'Well, I'm gonna get something to eat.' Next thing I know there's a beating at the door of my room... 'Meester Cockhair... Please... You must come with me... your friend – he is in terrible trouble!' 'Who? The drummer?'.... 'Yes. Please come quickly.' And he'd fallen asleep in his soup. It was alphabet soup and there's BJ – face down, he's lucky he didn't drown. As his nose is blowing, there's all these bubbles! We picked him up and he's got letters all over his face... B... K... A to Z... stuck all over him and falling out of his hair. These guys were so panic stricken they didn't know what to do. And I'm saying, 'Oh don't worry about him, he does this all the time' ... as there's like four of us carting him off to the elevator – pissed with all these letters all over his face."

Brooker's invitation for Wilson to guest on *Echoes In The Night* in 1985 possibly helped break his downward spiral and there were rumours that Procol would reform. After playing on Brooker's album Wilson drummed on Bob Siebenberg's *Giants In Our Own Room,* but then the gigs got scarce. The eighties were the era of 'the click track' and 'digital drums' – all of which were quite alien to BJ's idiosyncratic style.

At this juncture old friend Kellogs, determined to sort out BJ Wilson's drinking problems once and for all, invited the drummer to stay at his home in Kew, in west London. Kellogs had cleaned up his own act and, by 1987, was living the healthy life as a teetotal vegetarian who went jogging every day. He would recommend the same regime for his old friend Wilson but somehow it never happened. Wilson was now suffering from depression and he never made it over to Kew from Oregon where he had been living for some time. He had also become estranged from his wife, Sue.

In 1987 there were reports that Wilson had attempted suicide with a drugs overdose. In the event he lapsed into a deep coma as a result. Brooker immediately flew to his bedside, but his old mate did not wake up. On future visits Brooker brought a small electric piano to play at Wilson's bedside, singing some old Procol songs along with some new material that he'd recently written with Keith Reid. "You're going to get well and we're going to reform Procol," Brooker told Wilson. He made numerous visits to BJ's bedside in the hope that Wilson would recognise the familiar tunes and "somehow awaken". But he didn't stir. After three years in an almost vegetative state, Wilson contracted pneumonia and passed away on October 8, 1990.

Friends and colleagues in the music business lined up to pay tribute to Wilson on hearing that this biography would include a tribute to him.

Derek Sutton: "He always reminded me of the actor Tony Hancock: highly entertaining, witty – and greatly gifted as a drummer – but in the lightest of moments he could find the darkest of places..."

Robin Trower: "BJ Wilson? The loveliest, sweetest guy you could ever hope to meet in your entire life... What he did on the drums was unique. It was orchestral almost what he did on the kit. Quite unlike anything you'd hear anywhere really..."

Matthew Fisher: "I think a lot of people appreciate BJ's drumming *now* more than they did at the time. I mean *we* always knew that he was great..."

Joe Cocker: "I wrote 'Another Mind Gone' with Chris Stainton and Jeff Levine as a tribute to BJ Wilson. BJ worked with me for a long time; he was a friend of mine. It just angered me... There are a lot of rock tragedies, but that's a heavy one. The lyrics had a lot to do with (that)."

In 1999 a *Classic Rock* magazine reader's poll voted BJ Wilson as 'The Greatest Drummer Of All Time' – with Wilson polling a whopping 20% of the votes.

Jimmy Page: "BJ Wilson? There was nobody to touch him. He almost orchestrated with his drumming – with his uniqueness on the kit. And that's what he had. He was *very* special indeed. There was nobody in the world that could drum like BJ Wilson. And that's simply it."

In 1991 it was difficult to gauge whether the time was right for a Procol Harum reformation. Their progressive peers of yesteryear, among them Genesis (*We Can't Dance*), Jethro Tull (*Catfish Rising*) and Yes (*Union*), pushed out albums to loyal fans, particularly in America and Europe where it seemed like punk had never happened. In a rather moribund MOR-AOR climate, mainstream American rock provided a plethora of posturing poseurs, primarily in the shape of Bon Jovi and Guns 'N Roses. Both acts attempted to sell rebellion, but their performances were continually stage-managed under the watchful gaze of corporate culture. Then there was Seattle 'grunge' with new rebels Nirvana and cohorts of sound-a-likes all following in their wake. However, some old school acts who had previously cited Procol Harum's songwriting methods as being "an influence" were now celebrating their own former glories. So why shouldn't Procol Harum?

In the same year that Procol Harum chose to reform, Polygram's Mercury Records' imprint released the number one album *Two Rooms – A Tribute To Elton John & Bernie Taupin*. Numerous old school rock acts were enlisted to pay 'tribute to Elton & Bernie' on this lavish double album, including The Who and The Beach Boys. In turn Procol got Polygram Music Publishing, which handled Elton's Big Pig Music Publishing, to "look after" their BlueBeard Music Publishing, but opted to sign up with the Zoo Records label which was distributed by BMG

globally. Zoo's press agent was none other than old time Procol fan –
and sometimes their harshest critic – former *Rolling Stone* journalist Bud
Scoppa.

Gary Brooker explained how the reunion came about. "I had the good
fortune to do a few live London-based broadcasts from Bill Wyman's
cafe to American radio stations. Bill had a cafe called Sticky Fingers
in Kensington. Americans came over there and liked to run live radio
programmes, you know, 'We are here talking to you live from London
from Bill Wyman's Sticky Fingers and here is Gary Brooker!' ...They
had about five different radio stations in this cafe and they all broadcast
live to their own stations in Houston, New York, San Antonio, or
wherever. And they were acting like Procol were still going strong.
They played 'Conquistador' and 'The Devil Came From Kansas' and
not *just* 'A Whiter Shade Of Pale'. And I thought, 'It's like the band's
still going.' These people loved us. Fans started saying, 'You know we
miss this, we miss what you do. Our records are worn out now – any
chance of something else?'

"There were lots of little messages. I felt if there was the right kind
of marketing happening we'd definitely got an audience. A specific
audience – not necessarily a huge audience. So I phoned up Keith
[Reid], who was in New York, and I said, 'Would you like to write
some more songs, maybe with the idea of it ending up as a Procol
project?'"

Keith Reid: "I said, 'Well why don't you come over here?' In the old
days usually what happened was that I'd go and visit Gary in the country
and sit round his piano, and so I said, 'Well why don't you come over
to New York and sit round a recording studio?'"

Gary Brooker: "Keith and I worked with Matt Noble, who's an
engineer and writer from the New York area, and we were able to kind
of work out our songs and get them down on tape at the same time to
listen to how they were going. We had a good week of writing, we
wrote four or five songs."

Keith Reid: "We were very pleased with the results. We lived with
it for a while and we liked what we heard, and we decided to take it a
stage further, and Gary called on Matthew Fisher to come down and

join us. After that Gary and myself and Matthew began working on getting tunes together for the record and the question of guitar obviously started to appear. I think that we weren't sure whether Robin Trower would be interested in working with us; but anyway we took the tapes along and played them to him, and he loved it! In fact he said, 'Why didn't you call me sooner?' And we started playing them around for people to see if anybody liked it, or liked it as much as we did, and we got a very favourable response to it, and I think at that stage we seriously started to think, 'Well, this is going to be a record, we're going to go ahead with this.'"

Derek Sutton: "I was still managing Robin Trower [at the time] and there was a possibility that I might actually manage Procol Harum again... I was very excited about the band reforming. I was also officially a fan. And I still am to this very day..."

Barry Sinclair, Procol's former tour manager, was now resident in San Francisco and was still in touch with fellow Southend chum and Bay Area resident Mick Brigden, who worked for Bill Graham Productions. Sinclair suggested that Procol meet with Graham who had previously run the legendary Fillmore venues and Winterland where Procol had played so many successful gigs between 1967 and 1971. Graham also had a top PR team headed by Bud Scoppa who was well placed to look after Procol's spin doctoring – especially given that the 1991 version of the band contained the bulk of the 1967 to 1969 line-up generally preferred by Americans.

Reid knew that Lou Maglia, a former head of Island Records Inc., had just set up Zoo Records in New York, and approached Maglia with several demos featuring Fisher, Dave Bronze and Henry Spinetti playing 'The Truth Won't Fade Away', 'One More Time', 'A Dream In Ev'ry Home' (originally 'A Dream Without A Home') and 'Learn To Fly'.* With 'new' demos made under the watchful eye of Matt Noble, a deal was clinched with Zoo.

---

* Gary Brooker had previously enlisted Tim Renwick to demo four *Prodigal Stranger* songs as early as 1989.

In July the label announced: "It's been two decades since the nucleus of Procol Harum collaborated together [sic], but as the eighties came to a close the time seemed right to rekindle the magic. The rebirth of Procol Harum came out of a simple 'phone-call between two old friends'... Now for the first time in nearly two decades Gary Brooker, Matthew Fisher, Keith Reid and Robin Trower have reconvened for a musical feast. The results: *The Prodigal Stranger*. From those first few notes of 'A Whiter Shade of Pale' during the Summer of Love, Procol Harum's music has endured: the classical themes, the heavy R&B emphasis, the dual keyboards and ethereal lyrics, all combine to form a sound unlike any other."

Having played on the album Trower declined to tour. "Although I wanted to do it, I found it very hard to get back into that particular space," he explained in 2005. "I don't know if my brain had turned to mush, but I just couldn't... I'd got so used to doing what it is that I do that I had to continue doing *that* really... Once you've done your own thing it's very hard to go back to where you once were."

One character from Procol's past who was happy to go back to where they once were was Southend friend and former roadie John 'Kellogs' Kalinowski who returned to the fold, initially as tour manager and later as full time manager.

Sadly, a key factor missing in this new Procol Harum undertaking was BJ Wilson. But, as Brooker remarked in 1992, "We decided that if we couldn't do the new album *with* him – then we'd do it *for* him... It was our little tribute to him."

In 1991 the band undertook *The Prodigal Stranger* promo tour in the States from July to August followed by headline dates from September 23 to October 7. Tim Renwick (born August 7, 1949, Cambridge) filled Trower's shoes alongside a rhythm section consisting of former Robin Trower and Dr Feelgood bassist and fellow Southender, Dave 'Eric' Bronze (born April 2, 1952, Billericay, Essex) and Big Country's drummer Mark 'Michael' Brzezicki (born June 21, 1957, Slough, Middlesex) who had all played on the album.

Perhaps recognising the power of a new Robin Trower song, but this time written for Procol Harum, Zoo insisted that 'All Our Dreams Are Sold' became the single for airplay across American airwaves.

Robin Trower: "'All Our Dreams Are Sold' was the first song I'd written in many, many years that wasn't for one of my own things, you know, in other words it was for somebody else really. Although it's me that's playing it, I knew I had to come up *not* with a Robin Trower song, but a Procol Harum song. So that made it kind of a fascinating thing to work on."

However Reid and Brooker felt that Zoo had chosen the wrong song. "It was too guitar heavy – much more so than any of the other songs on the album and therefore not very representative of the band," said Reid. "It wasn't the Procol Harum people were expecting. Unfortunately with radio in America, they give you one shot. The record company had wanted 'All Our Dreams Are Sold'. I remember there was quite a lot of arguing about this. We wanted to go with 'The Truth Won't Fade Away'. The record company had their way – and the single did nothing! American radio is ruthless. You get one chance. If you don't do it first time out of the box, that's it. You don't get a second chance!"

In October the band were flown to New York to appear on *Late Night With David Letterman,* America's hippest chat show, jamming with the hot house band fronted by Paul Shaffer. In anticipation of this prestigious event, Q magazine, which had given *The Prodigal Stranger* a four-star review – "a return to form with a feeling of better to come", wrote Johnny Black – dispatched Tom Hibbert from London to report on proceedings.

"[We are] outside the studios of NBC Television in New York," Hibbert started in his droll style. "Some ancient group from England are appearing this night [and] there lurks a man, 40-ish, polo-neck sweater, jacket carrying food stains, great deal of hair, peculiar glint to the eye. He is clutching an old and much-thumbed book, an encyclopaedia of rock open at the 'Ps'. Pretty Things, The ... Previn, Dory ... Price, Alan ... Procol Harum.

"A party of middle-aged Englishmen arrive, the book-clutcher sidles forward, Mark Chapman-like, murmurs 'Er, hi. Which one are you?' Matthew Fisher, Procol Harum's organist, looks at the stranger with some alarm, 'Which one what? My name's Matthew Fisher.' The odd fellow consults his encyclopaedia – presumably to check that someone called Matthew Fisher was once a member of Procol Harum – and then wheezes with delight. 'Matthew! Yeah, oh Matthew! You're Matthew Fisher, right? Matthew, please sign my book right there on 'Procol Harum'! I love you guys!'

"Is this reunion just another cynical exercise in money-making through the powers of nostalgia, as practised in recent times by The Who and so many more? Procol Harum, who never got their royalties for 'A Whiter Shade Of Pale' – they were swizzed out of an unsmall fortune – might be forgiven for wanting to cash in on the pop memory boom. But that wasn't a motive at all, Keith Reid insists, 'We must have been asked to re-form at least eight or 10 times a year since we stopped but that was never a good reason to do it. This isn't memory lane.' Gary Brooker is less jaunty. 'We've got nothing else to do, this is the thing ...' The group have been playing 'A Whiter Shade Of Pale' on stage. It brings the house down, every time."

"I don't understand," says Fisher, who seems unable to get to grips with the modern pop process as the group sip tea and hang about waiting for their TV run-through. Fisher adds, 'Did you come especially to New York just to interview us? Really? Oh, that's odd. I find that very odd...'"

Letterman's show kicked off with much bluster. The dynamic house band appeared to be augmented by Brooker and Fisher. "Where are the rest of you guys?" enquired Letterman, "Or are there only two of you these days?" Brooker, wearing a bright red jacket, explained that the other three were "having a rest". Paul Shaffer quickly interjected, "Procol's lyric writer Keith Reid is in the audience," but the cameras failed to find him. Not a good start.

Brooker and Fisher played out to each commercial break with snippets of 'A Whiter Shade Of Pale', 'Conquistador', and 'The Devil Came From Kansas'. The concluding segment showed the pair seated centre stage in front of the house band. Brooker was now behind a handsome Steinway Grand next to Fisher's more modest Yamaha portable. Both launched into an anthemic uptempo version of 'The Truth Won't Fade Away'. Brooker delivered a solid vocal augmented by a punchy performance from Shaffer's beaming crew. Seemingly shocked by the intensity of the song, the dean of American chat lunged towards the mild

Englishmen, wrong-footing both by grabbing and vigorously shaking their hands. The proceedings concluded with some more 'knowing' damned Yankee banter and finally it was over.

With the departure of Tim Renwick who had only been temporarily filling in, the issue of a new guitarist came to the fore in autumn 1991. Kellogs knew Geoff Whitehorn by reputation – Whitehorn (born August 29, 1951, London) had toured and recorded extensively with Elkie Brooks and Roger Chapman, following on from stints with the jazz–rock band If and then Crawler, where he replaced Paul Kossoff. "Do I remember my very first gig with Procol Harum?" Whitehorn wryly recalled in 2005, "Yes... *The Johnny Carson Show...* No pressure!"

Thanks in part to Graham's management nous, Procol appeared on *The Tonight Show Starring Johnny Carson* live on December 13. For their introduction Carson and his sidekick discussed the correct pronunciation of the flower poinsettia as a lead-in to the actual 'pronunciation' of 'Procol Harum'. Carson sparred with the leader of the house band by giving three different types of intonation for Procol Harum – "Pro-Call Hay-Ram? Pro-Kill Hah-Rum? Procol Harum!" In so doing, the unequalled master of American chat neatly provided the band with not one, but three namechecks. Then amid a huge stage setting Procol launched into 'A Dream In Ev'ry Home', this time featuring the full five-piece band complete with a female backing vocalist and conga player – something of a first for Procol. Then it was straight into 'A Whiter Shade Of Pale', which received a standing ovation.

The Carson and Letterman appearances together with a special promo video conspired to push the next single 'The Truth Won't Fade Away' into the public's ear and brought *The Prodigal Stranger* to the attention of certain journalists. Two months later Jonathan Lewis, of US magazine *DISCoveries*, wrote, "*The Prodigal Stranger* has many peaks. 'The Truth Won't Fade Away' – a nineties folk rock anthem whose words could conveniently speak for the band and the sixties generation – 'It was black, it was white, we had so much to say/Right or wrong... The truth won't fade away.' On the last verse Fisher's Hammond propels the song along much in the way that Al Kooper drove Bob Dylan's faster tempo *Blonde On Blonde* material."

Steve Morse of *The Boston Globe* took a similar view on the song. "It's a glimpse of the Vietnam era when we had so much to say – right or wrong."

"Well with 'The Truth Won't Fade Away' Keith was thinking about Pompeii or Incas, I think?" Brooker countered. "He's a great master of words. I mean to be able to have a line or two which can be given a dozen interpretations, depending on how you feel and how you want to look at it, is quite a natural talent really."

Newly exploring the genre of 'World Music', Procol succeeded with 'Holding On', an anti-war song for the nineties with a message that still resonates.

Gary Brooker: "It was [directed] somewhere towards Ethiopia, to the best of my recollection, and we needed some girls to do some chanting. And these girls came along and they were South Africans and quite fluent in either Swahili or Zulu. I'm not sure what language it was, but they taught us all how to sing it and it ended up sounding interesting."

Keith Reid: "I wouldn't call 'Man With A Mission' typically Procol Harum at all. And yet when I've played the record to people they've said, 'Wow that's really Procol Harum.' It's a very positive song. It's putting things in a very positive light. We feel that our protagonist is indeed a 'Man With A Mission'."

In his *DISCoveries* article Jonathan Lewis suggested to Reid that "the morose and introspective 'You Can't Turn Back The Page' could be covered by Barry Manilow. 'Barry Manilow?' Reid hesitated for an unsure second and burst out laughing then put down the phone... 'Gary, this guy thinks that Barry Manilow could cover 'You Can't Turn Back The Page' 'Yeah – Gary's agreeing with you there!' admitted Reid."

'One More Time' is quite literally about Procol doing it all over again "one more time". With 'A Dream In Ev'ry Home' Brooker said that he liked the "ambiguity in that song. It could possibly be about television, the fact that some people are just alone in a room with a TV, or that everyone has hopes and dreams and they're not necessarily fulfilled, or maybe they are fulfilled, maybe the contents of one's home illustrate some of our dreams – there's all of that. Particularly ambiguous that one – it has *just* a touch of loneliness about it, too."

Matthew Fisher, "The basic groove of 'A Dream In Ev'ry Home' was just a riff that I thought up at home and I sequenced it up on my computer with a bass line and a drum part, which no real bass player or drummer would *ever* have played. It's not what *real* musicians would have done. It was a very synthetic thing, but which seems to work. It was typical of the way we work nowadays, what with the advantages of these computers and sequencers – you know, that you can toss ideas backwards and forwards and change things as you go."

'The Hand That Rocks The Cradle', opening with a Hammond phrase borrowed from Billy Preston's 'Will It Go 'Round In Circles', chugged along with an impassioned Brooker vocal reminiscent of Steve Winwood. "It's a very taxing one to sing," Brooker confirmed. While Reid admitted, "It was wrestled with long and hard in the studio, that particular tune. 'The Hand That Rocked The Cradle' had a lot of time spent on it." Later in 1992 the US football team the Miami Dolphins adopted Procol's song as their anthem. Cheerleaders danced along to it prior to and during the mid-game break. However, this was not entirely due to Procol. The Hollywood feature film *The Hand That Rocks The Cradle* (1992) was hugely successful and the Dolphins were involved with the movie. Unfortunately for Procol, the movie didn't utilise their song. The Dolphins did, however, feature Procol's song throughout their 1992 season, and 20 years later they gave it one more outing.

'The King Of Hearts' makes a subtle reference to 'A Whiter Shade Of Pale' with the repeated line '*So I wandered through my playing cards.*' Apparently it wasn't a conscious reference back, but it fitted perfectly.

Keith Reid: "The genesis of that song is the actual line, 'The King Of Hearts'. Really that song lyrically built up from the chorus; the king no longer being the king of hearts, but the king of the broken-hearted. And that's *really* where that song started, lyrically. And then that took me on a little voyage, just took me away. When we got to that point in the verse, the card game was going on, and the characters just seemed to speak out for themselves. They started talking about wandering through their playing cards. So I just wrote it down."

"Matthew Fisher plays the end differently almost every night," said Brooker when the song had entered their live set. "He lays down some beautiful arpeggios at the end. He has a particular lightness of touch!"

'All Our Dreams Are Sold' is about the bleakness of modern life. "The title isn't meant to be taken literally," Reid pointed out. "I mean that song isn't really saying 'all our dreams are sold', though that's a way that people might think. Another way of looking at that song is that all our dreams are sold to us. It is a feeling of being manipulated."

'Perpetual Motion' co-written with Matt Noble, features Reid's smoothest lyrics set to waltz time while 'Learn To Fly' was an uptempo AOR song only rescued from total blandness by Brooker's voice. As John McFerrin noted in his online review of Procol's output: "Arrgh, why did so many art-rock bands feel the need to go so blandly 'Adult Contemporary' around this time??!! The clichés abound here, both lyrically and musically."

'The Pursuit Of Happiness' pursues the bleakness of modern life and is another one co-written by Brooker and Noble. Continuing in the Procol tradition of reflective album closers, it features a simple hook from Brooker with a counter-melody from Fisher and an expressive Trower solo.

'Without A Doubt' *The Prodigal Stranger* served its purpose by reigniting interest among the faithful, and was clearly a return to form. Brooker summed things up. "We never knew if it would work out, but we did know one thing and that was that the basis of us making the new Procol Harum record would be if we could get together a good set of songs. And the next target we found, which we hadn't really expected, was, well, you just can't come and make a Procol Harum album after many, many years, because people nowadays may have only heard of 'A Whiter Shade Of Pale' or 'Conquistador' or maybe 'A Salty Dog'. They're quite substantial songs and records to live up to. So we had a bit of a goal there in that, if we're going to do anything, it's got to be at least as good, so we had a good target to head towards!"

Chapter 15

On The Road Again
1992–1997

"Procol reformed again recently and put out The Prodigal Stranger *their first album for I don't know how many decades. There's one track on it that is I think one of the three best tracks they've ever made – 'Holding On'"*
Douglas Adams

The European leg of a 24-date Procol Harum tour tied in with the belated European release of *The Prodigal Stranger,* taking in eight countries beginning in Augsburg, Germany on January 15, 1992 and concluding in Paris on Valentine's Day. The concert from the previous day's gig in Utrecht was later released as a live CD called *One More Time* (in 1997). "Whitehorn's interpretation of Trower's crunching power chords in 'Whaling Stories' shows why superstars such as Pete Townshend often ask him to join their touring bands," wrote journalist Frans Steensma of *OOR Magazine.* "When listening to the rocky 'All Our Dreams Are Sold' you hear a tight outfit, a great rock band with a lot of guts, which is amongst the best in the universe." Former *Melody Maker* journalist Chris Welch flew to the Paris gig and said of the show, "Procol

Harum were playing better than ever. For those fortunate enough to see them in Paris it truly was an exhilarating experience!"

Brooker was full of praise for Mark Brzezicki who had the unenviable task of filling the drummer's seat. "He had the late BJ Wilson off to a tee. Disgustingly good. He was so good at it, it was like BJ was sat there playing!"

With the band still hot from being on the road, a short North American tour was planned for May. By now Fisher had taken up studying for a Masters Degree in Computer Science as a mature student at Cambridge University. For the next four years his touring with Procol would be restricted to summer and Easter breaks only. As a consequence, Don Snow (aka Jonn Savannah, born January 13, 1957, Nairobi, Kenya) an old friend of Kellogs from his days at Stiff Records and formerly of The Sinceros and Squeeze, replaced Fisher for this particular tour.

On May 29 a memorable concert took place when Procol Harum were invited back to the Jubilee Auditorium, Edmonton, Canada for a 21st Anniversary Reunion with the Edmonton Symphony Orchestra. Helen Metella of *The Edmonton Journal* reported that, "The ESO General Manager Bob McPhee was watching *Late Night With David Letterman* one evening last October and exclaimed delightedly, 'Oh my God, they're back together!'" With the 3,000-seater auditorium selling out over two nights to punters across the whole of North America, producer and Procol aficionado Tommy Banks decided the show *had* to be televised. Banks negotiated a deal with the pay-TV channel Canadian ITV for multi-camera coverage of this special occasion. With a set planned to include many of the songs featured in the original Procol-ESO album from 1971 coupled with new *Prodigal Stranger* material Procol planned to deliver a set twice as long as the one undertaken 21 years before.

Brooker, Whitehorn, Bronze, Brzezicki, and Snow arrived in Edmonton on the day of the show amid much publicity. David Hoyt, the Greenwood Singer and the ESO along with the 3,000 in attendance all gave Procol Harum a standing ovation as they took to the stage. A few celebs, namely actor-comedian Richard Lewis and Hollywood star Annette O'Toole, were spotted in the audience as Procol launched into their set. Alan Kellog of *The Edmonton Sunday Journal* described the closing moments, "I wonder what the players thought when they received their fifth standing ovation on Friday? I guess I'd forgotten just how fond I used to be of the band, of a raft of songs that generally have withstood the vagaries of the decades, changing pop sensibilities. 'A Salty Dog', 'Shine On Brightly', 'Grand Hotel', 'A Whiter Shade Of Pale', the grand finale from 'In Held 'Twas In I' and other faves came off fresh and powerful."

Helen Metella in her review of May 30 pointed out a highlight of the concert, namely a brand new song receiving its first outing, "called 'Into The Flood' (a *Prodigal Stranger* outtake) causing the violins to fly like spirited country fiddles, the choir hit precise, gospel influenced harmonies with gusto and the horns dance with Geoff Whitehorn's lead guitar, it underscored how singularly innovative the sound is when rock and orchestra entwine". Reprising 'Conquistador' for its second outing of the night and the fifth encore Procol Harum were bowled over by the response to the whole show, which proved to be popular on Canadian TV, too.

Back in the UK the British media chose to ignore Procol Harum's rebirth and there were precious few reviews of *The Prodigal Stranger*. With no invite to appear on the BBC's newly inaugurated rock show *Later With Jools Holland* nor any promoter begging the band to play London, Gary Brooker chose to ignore Britain altogether until 1995.

In May 1993 Procol played four nights at the Casino Da Póvoa De Varzim, Oporto, at the personal invitation of the Portuguese president who had been a fan of the band since 1973 when *Grand Hotel* was 'the biggest selling album of the year' in Portugal. Keyboard player Josh Phillips(-Gorse) (born December 19, 1962, Rochester, Kent) formerly of Midge Ure's band and Big Country filled in for Fisher, while drummer Ian Wallace (born September 29, 1946, Bury, Lancs) who'd played with King Crimson, Don Henley and Bob Dylan, replaced Mark Brzezicki for the duration of the 1993 tours. By July Fisher was free from his studies and a short four-date tour took place between July 10 and July 18 when Procol kicked off with a private party in Dunsfold, celebrating Gary and Franky Brooker's silver wedding anniversary.

No doubt nursing sore heads Procol Harum and entourage (including this author) assembled at Stansted Airport at 9 a.m. the following day in order to fly to the Rock Summer Festival in Tallinn, Estonia where the band were headlining on the third and final day (July 11), over American Faith No More and the nineties answer to Alberto Y Los Trios Paranoias – The Funking Barstewards! One good reason for playing Tallinn was that MTV Europe would be televising their whole set and transmitting it to countless millions around the globe. That little detail aside, a visit to a former Soviet Republic, now free from the shackles of Russian imperialism, was something of a curiosity for all concerned.

Arriving at the airport barrier the press descended on Procol Harum in a way unseen since 1967. MTV Europe and Estonian TV and Radio pursued the band members to a fleet of Mercedes and minibuses. Each vehicle had a number plate saying "Rock 1, Rock 2, Rock 3", etc. Opting for a Mercedes, Brooker left the others to share a minibus to a former state owned hotel. The only cars to be seen in the streets were Ladas and the first sign of post Soviet decadence came in the form of brightly painted trolley buses the colour of Coca Cola tins – the white 'Coke' logo emblazoned across the side of each bus. Whizzing past a sea of grey concrete buildings Procol spotted a McDonald's before arriving at a hotel that looked like something out of a Len Deighton spy novel set in Moscow circa 1965. All the interior walls appeared to be covered in a dark brown coloured formica. "They should get Cadbury's to sponsor this place," Whitehorn quipped.

Taken into the old medieval walled city, which looked like something out of Hergé's adventures of Tintin, Procol spotted a man who looked alarmingly like Steven Spielberg. But as this was 18 years before *The Adventures Of Tintin* movie no further Tintin jokes were made.

After being fed lamb marinated in blackcurrant jam Procol were chaperoned in a minibus to the festival site where they were introduced to their personal guide, Rita. "Can we call you Bob?" asked Bronze. "Why do I look like a man?" enquired Rita." "No," said Whitehorn, "We'd just like to call you Bob for personal reasons. No offence intended." "You couldn't lend us a couple of bob, could you, Bob?" said Dave. Rita looked confused. "Is it because I wear my hair in a bob?" she enquired. Howls of laughter from Geoff and Dave, with Whitehorn adding, "As Jesus said to Moses, just carry on with the tablets..." Bronze then cracked a joke as old as father time, whispering into Rita's ear, "What's the difference between a buffalo and a bison? You can't wash yer hands in a buffalo..." Whitehorn smiled and said to the by now completely confused Estonian, "You'll have to excuse our pre-gig shenanigans. It's nothing personal."

Elsewhere Fisher studied the set list, which had only just been faxed over by Keith Reid from London. Kellogs explained that it is a tradition with the band "not to know the running order until sometimes just before they are due to go on stage". Reid had always chosen the set list's running order, "often adding songs" according to Brooker, "which the band hadn't rehearsed. Because the situation is unpredictable, it keeps us on our toes and provides room for change." Fisher appeared worried about the inclusion of 'As Strong As Samson', which to date he hadn't ever played with Procol.

At 9.45 p.m. local time the MC announced, "Mr Gary Brooker and Procol Harum". The band were followed on to the stage by swarms of MTV cameramen with yards of camera cable almost wrong-footing them. The anthemic nature of opener 'The Truth Won't Fade Away' had the crowd waving their arms in time. Having already witnessed Blur and The Shamen on previous days and with no preconceptions the young, twentysomething audience judged the band on the strength of music and performance and clearly loved them. Brooker was quick to rise to the occasion and stood chanting out the chorus. "Fade a-way" sang thousands of Estonians in perfect time. Procol had clearly not seen anything like it since their appearances at various sixties festivals and their performance went from strength to strength as a result.

A vastly reworked 'Whisky Train' began with Brooker singing, "Hey bartender, give me another gin" beginning as a slow blues and later following into a section with Bronze and Wallace playing together. Wallace, who had drummed on Bob Dylan's 1978 album *Live At The Budokan,* handled material in this particular setting in quite an exemplary manner. In an off the cuff moment Bronze punched the air and shouted out "Oi" to which some 45,000 Estonians suddenly shouted back "Oi" all punching the air in unison, clearly startling the band. At that very moment Procol Harum looked like they could have handled the likes of Glastonbury. This assertion was furthered by a rousing performance of 'All Our Dreams Are Sold'. Whitehorn gave it his all with a great reworking of Trower's original riffs adding a gutsy, ballsy punch to this underrated song. 'Man With A Mission' displayed Brooker's vocal range – from blues-to-soul-and-rock and back. It inspired dancing among the throng, more akin to epilepsy fused with a good old fashioned heads-down boogie.

For their first encore Procol launched into 'A Whiter Shade Of Pale' which the crowd appeared to know and sang along. Procol left the stage to thousands chanting "Pro-col Pro-col Pro-col". Returning Brooker asked, "I don't know if you can all understand me? But is it true that this is the land of the midnight sun?" Clearly fluent in English the audience shouted "Yes" back in unison. "Then could we do a couple of more songs?" Brooker stood at the piano and belted out Chuck Berry's 'Little Queenie' followed by 'Rip It Up'. The band left the stage and returned for another encore, delivering a spine tingling version of 'Repent Walpurgis'. Whitehorn played this better than any previous Procol guitarist had ever done, and the fusion of Brooker's melodic piano and Fisher's cathedral sounding organ took this into the realms of excelsis. As Whitehorn later remarked to Bronze backstage, "Matthew was looking quite Wagnerian tonight!" As Procol concluded the final crescendo, a mass of fireworks lit up the night sky.

Agreeing that the gig was an all round success Procol were chaperoned to an upmarket night club in the Gulf of Finland with huge panoramic windows looking out to sea. The entire venue stood and applauded as Procol entered the building. At 1:30 a.m. a huge sunrise lit up the morning sky, reflecting across the sea and bathing the entire venue in a golden light as the final drinks were served.

Six days later Procol played a homecoming to 200 friends, family and locals back home in Southend-on-Sea at the Zero Six Club, a small nightclub situated by Southend Airport – their first UK gig in 16 years.

"I can't wait to get the T shirt for this tour," Whitehorn joked with Kellogs, "Dunsfold Village, Tallinn, Estonia, Southend Airport, and Rosenburg, Austria!"

Still keen to push *The Prodigal Stranger* to American audiences Procol embarked on a six-week tour starting in August playing support to Jethro Tull. Tull still filled vast venues in the US at this point and had festival appearances in place, too. Ironically having supported Tull in the UK back in 1970 Procol were once again touring with their former Chrysalis labelmates 23 years on.

A regular feature of this tour was the encore of 'Pandora's Box' where Ian Anderson would join Procol to play flute prior to Tull coming on stage. However, this happened less and less as Procol appeared to be gradually stealing the limelight in the American press. Just one example of this came at Holmdel, New Jersey on August 28 when 'Uncle Mike' from the *Two Rivers Times* reviewed, "Now I realise that Jethro Tull as the headliner had put together a solid song list, played really well and Ian Anderson, as usual, was remarkable on the flute, but when it came to lead vocals and the entire presentation as a band, Gary Brooker was the man, and Procol Harum was the band. Needless to say they just blew me away and it wasn't just me. When Procol Harum didn't return to the stage for a richly deserved encore, the audience actually showed their disappointment by letting out a major league boo that echoed throughout the Garden State Arts Centre. Gary Brooker's vocals on 'Conquistador' and 'A Salty Dog' were haunting to say the least. They even managed to squeeze in a new [unreleased] song called 'Last Train To Niagara' which had heads bobbing throughout the crowd... Like the song says 'The Truth Won't Fade Away' and the truth is, neither has Procol Harum."

An added band feature for this particular tour came in the shape of bassist Matt(hew) Pegg (born March 27, 1971, Oxford), the son of Fairport Convention's Dave Pegg. Dave Bronze had been given the offer to tour with two bands back-to-back, namely The Hamsters followed by Eric Clapton – the latter being an opportunity he could not refuse especially given the irregularity of Procol tours. With Ian Wallace still on drums for Procol Harum's 21st American tour of 1993 the central line-up of Brooker, Fisher and Whitehorn remained fairly constant until 1994, when Ian Wallace moved on.

Following the US tour Brooker was personally invited by soul singer

Jocelyn Brown to perform Procol's 'Holding On' along with her 'big band' at London's hip Subterania club in Ladbroke Grove on October 13, 1993. Brooker then embarked on a two-week European tour as a part of the epic annual orchestral collaboration the Heineken Night Of The Proms. Concluding the tour in front of 10,000 at Rotterdam's Ahoy, following on from Barry Ryan, Colin Blunstone and the Proms Orchestra – and prior to a set by Sting – Brooker stole the show playing solo at a Steinway Grand piano in front of a 60 piece orchestra and choir singing 'A Whiter Shade Of Pale'. The show was later transmitted by Veronica TV across Belgium, Luxembourg, Holland and Germany to an audience of millions.

Also during this time Brooker made a guest appearance, alongside Jeff Beck and Eric Clapton, playing Hammond organ on Kate Bush's 1993 album *The Red Shoes*. Concluding the year, for Brooker's annual Christmas bash at Chiddingfold Club, near his home in Dunsfold, Procol performed a fine set that saw Mark Brzezicki back on drums. Special guest Frankie Miller joined in for what turned out to be his final live show, performing Wilson Pickett's 'In The Midnight Hour', Jim Reeves' 'He'll Have To Go', Allen Toussaint's 'Brickyard Blues' and Otis Redding's 'I've Got Dreams To Remember', leaving not a dry eye in the 800 capacity filled venue. The musicians were augmented by members of Gary's 'other band' No Stiletto Shoes, namely Andy Fairweather-Low (guitar), Frank Mead (sax), Henry Spinetti (drums), Peter Stroud (bass) and Maggie Ryder (backing vocals). A big band indeed and a night to remember, bringing 1993 to a triumphant close.

The first quarter of 1994 saw Brooker touring with former Rolling Stone Bill Wyman in his all-star outfit Willie & The Poor Boys. Two prestigious gigs took place during this period. Firstly, on February 13 at London's Royal Albert Hall in a 40-minute set as part of the Baby Lifeline appeal concert. Next up was the Mick Ronson Tribute gig at London's Hammersmith Odeon on April 29 with Willie & The Poor Boys doing a set and then Brooker performing 'A Whiter Shade Of Pale' solo at a Steinway Grand piano. A roster of names paid tribute to David Bowie's former collaborator, among them Glen Matlock, Mick Jones, Steve Harley, Bill Nelson, Joe Elliott, Roger Taylor and the Spiders

From Mars with Ian Hunter and Dana Gillespie. To the disappointment of all concerned Bowie declined to appear.

In the late spring BMG Classics New York invited Brooker to co-produce and sing on a proposed album, *The Symphonic Music Of Procol Harum,* to feature celebrity guests and the London Symphony Orchestra with guest conductors and arrangers. A 'celebrity fixer' promised much but delivered little, ultimately leaving the job of organising guests to Brooker himself. Brooker contacted his old friend George Martin who paved the way for the recording sessions – the first of which took place during April at London's AIR Lyndhurst Studios in Lyndhurst Hall – a former church in London's Belsize Park, among the finest recording studios in the world.

Former Curved Air violinist Darryl Way wrote the new orchestral arrangements for 'A Salty Dog' and 'A Whiter Shade Of Pale' while Brooker scored new arrangements for 'Simple Sister', 'Butterfly Boys', and 'The Long Goodbye' from *Echoes In The Night.* Classical arranger/conductor Nicholas Dodd scored 'Conquistador', 'Homburg', 'Grand Hotel', 'Pandora's Box', 'You Can't Turn Back The Page', and 'Strangers In Space'. Christian Kabitz scored 'Repent Walpurgis'.

With the exception of 'Simple Sister', 'You Can't Turn Back The Page' and 'Butterfly Boys', which were all recorded with the London Philharmonic Orchestra, and 'The Long Goodbye', recorded with The Sinfonia of London, all other recordings featured the LSO. Flute player James Galway guested on 'Pandora's Box', opera singer James Hadley sang 'Grand Hotel' while at a moment's notice and without rehearsal, Tom Jones, who Brooker had spotted in the Roundhouse Studio corridor while recording with the LPO, popped in to sing 'Simple Sister' in one perfect take. Brooker sang all the other tracks.

Brzezicki, Bronze and Whitehorn played on 'Conquistador', 'Homburg', 'Simple Sister' and 'Butterfly Boys', and for the final time (to date) the nucleus of the classic sixties line-up – Brooker, Trower, Fisher (alongside Bronze and Brzezicki) reconvened for 'Repent Walpurgis'. With Fisher playing a cathedral organ on 'Repent Walpurgis' and 'A Salty Dog', specially captured by the Virgin Manor Mobile Studio from inside All Saints Church in London's Margaret Street, the results were possibly the finest ever Procol Harum recording. Except it wasn't 'officially' a Procol Harum album even though it should have been!

With many months in post production the album finally got released under the banner of *The Long Goodbye – The Symphonic Music Of Procol Harum* in spring 1995 with little fanfare. Issued on the RCA Victor imprint the label did virtually nothing to promote a record that had cost a fortune to realise. To all intents and purposes RCA buried the album in the same way Mercury-Phonogram buried *Echoes In The Night* a decade earlier.

Much to everyone's surprise, in May 1995 former Eurythmics star Annie Lennox released an album called *Diva* featuring her cover of 'A Whiter Shade Of Pale'. Annie's 'Pale' became a UK Top 20 hit and *Diva* went triple platinum on both sides of the pond. This was good news for Procol who had *finally* plucked up the courage to book a series of UK dates some four years after *The Prodigal Stranger's* initial release. However, before returning to Blighty there was the small matter of Procol's 22nd coast-to-coast tour of America.

Meanwhile, Procol had lost another drummer as Ian Wallace went off to work with former Eagle Joe Walsh, while Mark Brzezicki returned to play with Big Country. So in July 1995 Graham Broad (born March 10, 1957, Hammersmith, London), formerly of Bandit, became Procol's third drummer since 1990. A 20-date tour of the US, Mexico and Canada, with Procol headlining over Steppenwolf and Jefferson Airplane (as well as in their own right), turned out to be something of an adventure for all concerned. Headlining on July 16 over a reformed version of The Doors (featuring Robbie Krieger, John Densmore, ex-Byrds bassist Skip Battin on keyboards, Krieger's son on vocals and a special guest vocalist who claimed to be Pearl Jam's Eddie Vedder) at the newly re-opened Fillmore in San Francisco, which was once again in the hands of Bill Graham (albeit briefly). The Doors turned in a strong set but Procol's truly excellent performance had the crowd calling out for more.

Two days later Procol headlined at the House of Blues on Hollywood Boulevard. Rising to the occasion Brooker added 'Alpha', an unreleased Procol blues number (from 1967) into the set with 'Fool's Gold' from

Procol's Ninth and a spine tingling cover of the standard 'Worried Life Blues', much to the delight of the younger LA-cool audience who appeared to make up the bulk of the crowd. Brooker's old chum, guitarist Albert Lee, came along especially to witness the show and was most impressed. The Steppenwolf gigs in the Midwest proved to be tricky. Hundreds of bikers at each gig would leave after John Kay & Co's set, leaving Procol to play to half empty theatres. Not an ideal scenario, but one they weathered well.

Arriving back in Britain for the annual Cropredy Festival, organised and run by Fairport Convention on August 11, 1995, Procol Harum embarked on their first British tour since 1977. Patrick Humphries' review appeared in *The Guardian* the following week: "Making their first UK [public] appearance in 18 years at Cropredy, Procol showed they had lost none of their mystery or imagination. Beginning with songs from their woefully ignored 11-album career, Procol really hit their stride with 'Quite Rightly So', their third single, which emphasises the band's piano and organ blend, binding their R&B roots to ethereal psychedelia. Gary Brooker is one of the great unheralded white soul voices, and he began 'Homburg' a cappella. Nearly 30 years on, the song still haunts and baffles. Geoff Whitehorn's guitar lent gothic gloom to 'Outside The Gates Of Cerdes', while Fairport's Ric Saunders added spritely [sic] violin to 'Conquistador'. 'A Salty Dog' came cruising out on to the night air, epitomising Procol's grandiose sweep, as the band set off on another voyage through the Sargasso Sea of rock'n'roll.

"Slowly and enticingly Brooker went into the genesis of 'A Whiter Shade Of Pale', a snatch of 'When A Man Loves A Woman', then it was that instantly recognisable Bach signature, and the 17,000 crowd were on their feet, lighters and matches flaring up in the night sky. Procol quit the stage just before midnight, proving emphatically that all these years on, they are still capable of skipping the light fandango."

With Harvey Goldsmith promoting Procol's return to the London stage at the Shepherd's Bush Empire on August 12 the press were out in force – and MTV turned up to video tape 'A Whiter Shade Of Pale' (only). Paul Sexton's half page *Times* article on August 14 was headlined 'Rock Dinosaur Still Alive And Kicking'. "Disillusioned by the reaction to their comeback, group leader Gary Brooker has put future recording plans in cold storage while gathering fellow-original Matthew Fisher and a band of sympathetic session players [sic] together for an eight date, for-the-hell-of-it tour to preview the release early next month of *Homburg and Other Hats – Procol Harum's Best Songs* [on Castle CD].

"The revival thus had all the unforced bonhomie of a pub gig. The Empire show was Procol's first London appearance since they taped a *Sight And Sound In Concert* show for BBC2 in this very location 18 years ago. I recall that on that final tour, a weary band could hardly be heard for the landlord ringing time on its career. Now, all shackles shaken loose, their playing was both taut and carefree and deserving of a larger audience than a sketchy turnout of mainly young males, vaguely aware that these men first recorded '*that* Annie Lennox song'.

"Brooker, now 50, may have acquired grey locks and a ponytail, but his voice remains a jewel, and Procol's performance of just about every well-remembered song in their catalogue was definitive. Instant soundbites such as 'Homburg' and 'Pandora's Box' mixed convivially with epic, episodic pieces such as 'Whaling Stories', 'Grand Hotel' and the still stirring 'A Salty Dog', while the overlooked mid-seventies single 'Nothing But The Truth' was one of several convincing rockers underpinned by Fisher on the organ. As that instrument led us into an unfeasibly fresh 'A Whiter Shade Of Pale', one savoured the sight of dinosaurs skipping the light fandango."

Max Bell in the *Evening Standard* added: "The eternally durable 'A Whiter Shade Of Pale' – John Lennon's favourite song of 1967 and an apparent influence on 'I Am The Walrus' – closed the main business with the singer pondering its ineffable nature. 'A lot of people have asked – what does it mean? Well, what does any of it mean?' he chuckled. I look forward with interest to Procol Harum being rediscovered by Blur and Paul Weller."

The advent of Britpop saw neither Paul Weller nor Blur pay any reference to Procol Harum whatsoever, but one wonders if the now largely forgotten Kula Shaker, complete with Hammond B3, may have been admirers?

★

Feeling strongly that *The Long Goodbye* deserved a proper live orchestral outing, in the summer of 1995 this author approached the head of public relations at the Royal Festival Hall on London's South Bank. The venue's PR representative set up a meeting with Graham Sheffield, the Music Director of the South Bank Centre, to gauge if there would be any interest. Sheffield suggested contacting the Managing Director of the LSO Clive Gillinson, which led to a meeting with him at his office on the sixth floor of Barbican Arts Centre, London. Gillinson revealed that he had also been a cello player in the RPO at Procol Harum's 1973 Rainbow Concert, whilst moonlighting from the LSO. He professed to "love the band" and it wasn't long before he had his diary open with a vacant spot. "I can make the booking now," he said. "What about February 8, 1996?" Gillinson now runs Carnegie Hall in New York.

The author moved quickly. "This is not my decision nor am I the band's agent, but here are the contact phone numbers of Gary Brooker and his manager John 'Kellogs' Kalinowski. I am sure they would both be very interested in your enthusiastic response ...!"

When Sheffield moved on to become the director of the Barbican Arts Centre, Nick Dodd was approached to conduct and oversee proceedings as musical director for the LSO-Procol Harum concert at the Barbican on February 8. The Chameleon Arts Chorus also came on board. With limited publicity but strategic advertising the main Barbican concert hall, with a capacity in excess of 4,000, sold out almost immediately. With electric anticipation of how good this event could be, an audience of music lovers and Procol aficionados gathered from all four corners of the globe for this one-off spectacular. Many sixties luminaries were spotted in the audience, including Pattie Boyd, the former wife of George Harrison and Eric Clapton, seen chatting excitedly prior to the show.

With Henry Spinetti (born March 31, 1951, Cwm, South Wales) chosen as drummer for the occasion, Brooker, Fisher, Whitehorn, and Pegg took to the stage after a short introduction from *Hitchhiker's Guide To The Galaxy* author and uber Procol Harum fan Douglas Adams. With the entire LSO, choir and band assembled onstage they launched into possibly the finest version of 'Conquistador' ever performed by Procol Harum with an orchestra.

"The fans watched the proceedings with a kind of analytical approval, as if aware that tearful outpourings of nostalgia would really not be appropriate for Brooker's men," wrote *The Guardian's* Adam Sweeting. "In full-blown classical style, the concert brochure listed the pieces to be played, while Brooker emerged from the wings in a dark suit with his grey hair in a tidy ponytail.

"But this was more than 'these you have loved'. The songs had been artfully refurbished and expanded. 'Grand Hotel' cut an elegant caper with its antiphonal vocal passages, accelerating waltz episodes and intimations of old Vienna. The instrumental piece, 'Repent Walpurgis', revelled in its Gothicky exclamations, while the newish 'The Long Goodbye' played off neat choral effects against a rowdy electric interlude.

"'A Whiter Shade Of Pale' inevitably drew the most rapturous reception, especially when Matthew Fisher's skirling organ sliced in underneath Brooker's supple vocals. Nevertheless, I suggest that Procol's finest song is 'A Salty Dog', freshly kitted out with an orchestral prelude. The song's stately cadences, poignantly incomprehensible imagery and droll nautical effects sum up the essence of Procol Harum. Long may she sail."

For the final encore Procol and the LSO ventured into an unplanned and unannounced version of Ray Charles' 'What'd I Say'. Brooker got the entire orchestra to stand as he too stood to sing quality blue-eyed soul in the spirit of his hero, whom he used to refer to as 'the man' back in the heady days of The Paramounts, some 30 years before.

Fresh from the Barbican orchestral triumph Procol Harum performed the Darryl Way arrangement of 'A Whiter Shade Of Pale' on French network TV for *Les Années Tubes De Jean Pierre Foucault* backed by full orchestra the following day.

Apart from a radio concert and gig in Denmark on February 18, 1996 and a Belgian performance on April 27, 1996 at the Sportpalais, Antwerp for *The Golden Years '96* Show (featuring The Equals, The Box Tops, The Spencer Davis Group, Slade II, The Troggs, The Turtles, The

223

Monkees, and a closing ensemble medley arranged by Gary Brooker) it was a quiet time gig-wise for Procol Harum. After *The Golden Years* concert The Turtles' Joe Stefko met Brooker and the concept for Keith Reid's *My Own Choice* lyric book anthology was born; it was published by Stefko as an expensive American-only limited edition hardback in 1998.

Brooker's next project was a stripped down version of the Barbican concert in a 700-year-old stone church where Procol's music was interspersed with everything from Lee Dorsey to Vaughn Williams. On September 28 a small crowd gathered on the pews of the 13th century church of St Mary & All Saints, Dunsfold, situated just outside Godalming, Surrey. Comprising 150 locals and rock fans the congregation snuggled next to the musicians and singers who numbered a further 25.

"It was like sardines in there," says Brooker, "so there wasn't much scope for raising a huge amount of money, but we did two concerts on the same evening."

The musicians included Mark Brzezicki and Dave Bronze alongside guitarist Robbie McIntosh and Michael Bywater on church organ. Brooker arranged all the music for both strings and choir, featuring a stripped down version of The Chameleon Arts' Choir numbering 16 and Chameleon Arts' String Quartet.

Gary Brooker: "I wrote two [new] special pieces for the concert including 'Within Our House', which I wrote with Keith Reid. We also did the old Elvis Presley song 'Peace In The Valley'. On the Procol Harum pieces 'Holding On' and 'A Salty Dog' we added some Latin text. We also did 'A Whiter Shade Of Pale', of course!"

The concert was recorded and after mixing the results, Brooker decided to press up a limited edition of a thousand CDs in time for Christmas, which sold quickly via the Internet. *Within Our House* then came to the attention of Germany's Repertoire Records, which decided to issue the material across Europe. "We had a good night of excellent music and we raised some money for the village church, which was the objective," Brooker confirmed.

★

At some point in 1996 Brooker was asked to co-star in Alan Parker's epic feature film adaptation of Andrew Lloyd Webber and Tim Rice's *Evita,* starring Madonna, Jonathan Pryce and Antonio Banderas, which was released globally shortly before Christmas. Playing the part of Juan Atilio Bramuglia, he sang the song 'Rainbow Tour' with Peter Polycarpou and Antonio Banderas.

Alan Parker: "Gary Brooker was quite astonished when I called him about *Evita*. He's a very humble man. I think he was surprised that he was asked to do something that was outside his normal world. I was flattered that he came to audition as I had already looked at quite a lot of people to play that role. I mean he's not the kind of person who needs to do any audition, but I think he was very pleased to do it.

"When I was casting *Evita*, I said, 'You wouldn't believe who I've got to play this particular role Gary Brooker!' They [the executives] said 'Who?' I said, 'From Procol Harum – 'A Whiter Shade Of Pale'. I think the world has not yet discovered him. It's a complete mystery to me why he isn't the biggest star in the world. He's hugely talented and I love the way he sings and it's not just 'A Whiter Shade Of Pale', I think the guy could sing anything and it actually gives me goose pimples every time he sings.

"On the day we started filming he was probably a little nervous. The extraordinary thing was what a natural actor he was. I'm amazed he's not done more. He took to it like (*snaps fingers*). The minute the playback started he seemed very comfortable with it all and was extremely easy to work with.

"Madonna wasn't actually in his scenes. She was listening to a playback one day of songs she wasn't involved with and she suddenly heard his voice come out of this *other* song – so clear and so special. She said, 'Whose voice is that?' I explained to her and then obviously she *knew* because his voice is so clear and characterful. It's so very obvious that it's him."

With the departure of manager John 'Kellogs' Kalinowski at the end of 1996, an old friend of Brooker's, Diane Rolph, suggested a Procol Harum 30th Anniversary Reunion Concert which was to take place on July 19,

1997 at the Redhill Theatre in Surrey. With the able assistance of Procol Harum's *Shine On* fanzine editor John Grayson the concept quickly came to life. The idea was to have every period of prime Procol output represented live by the original members. However, the sixties line-up would *only* feature Brooker and Fisher, who would be augmented by Graham Broad on drums and Matt Pegg on bass. The seventies line-ups would feature both keyboard players, with Chris Copping and Pete Solley jetting in from Melbourne and Florida respectively. Mick Grabham and Alan Cartwright would re-join, too, for one night only. There was much anticipation in the air that night with everyone performing for the sheer love of it.

The pinnacle of the evening was the rarely performed epic 'In Held 'Twas In I', which featured Broad, Bronze, Brooker, Fisher, Grabham, Pegg, Solley and a recitation from author Douglas Adams in place of Keith Reid. Other highlights were some seldom performed songs in the shape of the seventies line-up delivering 'Piggy Pig Pig' from *Home* (featuring Copping on Hammond organ), 'Thin End Of The Wedge' and 'The Idol' from *Exotic Birds & Fruit;* 'Robert's Box' and 'A Rum Tale' from *Grand Hotel* and the 1977 unreleased rarity 'This Old Dog' featuring everyone on stage with Solley playing a Poco-like tempo violin solo. A rousing version of 'A Whiter Shade Of Pale' naturally proved to be the most popular rendition of the evening.

The musicianship throughout was faultless. In terms of scale the fact that many band line-ups all appeared on *one* stage throughout the course of *one* night for *one* concert, this must surely remain unparalleled in the annals of rock history.

Following the concert Procol Harum took a long sabbatical. Once again, in the eyes of many, it appeared that the band had simply called time.*

---

* Between the remainder of 1997 and 2001 Gary Brooker joined Ringo Starr's All-Starr Band for several world tours, while also participating in gigs with Bill Wyman's Rhythm Kings. Besides this Brooker was also heavily involved in celebrity rock-star charity gigs under the banner of 'Band Du Lac'.

Chapter 16

A New Millennium &
The Well's On Fire

2000–2004

"The Well's On Fire is quite suggestive: it vividly refers to burning Kuwaiti oil wells. It can also evoke the metaphor of the 'wishing well', thus suggesting that we can no longer wish for anything. It may also simultaneously be referring to the world itself, as revealed by the album cover. Indeed, the World Is On Fire. One could hardly be more relevant, since the album came out during the war against Iraq…"

Michel Seymour, Department of Philosophy
at the Université de Montréal, Canada.

Gary Brooker's contribution to the millennium celebrations was to reconvene Procol Harum for the Web Festival a special one-off concert in Stoke Park, Guildford, Surrey on September 17, 2000 in conjunction with the New London Sinfonia, the Guildford Choral Society and the Occam Singers.

With Graham Broad now a part of Bill Wyman's Rhythm Kings, Mark Brzezicki returned to fill the drum seat. Regulars Brooker,

Fisher and Pegg were augmented by Mick Grabham and 'special guest guitarist', Geoff Whitehorn, Procol's regular axeman since 1991.

The night before the gig a newly formed Procol Harum Tribute Band called The Palers performed at Guildford Civic Theatre with their special guest, former Procol guitarist Dave Ball flying in from Australia to play alongside the group, which also featured Brooker playing a couple of guest spots as a warm-up for the following day's concert.

With over 3,000 in attendance at Stoke Park, Procol's new orchestral collaboration saw them utilise arrangements written entirely by Brooker that nodded back in the direction of the Edmonton Symphony Orchestra and Los Angeles Philharmonic Orchestra gigs of 1971 and 1973. The band delivered a strong set with the orchestra almost as their backing band, but a very different deal from the LSO Barbican collaboration of 1996.

In 2001 after a six year sabbatical from touring Procol Harum reformed once again to undertake 14 gigs across Europe throughout May, June, September and December. The line-up featured Brooker, Fisher, Whitehorn, Pegg and Brzezicki. The intermittent tour spanned Denmark, Norway, Russia (for the first time ever) a return to Poland, and England. However, the pinnacle of the year turned out to be Procol's second live collaboration with Nick Dodd with the Hallé Orchestra and Hallé Choir on June 17 in Manchester. Unlike Guildford this concert featured the arrangements written specifically for *The Long Goodbye: The Symphonic Music Of Procol Harum* in a performance that would clearly better Procol's triumphant appearance at the Barbican in 1996.

"Brighter Shades Of Pale At Bridgewater Hall" headlined Paul Taylor's *Manchester Evening News* review of June 18. "As the white tuxedos of the orchestra stood stiffly to attention, Procol Harum guitarist Geoff Whitehorn ambled on in rockers' regulation black tee shirt, tossed back his *Spinal Tap*-style coiffure and hoisted a thumb aloft... It could have seemed an over grand affair, but Brooker's gruff yet chummy Southend tones between each song brought things down to earth. This was not the ghost of progressive rock returning to haunt us. It was that rarest of occasions when rock and classical coupled to produce an offspring you could really love."

On November 29 Gary Brooker was among a stellar array of musicians and singers participating in the Concert for George at London's Royal Albert Hall a year on from George Harrison's passing from cancer. Paul McCartney, Ringo Starr, Eric Clapton, Jeff Lynne, Tom Petty & The Hearbreakers, Joe Brown, Billy Preston and Klaus Voormann were among those lining up to pay musical tribute to their good friend. Brooker sang lead on a version of 'Old Brown Shoe'.

A fairly average Procol Harum gig from Copenhagen of December 15 was videotaped for DVD by *Classic Pictures* for global distribution, neatly drawing 2001 to a conclusion in anticipation of better to come. The following year saw Procol undertake 11 gigs across Denmark, Holland, and Poland including a five-date December tour of Italy that took in a special concert in Florence as well as two UK gigs at Fairfield Halls, Croydon on May 25 and the Bramhall Festival on June 2. The rest of the year was taken up with writing new material for Procol's twelfth album scheduled for a global release in early 2003 on Eagle. The invitation to record on this particular label came from company executive Terry Shand, who was a nearby neighbour of Brooker's. An old industry heavyweight he co-fronted the label which distributed and funded the *Classic Albums* series among a host of other CD and DVD titles.

The year 2003 saw Procol Harum's busiest touring since 1976, starting in March and continuing right through until December. Procol's exhausting schedule spanned 11 countries with over 60 shows across three continents, taking in America, Germany and Japan. Eagle Records, however, failed to deliver *The Well's On Fire* CD into either Tower Records or Virgin Megastores anywhere! The financially ailing Tower and Virgin chains were *only* championing chart related product and said, "We will not be stocking Procol's latest CD," despite high level intervention from Eagle executives. "It's taken us almost 12 years to release this album and you can't even get it in the shops?" said Reid with an air of resignation in 2003, before adding, "We better not wait another 12 years [to make another album] or it *really* will be too late!"

Produced by Rafe McKenna (UB40, Big Country, Ash) *The Well's On Fire* was recorded throughout October and November 2002 at Queen drummer Roger Taylor's Cosford Mill Studio in Surrey. The opening track, 'An Old English Dream', had some previous input from former Procol producer Chris Thomas prior to Rafe taking the helm. The song has a strong melody line and haunts the listener from its first outing, moving from a slow ballad-like opening to anthemic rock. According to English scholar Roland Clare the song lyrically derives from WH Auden's poem 'Refugee Blues'.

With its clever wordplay some thought 'Shadow Boxed' was Reid looking back at his lyrical output over the decades. But Reid is having none of it. "I was thinking about John Lennon when I wrote that – hence the 'Instant Karma' reference!"

'A Robe Of Silk' was a reworking of an old song derived from a *Shine On Brightly* outtake and was undertaken to appease diehard fans in their quest for unissued Brooker/Reid output. So obscure was the song that drummer Mark Brzezicki was unaware of its particular vintage. "It's a new song," said Brzezicki in 2003. An untypically romantic Reid song, it's probably the weakest number on the album. Matthew Fisher was in total agreement, "I didn't care for it much then and I don't much *now*! But Brooker nails the direction that this song nods towards, 'She Wandered Through the Garden Fence' [from the band's first album] with the drums starting up the rhythm."

With the benefit of nine years' hindsight 'The Blink Of An Eye' numbers among the best songs about 9/11 ever written; completely devoid of the kind of redneck jingoistic stance so prevalent in American songs written about the tragedy. Perhaps Reid being 'An Englishman In New York' helped here? "The song is more me responding to the events," he said, "and also to a lot of people around me who went through that experience." Brooker also asserts that, "It could also be about the moment when the first V2 rockets slammed into London [during the closing stages of World War II]. Keith's lyrics are typically more evocative than concrete, open to interpretation. On the new album, though, they tend to be more literal."

Brooker went on to tell *The Washington Times'* Dan Campbell, "The words to 'Blink Of An Eye' are quite direct... Keith lives in lower Manhattan. He couldn't get into his place for a long time... Just as an interesting point, when he was allowed back in, there was a strange smell in the air, which he actually recognised in some way. After a few weeks, he suddenly realised what it was: it was from [Mile End] the place [where he lived as a boy] in London's East End; it was the smell of the bomb sites. You could also play around bomb sites – that's what kids used to do. When I was growing up, we used to play in a German bomber that had crashed at the top of our road in a field. That's what we used to play in. They had obviously taken the pilot and crews out. But everything else was still there. It hadn't really been smashed up. We used to have a marvellous time in that.

"The other week we were travelling to Norway, and Heathrow Airport was surrounded by tanks. They had a warning that some terrorists were going to shoot down a commercial airliner with missiles. They seem to have had fairly firm intelligence on that. But we didn't *not* go to Norway. No, there were people out there waiting to see us. They had paid their money. No, it doesn't really stop us. It would have to be pretty dire circumstances, touch wood you know, and hope all goes well."

On 'The VIP Room', a great rocking Procol standard, Brooker exclaims that when the time comes for him to check out, "it's going to be in the VIP Room, away from the unwashed masses, with a bottle of champagne in hand". Dry Procol humour all the way.

'The Question', a Matthew Fisher song, rocked in a way that many other Fisher songs hadn't up until this particular point. "Back in 2002 I bought myself a Red Submarine laptop [for music programming] and a portable Midi Keyboard," said Fisher recently. "Although Carol [Bellantoni] and I had got married on May 3, 2002, she was still living in the USA as she hadn't yet retired from her job. I went out there in the summer to spend some time before returning to the UK to start work on the album. I'd brought my laptop and keyboard out with me. I'd also got some words from Keith. While I was staying there I used the laptop to demo 'The Question', 'The Signature', 'Every Dog Will Have

Its Day' and 'Fellow Travellers', as well as a few more ideas that didn't get used."

'This World Is Rich (For Stephen Maboe)' took its name from a quote "The World Is Rich But It Is Not Mine" appearing in the British newspaper *The Guardian* by South African Stephen Maboe from September, 2003. Shortly before the song was recorded in October, Reid told Roland Clare: "Actually I think what happened was that I saw that in the paper and it struck a very strong chord with me, and I think it was shortly after that that I went down and spent a day with Gary, and he had some chords and he was playing around with them, and I said, 'Well I think I've got something that will fit with that.'"

"Stephen Maboe is the South African activist," Brooker told Dan Campbell. "Actually [there's] probably an anti-America song [there] in that there was a meeting last year in South Africa, of the rich nations, to see how they could help the poor nations. And nothing happened. America has, on various occasions, through its own power and grandeur, said 'No, we're not doing this. We're not going to back… [the Kyoto Agreement].

"Often these are very important to the smaller countries in the world and to the poorer people that something be achieved, and it hasn't. And the reason that it hasn't has been mostly on the part of American Big Business, looking after its interests. 'We're not going to cut down this, just to stop a bit of pollution. Our oil producers are going to get upset.' That has happened on several occasions. I think in the end it has weakened America's moral position. 'The world is rich, it is not mine.' [It is a] very rare song for Procol Harum, because it's sung from that point of view. I have to put myself in Steve Maboe's shoes, and sing as if he was going to sing it."

'Fellow Travellers', a Fisher/Reid co-write, has a hymnal quality to it and perhaps fits well next to its near cousin 'Pilgrim's Progress', also by Fisher, from 1969's *A Salty Dog*. "'Fellow Travellers' was different in that Keith hadn't yet written the words," explains Fisher. "The inspiration for this dates back to an earlier time when Carol and I spent a weekend in Cannes during which we attended a concert featuring the

British countertenor James Bowman. During this concert, he performed the Handel aria 'Lascia ch'io pianga'.

"I'd never heard this song before, but it made a huge impression on me and I was convinced it could be adapted to a 'rock' format by changing the time signature from 3/4 to 4/4. When I got back to England I presented Gary with a recording of the original together with my proposed 'backing track', which featured a piano playing the vocal line. He seemed to like the idea and so we sent the backing track to Keith, who I remember saying didn't want to hear the original – just the backing track.

"When Eric Clapton heard the finished album 'Fellow Travellers' and 'The Emperor's New Clothes' [detailed below] were his two favourite tracks – I know this because Gary played us all back the message that Eric had left on his answer machine!"

'The Emperor's New Clothes' is reminiscent of 'A Salty Dog' and is certainly up there with that great Procol standard. Keith Reid is clearly attacking politicians who try to pull the wool over our eyes with 'spin doctored statements'. Maybe he was thinking of Tony Blair here and his 'weapons of mass destruction' statement vis-a-vis Saddam and Iraq.

The subject matter of 'Wall Street Blues' is self-evident. When reviewing Procol's 2003 Cropredy Festival appearance *Time Out's* 'Insider Column' wrote, "All You Need Is Cash … hippie stuff at Fairport Convention's annual Cropredy reunion gig, where we ran into the magnificently misanthropic prog rockers Procol Harum. 'We're only doing this tour and album because all our pension funds collapsed over the last year,' Harum frontman Gary Brooker growled at us as the band lurched into 'Wall Street Blues'. And who said the spirit of '69 was dead?" As a retort to this *The Boston Herald's* Dean Johnson wrote the following with regard to Brooker's similar statement after another 'Wall Street Blues' performance at a May 7 House Of Blues gig in Cambridge, USA: "It all would have seemed like so much whistling past the graveyard if Brooker and the band hadn't sounded so vital."

Gary Brooker: "Chris Copping reminded us of a song we did in 1975 and 1976 at gigs, which we never recorded on *Procol's Ninth,* called 'So Far Behind'. I went to Australia in 2000 and he kind of resurrected

this song. 'Do you remember this one?' When Chris found out that
we were going back into the studio to record *The Well's On Fire* he
sent an e-mail saying, 'Make sure you do 'So Far Behind'. Yet again I
had forgotten about it. So the slightly ambiguous credit in the album's
booklet was a way of thanks to Chris for reminding us ...''

'Every Dog Will Have His Day', credited as a Brooker/Fisher/Reid
collaboration, is possibly the best rocking song on the album and has
Brooker literally howling like a dog. This song worked even better in a
live setting and caused much amusement among audiences throughout
2003 and 2004.

The album closes with Fisher's instrumental 'Weisselklenzenacht'
(aka 'The Signature)' a grandiose sign-off very much in the realm of
Fisher's other instrumental showcase 'Repent Walpurgis', which closed
Procol's eponymous debut disc in 1967.

Gary Brooker: "Diane Rolph, an old friend of ours who helped
us out from time to time, said to Matthew Fisher, 'Why don't you
write another 'Repent Walpurgis', it's about time. Or at least another
instrumental.' So he thought, 'Yes. It's been a while,' so 35 years later he
followed it up. It's very popular. On stage it's absolutely unbelievable...
It was getting standing ovations wherever we played ...''

By the time *The Well's On Fire* was released, Geoff Whitehorn
had been playing with Procol for over 12 years and Matt Pegg for 10
– yet both had never actually gone into a studio to record any new
Brooker/Reid songs. "That's a decade they've spent re-creating parts
[that] another musician originally played," Brooker told Dan Campbell,
adding, "but with this album, they finally had free rein. I did say to
them before we started, 'Up until now you've done a great job playing
Procol Harum's repertoire for the last 10 years. But forget about that;
forget about BJ Wilson – although it sounds cruel – forget about Robin
Trower or Mick Grabham. Just be yourselves and put what you've got
into it. And they nailed it. I think *The Well's On Fire* benefited a lot
from that sort of feeling...

"Matthew Fisher had very strong ideas, but at the same time, he is
very open to what I am feeling or wanting to do and the direction
that the band might take. He's a great musician. You know when

he plays the Hammond, it's going to sound like him – not just like a Hammond, but him. And he is THE Hammond sound of Procol. Everyone else is an imitator. I mean, Chris Copping played organ in the band for years, but he was only playing it like Matthew would have played it!"

In 2004 Fisher said that *The Well's On Fire* was "the best Procol Harum album since *Home*", and Whitehorn described it as "Totally Procoly" while Brooker said, "It felt like a solid album made by a band that had been touring for 10 years."

The Prodigal Stranger had suffered from being over-produced and felt more like 'a production job' rather than an album made by a band. The somewhat dated eighties wall-of-percussion sound replete with double-tracked digital drums did not help *The Prodigal Stranger* to stand the test of time, whereas *The Well's On Fire* still sounds as fresh today as it did back in 2003.

But two Procol Harum albums across 20 years? Not a huge amount of 'original' output. Nevertheless, it must be said that *The Well's On Fire* CD would have certainly filled up four sides of 12-inch vinyl had it been pressed up, thereby potentially compensating for a 12-year hiatus.

"Credit the band for not watering down its legacy with 20 years of weak or mediocre albums," Dan Campbell wrote in *The Washington Times* in April 2003, "the way the Stones, Paul McCartney and Yes did throughout the eighties and nineties." "When you make an album, it should be new and important," said Booker, adding that "a lot of thought and creativity needs to go into it."

Doing their damnedest to get *The Well's On Fire* out to audiences globally, Procol toured continually throughout 2003. Key UK gigs also took place at the Cropredy Festival, Milton Keynes, Catford Town Hall, London and the Union Chapel, London. The Union Chapel show was recorded for Eagle DVD and Eagle CD.

The first half was slightly below par and it was not until the band had returned from the intermission (after some liquid sustenance) that they were back to top form. As a result the DVD cunningly re-arranged the running order in order to disguise the fact. With the benefit of hindsight there is also a potential unease in the shape of Fisher's body language throughout this performance. It would appear that after almost a year of touring with Procol Harum a certain amount of strain was beginning to show.

Chapter 17

The Legacy Of
A Whiter Shade Of Pale

1967–2012

"A Darker Shade Of Black"
        Headline in *The Daily Telegraph*, December 21, 2006

When launching their reunion album *The Prodigal Stranger* in 1992 Procol Harum had elected not to undertake *any* concerts in their homeland. "Why was this?" enquired some eager music journalists. The answers from Gary Brooker were not entirely straightforward.

When Procol finally chose to tour Britain some three years later, their London gig at the Shepherd's Bush Empire elicited the interest of MTV and the reason for its presence soon became abundantly clear. The TV crew simply lingered in the wings until Procol launched into the opening bars of 'A Whiter Shade Of Pale', then leapt out to videotape the performance before beating a hasty retreat.

Asked about 'the unmentionable song' in 1992 and its very particular global legacy, Brooker replied, "You said, 'What countries was it number one?' Well six months after it was number one in Britain and France, it was *still* number one in Venezuela. You know if it was number one in Venezuela for six months it was probably number one in a lot of places."

When Matthew Fisher issued his first solo album, *Journey's End*, he became embroiled with *Melody Maker* throughout 1973 in an ongoing correspondence via the letters page in which he first claimed – publicly and in print – that it was he who wrote "the opening bars" that were recognised by all as the central motif of 'A Whiter Shade Of Pale'.

By 1992 Fisher was back in the new line-up of Procol, on their album and touring with the band. Matters relating to the authorship of 'Pale' were swept under the carpet. But the ghost of 'A Whiter Shade Of Pale' – without a shadow of a doubt – was the root cause behind Procol's belated return to their homeland. Maybe the 'unmentionable' would be mentioned? Perhaps, in 1995, they would simply surrender to the inevitable? In the end 1995 saw the release of *The Symphonic Music Of Procol Harum* and a new symphonic version of 'Pale', which went largely unnoticed.

There was another reason why 'A Whiter Shade Of Pale' was now unmentionable: it had accumulated a vast treasure chest for all concerned. So what was this particular legacy?

In April 1994 Prime Minister Tony Blair wrote to Phonographic Performance Limited to congratulate this august British record industry affiliate on its 70th birthday. After assessing literally thousands of songs played on both British radio and jukeboxes, a PPL chart finally provided a definitive listing showing 70 songs from 70 years. At the top of the chart was Procol Harum's 'A Whiter Shade Of Pale' listed as "the most played record of the past 70 years".

This must have delighted Tony and Cherie Blair as 14 years earlier they had chosen 'A Whiter Shade Of Pale' as the song that accompanied their walk down the aisle at their wedding on March 29, 1980. Former Conservative Party Leader and Home Secretary Michael Howard said that 'A Whiter Shade Of Pale' would have been the song to be played at his wedding, too, but for the fact that his local Registry Office didn't allow music inside the building. Oh, how times have changed. According to a recent ecumenical survey, 'A Whiter Shade Of Pale' is now 'the most played wedding theme' next to Mendelssohn's Wedding March. Cyndi 'Girls Just Wanna Have Fun' Lauper had Patti 'Lady Marmalade' Labelle sing it at her celebrity wedding, fuelling the fashion for 'Pale' nuptials. Ironically the trend started from within the band itself: in 1968 when Gary Brooker married his Swiss girlfriend, Francoise 'Franky' Brun, on July 13 at St David's Church in Southend. Robin Trower, David Knights, and BJ Wilson all attended. In a further irony Matthew Fisher played 'A Whiter Shade Of Pale' on the church organ from inside a gothic crypt situated high above the congregation as the happy couple walked down the aisle.

Conversely the song has also became a favourite theme to be played at funerals. Playwright Joe Orton requested that it be played at his funeral alongside The Beatles 'A Day In The Life'; Spike Milligan also requested it for his [it wasn't played] and Cher has allegedly asked for it to be played at hers too. The song became the soundtrack to many TV commercials, but most famously in the late nineties for Dulux paints with 'A Whiter Shade Of Pale' being the famous 'buy line'. The Ford Mondeo campaign also utilised this theme and referred to the varying "shades of pale" that the car was newly available in.

When the missing verse of the song was uncovered by British journalist Mike Butler the discovery led to a two-page feature about 'A Whiter Shade Of Pale' in *The Independent On Sunday* on September 18, 1994. Three more UK newspapers ran with the story the following day. 'A Lighter Shade Of Pale' said *The Daily Mirror* in a double page spread, 'Now A Brighter Shade Of Pale' said *The Daily Express*, beginning two decades of headlines that would utilise the words 'Shade Of Pale' in many varying contexts. Advertising copyrighters were quick to follow suit and came up with one-liners for all manner of consumables, including 'A Lighter Shade Of Ale' and 'A Darker Shade Of Chocolate'. Perhaps this is Procol Harum's contribution to the ever evolving lexicon of post-modern English.

Butler's article on 'Pale' gave birth to a book called *Lives Of The Great Songs,* edited by Tim De Lisle and published by Pavillion Books in 1994, which included Butler's 'Pale' feature. "Is it about getting pissed and fancying the person opposite you?" Butler asked Keith Reid. "I never understand when people say they don't understand it," said Reid. "We skipped the light fandango'. That's straightforward. "Turned cartwheels across the floor." It seems very clear to me..."

Butler further asserted that the song "explores what it means to be wrecked, in more than one sense of the word. A nervous seducer sustains his courage with alcohol. As he becomes more drunk, his impressions of his unfamiliar partner become confused by stray thoughts, fragments of childhood reading and his own faint-hearted aspirations. The song's recurring metaphor is of maritime disaster, and a parallel is drawn between romantic conquest and the allure and peril of the sea. The hero is a callow juvenile, far happier with a book than risking the emotional bruising of relationships. This ambivalence is underscored by frequent allusions to nausea.

"As befits a night of excess, there are gaps in the telling. The evasive 'And so it was that late ...' is given weight by repetition and its positioning just before the hook ('Her face at first just ghostly/Turned a whiter shade of pale'). The listener is invited to fill the gaps with his or her own (prurient) imagination. An entire verse was dropped early in the song's gestation. Another is optional ('She said, 'I'm home on shore leave/Though in truth we were at sea') and was excised from the recorded version at the insistence of producer Denny Cordell, to make the record conform to standard single length.

"For a pop song, 'A Whiter Shade Of Pale' carries an unprecedented amount of literary baggage. Although, Reid reveals, the reference to Chaucer is a red herring. 'One thing people always get wrong is that line about the Miller's Tale. I've never read Chaucer in my life. They're right off the track there.' Why did he put it in then? (In mild dismay at the peremptory demolition of this intellectual prop.) 'I can't remember now,' said Reid. The analogy with *Canterbury Tales*, whether welcomed by Reid or not, holds good. Both are quintessentially English works, the one established in the canon of literature, the other a pop standard. Both have associations of piety and decorum – '[I] would not let her be/One of sixteen Vestal Virgins.'

"Vestal Virgins were handmaidens of the Roman half-goddess Vesta (meaning hearth), whose job was to maintain a sacred and perpetual fire. The number of them is significant, invoking the biblical parable of the five wise and five foolish virgins, and, less edifyingly, the barrack-room ballad of 'Four-and-twenty virgins ... down from Inverness'. Why Reid's lot should amount to 16 is one of the song's more imponderable details. Maybe it has something to do with 16 being the youngest a girl can be lusted after by a rock'n'roller with impunity ('You're Sixteen', 'Sweet Little Sixteen', etc). The passing allusion to Lewis Carroll in the preceding couplet – 'I wandered through my playing cards' – suggests that some of the obscurity of 'A Whiter Shade of Pale', as in Alice, may be due to the broaching of a taboo. The hesitant lover in the song is caught midway between the chivalry of 'When A Man Loves A Woman' and the carnality of Jane Birkin in 'Je T'Aime' – a smash hit of the following year [sic], blatantly modelled on the Procol Harum song." (21)

The song's finest movie moment was in Alan Parker's 1991 feature film *The Commitments,* which utilised 'A Whiter Shade Of Pale' as a central motif in a story about a bunch of young Dublin-based musicians and their quest for fame and fortune in a screenplay adaptation by Dick Clement and Ian La Frenais of Roddy Doyle's novel.

"I put 'A Whiter Shade Of Pale' in *The Commitments* because of a combination of things," says Parker. "We had this scene where this rather fuddy duddy member of the band was very religious and played the organ. It was also due to the fascination and bewilderment as to what the lyrics actually mean. It allowed us to write quite a funny scene around what the lyrics *actually* mean and to then follow it through right until the final scene. In fact we used the lyrics of the song to conclude a number of other final thoughts."

"They nicked it from Bach," says one of the film's characters from the organ loft of a Dublin cathedral. Commenting upon this scene in the movie The Pogues' lead singer, Shane MacGowan, is quick to counter this popular assertion "Yeah man, people [often] say they nicked it from Bach. But it doesn't matter, because what they did with it was much better than what Bach did with it."

241

"'A Whiter Shade Of Pale' wasn't in the original script," continues Parker. "The first scene in the film [in the organ gallery] was written around the song. Once we started to talk about the song it was too good a thing not to pay off! So once we'd chosen the song and were doing a script meeting with the writers Dick Clement and Ian La Frenais we'd often just end up talking about 'what did those lyrics actually mean?' It's an ongoing thing that happens every five years. (The song's key lyrics are stated in the film's concluding moments.)

"When we made the film *Evita* and Gary Brooker had just finished filming his scenes, traditionally, as an actor would finish, we would play a piece of music relevant to the person and give him a round of applause out of respect. So on the playback across the set we played 'A Whiter Shade Of Pale' and it came out very loudly. Gary was very humble and started saying goodbye to everybody. Saying goodbye to a film crew is not really his world. And the whole film crew gathered around in a circle talking to him about 'A Whiter Shade Of Pale'. Gary said, 'The words are not *that* complicated really, because there were verses that were missing that were not included on the record. It's the other verses... If you hear them you would understand everything.' So I said, 'Well, will you sing them?' as he had a lot of fans around him – technicians, electricians and so forth. So he said, 'Oh, it's not the right time of day for that!' So instead he spoke the words to the additional verses and said, 'Now it's all clear ...'"

The Missing Verses of 'A Whiter Shade Of Pale'

She said, 'I'm home on shore leave'
Though in truth we were at sea
So I took her by the looking glass
and forced her to agree
saying, 'You must be the mermaid
Who took Neptune for a ride.'
But she smiled at me so sadly
that my anger straightway died

If music be the food of love
then laughter is its queen
and likewise if behind is in front
then dirt in truth is clean
My mouth by then like cardboard
seemed to slip straight through my head
So we crash-dived straightway quickly
and attacked the ocean bed

"All of us were even *more* confused by the additional verses but it was quite a moment actually," adds Parker. "It's like a detective story really, because it's so important in all our lives. Yet none of us truly know what it truly means. And there are not that many songs in history that have that effect on you – when you're completely in the dark about what they're singing about..."

Not knowing the meaning of the lyrics didn't hinder those who covered the song. 'A Whiter Shade Of Pale' is one of the most covered songs of all time with over 1,000 versions registered on the UK's MCPS database. It must be said, however, that 95% of these covers are truly awful. Nevertheless, there are at least 25 good versions. The strength of the original song comes through when you hear how well it translates into many differing genres and there are very few songs that lend themselves to such a variety of interpretations.

According to Keith Reid, Denny Cordell had originally offered the song to Otis Redding. Redding, however, wanted an exclusive, which would have meant ditching Procol's debut disc. Percy Sledge then went ahead and covered it as a single anyway. This 1967 cover had to be withdrawn for fear of it usurping Procol's debut. (Sledges's version would later surface on an obscure *24 Greatest Hits* album.)

Among the first wave of 'Pale' covers came from the Jamaican underground from the studios of Clement 'Sir Coxsone' Dodd, the legendary godfather of reggae music. Jackie Mittoo's 1967 instrumental cut was a ska take with a backing track potentially later re-used by Byron Lee & The Dragonaires on their vocal version. Reggae hero

Jimmy Cliff covered it on his 1967 Island Records album *Hard Road To Travel*, but Alton Ellis and Pat Kelly provided the best Jamaican covers, with Kelly's version boasting invented lyrics in the shape of 'We skipped the light and *bang go!*'

Two dreadful 1967 'Pale' covers that tried too hard to be 'hippy' came from The Merseybeats' *Super Hits From England*, a cash-in LP with no relation to the original Liverpudlian group, and Don Everly on the Everly Brothers' album *Sing*. Much better was Alex Chilton's blue-eyed-soul interpretation on The Box Tops' album *The Letter/ Neon Rainbow*. Beating this version hands down was Nicoletta Grisoni's 'Les Orgues D'Antan', a French chanson version featuring Nicoletta's full-on Edith Piaf vocalising with entirely new lyrics. The 'new' lyrics spoke about 'a man crying alone in a church; crying about his past; and crying because he felt alone, whilst apparently listening to a church organ recital ...' Not exactly the recipe for a big hit – not even in France where existentialist angst was de rigueur.

The first truly epic orchestral version came from Johnny Rivers on his 1968 album *Realisation*. This was soon to be eclipsed by several blinding soul versions. Saxophone giant King Curtis recorded it twice, firstly in 1967 on *King Size Soul* and again magnificently in 1971 on *Live At Fillmore West* with The Kingpins and Billy Preston. This latter version was recorded some five months before his murder. Topping this are two more soul covers – Shorty Long's 1969 Motown version on *The Prime Of Shorty Long*, which replaces the song's familiar organ figure with a full brass section played magnificently in the spirit of an Ennio Morricone spaghetti western theme tune. Zulema's powerful 1975 soul take is handled as Aretha Franklin might have sung it had she covered it circa her 1968 album *Lady Soul*. With more than a nod towards pure gospel vocalising Zulema's dynamic cover is an overlooked masterpiece.

Three jazzy versions are worth noting, but all for different reasons. Elvis Presley's original bass player, Bill Black, covered 'Pale' on his 1968 easy listening album *The Beat Goes On*. Dick Heckstall-Smith & Colosseum covered it on their 1969 jazz-fusion debut *Those Who Are About To Die We Salute You*, and top jazz flautist Herbie Mann interpreted it on his 1974 album *The London Underground*.

Procol Harum, backstage prior to performing 'Homburg' on BBCTV's *Top Of The Pops*, October 1967, wearing the costumes designed by The Fool; left to right: Robin Trower, Matthew Fisher, Gary Brooker, BJ Wilson and Dave Knights. COURTESY OF FLY RECORDS

Prior to a Procol Harum gig in Birmingham, Alabama in 1972, Gary Brooker sports a Hawaiian shirt in a photo taken by fellow band member and 'Conquistador' guitarist Dave Ball. DAVE BALL

It's white ties and tails for Procol Harum's *Grand Hotel* album cover shoot in Malibu, California in the summer of 1972; left to right: Gary Brooker, Alan Cartwright, Keith Reid, Chris Copping and Dave Ball pointing at BJ Wilson. IRIS JORDAN

Chrysalis Records' *Grand Hotel* campaign reaches Hollywood, California. Parked underneath the hording is Chrysalis MD Chris Wright's Rolls Royce Silver Ghost and next to it Gary Brooker's red Jaguar. On the poster, left to right, are Keith Reid, Gary Brooker, Mick Grabham, Chris Copping, Alan Cartwright and BJ Wilson. COURTESY OF HENRY SCOTT-IRVINE

Procol Harum In Concert With The Edmonton Symphony Orchestra & The Da Camera Singers at the Jubilee Auditorium in Edmonton, Canada, in November 1971. COURTESY OF CHRYSALIS RECORDS

Procol Harum sing 'A Souvenir Of London' on stage at the Hollywood Bowl with the Los Angeles Philharmonic Orchestra in 1973; left to right: Mick Grabham, Alan Cartwright, Gary Brooker, Chris Copping and BJ Wilson. ANDREW KENT

Procol Harum rehearsing *Exotic Birds & Fruit* in 1974 inside 'Dungeon Number 2' at AIR Studios, Oxford Circus, London: Gary Brooker on piano, Chris Copping on Hammond organ, Alan Cartwright on bass, Mick Grabham on guitar and BJ Wilson drums.

Procol Harum in 1977; left to right: Pete Solley, Gary Brooker (wearing a 'The Worm In The Tree' T-shirt), Chris Copping, BJ Wilson and Mick Grabham (seated).

Procol Harum's *Prodigal Stanger* tour concludes backstage at Elysee Montmartre, Paris, on Valentine's Day 1992; left to right: Geoff Whitehorn, Matthew Fisher, a fan, Dave Bronze, Gary Brooker and Mark Brzezicki. HENRY SCOTT-IRVINE

Procol Harum—'the headline act'—backstage at the Rock Summer Festival in Tallinn, Estonia, July 11, 1993; left to right: Geoff Whitehorn, Dave Bronze, Gary Brooker, Matthew Fisher and Ian Wallace. HENRY SCOTT-IRVINE

Procol Harum in concert with the London Symphony Orchestra at the Barbican Theatre, London, on February 8, 1996, with Gary Brooker at the Steinway grand piano. HERMANN BAUNSCHMIDT

Nine present and past members of Procol Harum take a bow at the 30th Anniversary Re-Union Concert, July 19, 1997, at the Redhill Theatre, Surrey; left to right: Graham Broad, Chris Copping, Pete Solley, Matthew Fisher, Mick Grabham, Alan Cartwright, Gary Brooker, Matt Pegg and Dave Bronze. COURTESY OF JOHN GRAYSON

Left: Matt Pegg on bass and Josh Phillips on Hammond organ, in the US in 2010. BERT SARACO Right: Gary Brooker and Keith Reid caught sneaking out of the back entrance of St John's Church, Smith Square, Westminster, London, on July 20, 2007, after Procol Harum's 40th Anniversary Re-Union Concert. ROLAND CLARE, COURTESY OF SALVO RECORDS AND UNION SQUARE LTD

Procol at the Isle Of Wight Festival on June 11, 2006—36 years since their 1970 IOW debut. Gary Brooker is wearing the tunic he wore on BBC's *Top Of The Pops* when 'A Whiter Shade Of Pale' reached number 1 in 1967. SIMON SARIN/RETNA UK

Gary Brooker, MBE, keyboards and vocals, the rock on which Procol Harum was built and the central figure in the group's longevity.

Joe Cocker had three attempts, the best being his first in 1972 as featured on a live bootleg CD *Shut Out The Light*. At the height of the European disco boom Donna Summer's producer Giorgio Moroder took the song into a disco orbit with Munich Machine featuring Chris Bennett, while in 1982 country legends Willie Nelson and Waylon Jennings duetted 'Pale' on Nelson's *Always On My Mind*.

From 1983–1984 Sammy Hagar and Neal Schon formed a heavy rock supergroup Hagar, Schon, Aaronson & Shrieve with former Foghat bassist Kenny Aaronson and former Santana drummer Michael Shrieve. Their cover of 'A Whiter Shade Of Pale' received some airplay, peaking at 94 in the *Billboard* singles chart. Another hard rock interpretation of 'Pale' came via former Deep Purple bassist Glenn Hughes on his 2003 album *Stormbringer Live In Italy*.

The most recent cover version to actually become a hit was Annie Lennox's interpretation on the 1995 double platinum selling album *Diva*. Released as a single her version of 'Pale' reached number 15 in the UK as well as featuring in the Hollywood movie *The Net,* a cyber thriller directed by Irwin Winkler that featured Sandra Bullock, Jeremy Northam and Dennis Miller.

'A Whiter Shade Of Pale's' first foray into the movies came as early as 1967 in the Italian *Peggio Per Me...Meglio Per Te* when Little Tony – Italy's very own Elvis lookalike – covered the song in a surreal Fellini-esque party setting. However, Procol Harum's version did not appear on the soundtrack of any *significant* feature film until the 'baby boomer' generation of Hollywood directors began to make their mark some 15 years later.

Purple Haze, a 1982 US drama about a college student expelled for smoking cannabis and subsequently drafted to Vietnam in the summer of 1968, disappeared completely. The song's next two outings in 1983 were more significant. *Baby It's You* was John Sayles' first major Hollywood film about a romance between an upper middle class Jewish girl named Jill Rosen played by Rosanna Arquette, and a blue-collar Italian boy nicknamed 'the Sheik' played by Joe Spano. Set in late 1966 in New Jersey, Sheik aspired to follow in Frank Sinatra's footsteps in the summer of 1967 when 'A Whiter Shade Of Pale' was riding high in the charts.

The Big Chill, an American comedy-drama directed by Lawrence Kasdan, starring Tom Berenger, Glenn Close, Jeff Goldblum, William Hurt, Kevin Kline, Mary Kay Place, Meg Tilly, and JoBeth Williams told the story of a group of 'baby boomer' college friends who reunite briefly after 15 years due to the suicide of a friend. 'A Whiter Shade Of Pale' featured on the soundtrack of this hugely successful movie, which later inspired the creation of the popular US network TV series *Thirtysomething* during the eighties.

Withnail And I was former actor/screenwriter Bruce Robinson's 1987 black comedy produced by George Harrison's HandMade Films. Based on Robinson's life in London during the late sixties, the film was ignored at the time, but is now rightly regarded as a great time capsule. King Curtis' live Fillmore cover of 'A Whiter Shade Of Pale' is a key narrative motif that signifies the sunset on a golden age.

Martin Scorsese's *Life Lessons* is one of three 30-minute shorts from 1989's *New York Stories*. 'A Whiter Shade Of Pale' and 'Conquistador' both featured heavily in the film. 'Pale' opened the film, which was loosely based on Fyodor Dostoevsky's short novel *The Gambler*. Nick Nolte played Lionel Dobie an acclaimed abstract artist who found himself unable to paint during the days before a major gallery exhibition featuring his new work. 'A Whiter Shade Of Pale' was used again as the soundtrack to Dobie's gallery reception – and to great effect – signifying the cyclical nature of his relationships and thereby providing a fitting conclusion to a fine film.

As noted, Alan Parker's 1991 film *The Commitments* came next. This was followed by Nils Malmros' *Kærlighedens Smerte* aka *Pain of Love* a dramatic 1992 Danish tragedy starring Anne Louise Hassing and Søren Østergaard in a beautiful, but bitter story about a young college student whose small setbacks at school and in her relationships led towards her inexorable descent into suicidal depression.

Heaven & Earth (1993) was the final movie in Oliver Stone's 'Vietnam Trilogy' and 'A Whiter Shade Of Pale' was utilised extremely well in this moving epic film made by Hollywood's enfant terrible.

Gazon Maudit aka *French Twist* was a 1995 French comedy film written and directed by co-star Josiane Balasko. The film was both a critical and commercial hit in France gaining 3,790,381 admissions as well as winning a Cesar Award and grossing $1,400,000 in the United States, too. A cover of 'A Whiter Shade Of Pale' performed by Francis Agbo featured on the soundtrack.

Breaking The Waves was Lars Von Trier's award winning breakthrough movie of 1996. It starred Emily Watson and was set in the Scottish Highlands in the early seventies. The film told the story of an unusual young woman, Bess McNeill, of the particular love she had for Jan, her husband, and of the influence that the retrogressive Calvinistic 'Free Church of Scotland' had on her. Again 'A Whiter Shade Of Pale' played its particular part within the film's story.

Shade Of Pale was a 2005 romantic Hollywood drama that featured narrative elements from both *Vertigo* and *Lolita*. *The Boat That Rocked* (re-titled *Pirate Radio* in North America) was a 2009 British comedy film written and directed by Richard Curtis. The fictional story was inspired by the now infamous pirate radio ships Radio London and Radio Caroline that anchored off the UK's shores during the mid-sixties. 'A Whiter Shade Of Pale' featured as the last song to be played on the 'fictional' pirate radio ship as it sank beneath the waves. 'Pale' of course originally received its on-air debut on Radio London back in 1967. The film had an ensemble cast featuring Philip Seymour Hoffman, Bill Nighy, Rhys Ifans, Nick Frost and Kenneth Branagh.

The mainstream retro British police series *Heartbeat* had an episode entitled 'A Whiter Shade Of Pale' in Season 18, Episode 16, which was first transmitted on network ITV on July 18, 2010 as a part of the final series; the song featured throughout.

In January 2001, Channel 4 TV UK placed 'Pale' at number 19 in its chart for 'The Top 100 Songs Of All Time'. In 2004 *Rolling Stone* magazine placed it at 57 in its '500 Greatest Songs Of All Time'. Later that year it was named as the most-played record of the past 70 years. The song also topped a BBC Radio 2 listeners' Top 100 poll in 2009.

In early 2012, '60 Years of *NME*' voted it number 19 in its 'Top 100 sixties Songs'. On July 17, 2012, ITV UK transmitted 'The Nation's Favourite Number 1 Single', which featured 'Pale' at a position of number 16.

In today's modern digital age 'A Whiter Shade Of Pale' is now a hugely successful downloadable mobile telephone ringtone as well as being a Wii computer game, where the user can remix and remaster the song by utilising parts from the original 1967 'four track' quarter inch tapes, no less.

British 'Pay Per Play' ('PPL') payments from jukebox and airplay receipts for 'A Whiter Shade Of Pale' are alleged to have earned in excess of £6 million. "No, not six million," asserts Simon Platz, "but certainly millions." The British sales of the original single alone are alleged to have earned in excess of £10 million. "No, not that much," corrects Platz, adding again "but certainly millions."

Platz also points out that lyric writer Keith Reid was on "an equal 50-50 split with composer Gary Brooker across Procol Harum's entire song catalogue throughout the years represented by Essex Music [later trading as Onward Music Publishing Ltd]". So if a lyric appeared in a book Brooker got half the royalty. And if a tune minus a lyric appeared in, say, a movie, then Reid got half. It was an unusual scenario, but one which summed up the strength of their writing partnership.

In the light of all this, however, it isn't hard to understand why Matthew Fisher decided to stake his claim to a share in the authorship of 'A Whiter Shade Of Pale' nor why Gary Brooker and Onwards Music were keen to defend their interests.

Accordingly, during mid-March 2004, Fisher's lawyers filed a claim against Gary Brooker and Onward Music Publishing Ltd for a song writing co-accreditation claim vis-a-vis 'A Whiter Shade Of Pale'.

Matthew Fisher quit Procol Harum the day the writ was issued in preparation for a court case that would turn out to be one of the costliest, longest, and most bitterly fought battles in British legal history.

Chapter 18

Pale Goes To Court

2005–2009

"A Wider Share Of Cash."
       Headline in *The Daily Mail*, November 14, 2006

When lightning strikes it is usually unexpected and shakes one to the very core. Matthew Fisher's actions in 2004 had the same kind of impact upon Procol Harum. The previous year had been important for the band. They had made a strong new album and undertaken a huge world tour. Furthermore, Brooker was awarded the MBE for his tireless charity work. On July 14 he wrote an open letter to the Procol Harum fan website Beyond The Pale:

"My dear friends, I would firstly like to say what a great day this is for me in being honoured by my Queen in her birthday honours list. I have not seen the newspapers yet but believe it is for 'services to charity' and I would like to thank my wife and my friends and associates who must have put my name forward. All we need now is a 'Grammy' for *The Well's On Fire* to make 2003 a year to remember.

"We have had a fantastic time with the band since starting concerts on 03/03/03 and I would like to thank all the people who came to see us and those we were lucky enough to meet in a hectic schedule. Of course, we have visited Europe in the last couple of years so to be in the USA for the first time since 1995 was very exciting. We're still not sure if we played to 3,000 people or if it was the same 300 every night! There were some wonderful faces out there and it was a pleasure to play for you.

"I personally feel that this year Procol Harum has come of age and is solid. There is a great commitment and I believe that ghosts have been buried this year and we can move forward...."

During the 2002 recording of *The Well's On Fire,* Fisher felt a distinct change in attitude towards him from the other band members and Chris Cook, Procol's new manager in particular. "Since Chris Cook took over from Diane Rolph right away I felt that I had suddenly been 'demoted'," said Fisher, "and was no longer being treated as the *other* original member – I was just *one* of the band."

According to Fisher, the success of extended touring as part of Ringo Starr's caravan of well-known musicians coupled with the newly found recognition that came with Procol Harum's revival alongside an upsurge in tour receipts had all potentially gone to Brooker's head. Fisher specifically cited "Procol Harum's 30th Anniversary [concert] and the rise of the Procol Harum website" [one of the most successful fan sites of its kind in the world] as both having [allegedly] "played their part".

A letter from Cook which, like the bulk of the correspondence relating to the subsequent trial, would later be made publicly available, was sent to Jens Hills, Fisher's solicitors, by fax on May 4, 2005 – a salient excerpt of which read: "Matthew came to me in October 2002 at Cosford Mill Studio, and asked for my assistance in ratifying a matter for him. He was concerned that his royalties existed on an ex-gratia basis, and that should Gary Brooker or indeed Matthew die, then his children would not have the benefit of this income.

"Although these discussions didn't start in earnest till September 2003 the points raised at this time were generally reasonable, and the main sticking point related to the established share attributed to Keith Reid. A point which I could not answer for Matthew or his representative, they would need to obtain an agreement from Keith, which was not pursued. This delayed any ratification of an acceptable agreement.

"At no point during any of these discussions did Matthew refer to the song ['A Whiter Shade Of Pale'] or his contribution to it. Only in a fax from Dennis Cooper [Fisher's then legal representative] dated March 19, 2004, did the matter of a writer's share of the song occur as a new item…"

Fisher would claim that his legal representative Dennis Cooper had tried to open up some kind of dialogue, "to discuss various matters with Chris (Cook) and Gary (Brooker) but it soon became obvious that the general attitude was one of, 'The answer is *no*… What is the question?'"

As a consequence, on April 14, 2005, Fisher's lawyers Jens Hills & Co wrote to both Brooker and Onward Music's Simon Platz: "Our client raised the issue of writer's credit with Mr Reid in 1967, pursuant to reviewing the sheet music of the song at the offices of Essex Music in 1967 and concluding that as his part had been reproduced, he should be entitled to a credit. We are instructed that Mr Reid referred the matter to you and you stated erroneously that our client's contribution did not give rise to an entitlement to a share of copyright.

"Open Proposal Notwithstanding, the aforementioned our client does not want to get embroiled in litigation and wishes to approach the matter pragmatically. The principle objective for our client is to be recognised as a joint author, monetary issues are secondary. Accordingly, our client is prepared to settle on the following terms. Our client requires:

1. A declaration that he is the joint author of the Song;
2. An entitlement to twenty-five percent (25%) share of the ownership (calculated by reference to half of musical composition of the song);
3. An entitlement to a 25% share of all future income in respect of the Song;
4. A credit to be agreed on all future pressings, licensing and label copy of the Song duly recognising our client as joint author;
5. Payment of our client's legal costs to be assessed if not agreed.

"You will note this proposal is a significant concession by our client as he is offering to waive his entitlement to past royalties."

Brooker and Reid were flabbergasted by Fisher's actions. For them the *key* question at this juncture still remained unanswered, specifically how could Fisher remain silent and not raise the matter for some 38 years?

They had a point. Fisher had recorded three albums – *Echoes In The Night*, *The Prodigal Stranger* and *The Well's On Fire* with Brooker and Reid in a collaborative fashion. Furthermore, he had rejoined Procol Harum in 1991 and toured on and off with the band until taking decisive action in 2004. However, lurking beneath the surface during those years was the spectre of 'A Whiter Shade Of Pale', which evidently suppurated like a festering sore within Fisher's wounded psyche.

No doubt he was aware that if the name Procol Harum cropped up in a word association game, 'A Whiter Shade Of Pale' always followed. In references to the group, the media would perpetually return to *that* song and, as a result, it remained foremost in the minds of those who tended to view Procol Harum as a 'one hit wonder', even though their sizable catalogue boasted well over 100 songs. This had always been a source of continual annoyance for both Brooker and Reid, especially when 'new' Procol Harum material was on offer. At a glitzy American music industry function in 1985, former Chrysalis Records executive Ann P. Munday introduced Keith Reid to a fellow VIP as "the man who wrote 'A Whiter Shade Of Pale'." Deeply angered by this, Reid later chastised Munday saying, "*Never* introduce me to anyone like that *ever* again," before storming off, according to Munday.

Over time 'A Whiter Shade Of Pale' had become 'the crowd pleaser', 'the pension plan', 'the masterpiece', 'Procol's *Citizen Kane*', 'the unmentionable hit'. Yet it was still the song that stirred the most reaction, good or otherwise. Ultimately, 'Pale's' contradictory lyrics came to mirror a rather contradictory ethos within Procol Harum's inner circle. Perhaps this was why the song became such a tetchy matter for all of the original surviving members. Or was it simply down to money?

Fisher felt that the familiar melody as heard in the opening bars of the song, and again in the middle, had *always* been his uncredited creation. But Brooker solely claimed the credit for composing the music. 'Pale' had clearly earned the songwriters a tidy fortune, despite them being on a royalty deal that was originally deemed to be "not that great". This begged the question, why had there also been a 'band debt' issue that lingered from the late sixties into the early seventies, especially considering the amount of money the song must have earned for both the composer and lyricist?

Brooker even joked about the band's money problems in a 1971 A&M American radio interview disc when alluding to legal issues Procol Harum had experienced with former managers. Furthermore, they had also got rid of original guitarist Ray Royer and drummer Bobby Harrison when 'Pale' was still at number one back in 1967. "All this involved great lawsuits and expense," Brooker confirmed to Andrew Bailey in a 1971 *Rolling Stone* interview. Then of course there were the badly run tours of the sixties, which resulted in a succession of managers being fired, leading to more financial chaos. In every instance Procol Harum had settled out of court.

Matthew Fisher: "I think the whole issue was quite ridiculous. Was it *my* fault that the band was perpetually in debt? No one has ever suggested that the band debt was in some way a consequence of my deficiencies as an organist. I would argue that it was a consequence of inept mismanagement by a whole succession of managers: Keith Reid, Jonathan Weston, Tony Secunda, Bennett Glotzer and Ronnie Lyons. I would further argue that the band had always been managed with the aim of providing a vehicle to exploit the Brooker/Reid song catalogue, rather than to represent the interests of the band as a whole. Once Chrysalis took over, the whole thing got on a more professional footing, but I was long gone by then.

"I had decided to leave the band in 1969, and Ronnie [Lyons] said he'd like to manage me. Not knowing any better, I agreed to this. He was still managing Procol and relations between the three entities were quite friendly at first. It was Ronnie who had his lawyer draw up a rather amateurish agreement between me and the band on the terms of my departure. [Bassist] Dave Knights signed an identical agreement. This was a very bad agreement, which nobody seems to have a copy of any more, so I would argue that insofar as it concerned me, the whole 'band debt' issue was created by Ronnie Lyons. Within a few months, Ronnie and I had independently terminated our respective business relationships with Procol, but our mutual business involvement carried on until 1984."

Fisher's website announced that "Jens Hills & Co., specialist media and entertainment litigators, have issued proceedings in the Royal Courts of Justice, Chancery Division on behalf of Matthew Fisher against Gary Brooker and Onward Music Limited for inter alia a declaration that Matthew Fisher is the co-author of the music in the song entitled 'A Whiter Shade Of Pale'. The Royal Courts of Justice served the Claim Form and Particulars of Claim on Gary Brooker and Onward Music Limited on the May 31, 2005."

A response on behalf of Brooker from the law firm Harbottle & Lewis was forthcoming on June 17: "Matthew Fisher has regrettably issued court proceedings against Gary Brooker and Onward Music Limited claiming a share of the copyright in 'A Whiter Shade Of Pale'. Gary Brooker today said that ''A Whiter Shade Of Pale' was written by Keith Reid and me before Matthew even joined the band. I am shocked and dismayed that after Matthew had worked with us quite happily over the course of 40 years without him once alleging that his role on 'A Whiter Shade Of Pale' was anything other than as a musician, it is only now that he claims he recalls writing part of the song. I think people can draw their own conclusions from this'."

As early as 1966 Brooker had admired Jacques Loussier's version of Bach's 'Air On A 'G' String' (aka 'Aria Number 3 In D Major') as performed by The Jacques Loussier Trio from the 1960 Decca album *Play Bach Volume 2*. But where had he first heard this particular version? The answer was as part of the soundtrack to the cult British television commercial for Hamlet cigars, which featured this said aria. Brooker even wrote to Hamlet, which sent him a single with Hamlet Cigars printed on the label. So, according to Brooker, this particular commercial was the inspirational source for 'A Whiter Shade Of

Pale' and written long before Fisher had even auditioned for Procol Harum.

A demo featuring Brooker singing and playing piano was recorded as early as 1966 and led to job-for-hire musicians being employed to rehearse and then record 'A Whiter Shade Of Pale' on two separate occasions: firstly in November 1966 and again in January 1967 as part of two individual sessions that were produced by Guy Stevens. A handful of acetates were made for distribution to potential record labels, but none appeared to have survived. This was crucial as no comparison could be drawn between the pre-Fisher version and the hit single containing his work. By a twist of fate Stevens' widow Diane mentioned that she had a copy of the original acetate in an old trunk in her loft. Brooker was made aware of this and contacted her to see if he could access the disc. Despite having suggested to a third party that Brooker should get in touch with her in 2005, Diane appeared to be annoyed with Brooker when he finally made contact by telephone. This was apparently because nobody from Procol Harum had been in touch with Diane, or Guy, since 1967. Diane also felt that "Guy had been wronged by Brooker and Reid", and that this was something that "he *never* got over".

Stevens had coined the phrase 'A Whiter Shade Of Pale' and named the band Procol Harum, and, according to Diane, "Guy suggested the Hammond organ and piano format, too," which was the very basis of the song. Yet Procol had ditched her husband after his drug misdemeanour and he apparently never saw a penny from his early involvement in their career. Accordingly, Diane, who died in early 2012, decided that Brooker was "not going to get the acetate".

With no original 'Pale' demos apparently in existence, or forthcoming, the upcoming court case was going to be a tough ride from day one: a fact that the defendants had neither anticipated nor realised until vast legal bills had been run up. A High Court case with top notch legal teams in place throughout meant that proceedings might cost something in the region of a hundred pounds per second. Was it all really going to be worthwhile for the claimant? And were the defendants being unduly optimistic by considering victory to be their entitlement?

In a press release made by Harbottle & Lewis who acted for the defendants, it was announced that proceedings in the Chancery Division would commence on Monday, November 13, 2006. Under the headline "Money Spinner" Adam Sherwin wrote in *The Times* three days before: "The dispute is complicated because all sides agree that Johann Sebastian Bach originally inspired the song's mournful melody." Unwittingly appearing to take sides, the journalist added, "Brooker first wrote the song as a straight R&B tune, based on Bach's 'Air from the Orchestral Suite No 3 in D', which he had heard on a Hamlet cigar advertisement, and the composer's 'Cantata No 140', known as 'Sleepers Awake'. His organ melody includes lines running in counterpoint to the vocal melody and also the memorable eight-bar solo that appears between verses. He transformed the tempo and rhythm of the cantata 'lift', cleverly disguising its classical source. Brooker, who strongly contests the claim, concedes that Fisher, who left the band in 1969, 'refined' the song's use of Bach. But the organist believes he created an original melody.

"Fisher has hired Jens Hill & Co, the company that represented Pete Best when the axed Beatles drummer successfully sued his former bandmates for royalties. Brooker, 61, has engaged Harbottle & Lewis, which acted for Simon Fuller, the *Pop Idol* mogul, in a recent dispute with Simon Cowell."

In the absence of both Guy Stevens and producer Denny Cordell witnesses close to the source offered their memories instead. Gary Brooker's wife, Francoise (aka Franky), recalled, "The song, as Gary played it to me on the piano, was the same as the recorded version and included the now-famous introduction."

"Skipping the fandango in Court 56" ran the front page headline on *The Guardian* above Duncan Campbell's incisive feature of November 14. "It may be nearly 40 years since the song was first recorded in the Marquee studio in Soho but the judge, Mr Justice Blackburne – with an 'e', first name not Tony – made it clear that he was perfectly familiar with it. 'I'm of an age,' he replied when Mr Fisher's counsel, Iain Purvis QC, checked apologetically with him that there would not be 'any risk of a "What are the Beatles?" moment'.

"Why had it taken so long for the case to come to court? 'Mr Fisher raised the issue in 1967,' said his barrister, Mr Purvis. Mr Brooker was 'totally unsympathetic' and, as Fisher had just joined the band, 'he didn't want to rock the boat... He felt he had a major gripe, it wasn't at all clear he had a legal claim.' He left the band in 1969 but had always felt he was wrongly denied a credit. It was only when similar cases came to court (eg session violinist Bobby Valentino versus The Bluebelles with a claim over the song 'Young At Heart') more recently that he had decided to seek what he felt was due."

Co-defendant music publisher Simon Platz, who was present to represent Onward Music, felt the case was lost when Brooker got up to demonstrate the song in court, giving those present an exclusive performance of the music that he claimed to have originally written based upon Bach's arias. The results did not sound anything like the issued record at all despite Brooker's efforts trying to prove it did. It really was 'game over' there and then for all of the co-defendants. Fisher claimed that his opening bars – originally *only* the solo in the middle – gave the song its distinctly recognisable tune.

After six days in court (November 13-24), in his summing up on December 20, Mr Justice Blackburne said in Clause 11: "The organ solo is a distinctive and significant contribution to the overall composition and, quite obviously, the product of skill and labour on the part of the person who created it." He went on to outline the key issues in Clause 12 of his summing up: "It is not in dispute that Mr Fisher participated in the evolution of what became the Work by his contribution of the organ part, including the organ solo. What is in issue, however, is the extent to which the organ part, especially the organ solo, is to be viewed as Mr Fisher's invention and, even if it was wholly his invention, whether his contribution of it was such as to entitle him to a share in the authorship of the overall Work. The matter can be broken down into the following issues: (1) the extent of Mr Fisher's contribution to the Work; (2) whether that contribution was capable of conferring on Mr Fisher an interest in the musical copyright in the Work and (3) whether any copyright interest in the Work to which Mr Fisher would otherwise be entitled is defeated by

(a) the existence of a copyright interest (otherwise than in Mr Fisher) in an earlier version of the Song and the consequences that flow from that."

In Clause 36 Mr Justice Blackburne considered that "Matthew Fisher, found inspiration for the organ solo in another of JS Bach's works, namely 'Wachet Auf, Ruft Uns Die Stimme' ('Sleepers Awake, The Voice Is Calling'). Having decided that he wanted to incorporate something which reflected that piece in the organ solo, he adapted it, by small changes in note value and pitch, so that it could be combined with the descending bass line provided by Mr Brooker with its echoes of 'Air On A G String'. The working in of this reference to 'Wachet Auf' led to Mr Fisher making, he said, a small alteration to the bass line in bar 8, namely the substitution of a root position G chord for a bass C on the first beat of the eighth bar and the substitution of two first-inversion chords, F and G7, in place of a bottom G in the second half of the eighth bar."

In his penultimate Clause (98) of summing up Mr Justice Blackburne made reference to a 'musicologist' called Mr Oxendale who had been brought in to assist in assessing both Fisher's and Brooker's contributions. "I had the impression that what he had to say on the matter was very much thought up as he went along. The question ultimately is a highly subjective one. Doing the best I can I have come to the view that Mr Fisher's interest in the Work should be reflected by according him a 40% share in the musical copyright. His contribution to the overall work was on any view substantial but not, in my judgment, as substantial as that of Mr Brooker. As between the two it seems to me that Mr Brooker should be accorded the greater share."

Against all expectations, Matthew Fisher had won his case. "Beyond The Pale – singer seethes as organist wins fight over 60's classic," stated the headline above Duncan Campbell's December 21 *Guardian* feature. "I'm dazed," said Fisher after the judgment. "It will take a week or two to sink in." He said he imagined he would be "crossed off Gary and Keith's Christmas card list, but that's a small price to pay". Fisher added that the action had "nothing to do with money", but was to establish his right to be recognised as part-author of one of the most famous pop songs of all time. Every effort had been made to reach an amicable solution before going to trial, but without success, he said. The court heard that Brooker's lawyers had threatened to pursue Fisher 'to bankruptcy' if he persisted with his action.

"I'm relieved that the trial is over, but my faith in British justice is shattered," said Brooker in *Guardian* writer Duncan Campbell's feature, concluding, "If Matthew Fisher's name ends up on my song, mine can come off! I have to respect and acknowledge the people I write songs with. After all this time, the case should never have got to court. Johann Sebastian Bach deserves the credit for his inspiration to all musicians."

Lucy Bannerman reported in *The Times* of December 21, "It was his creative contribution as a composer rather than just a performer that made the song a hit, Mr Fisher argued. Mr Justice Blackburne endorsed this, awarding him a co-authorship credit and a share of future royalties. Mr Fisher will be entitled to 20 per cent of royalties backdated to May 2005 when he made the claim, while the 50 per cent cut that Mr Brooker has enjoyed for 40 years will be reduced to 30 per cent. It is believed that Mr Fisher will receive a five-figure sum.

"Mr Brooker, 61, who was unable to attend the hearing because he had just returned from tour, said in a statement that it was a dark day for the music industry. He said: 'Any musician who has ever played on any recording in the last 40 years may now have a potential claim to joint authorship. It is effectively open season on the songwriter. Songwriters and publishers will now have to view all musicians with suspicion as potential claimants to a share in their copyright. This creates a ticking time bomb ready to explode whenever the musician chooses and when, possibly, material witnesses have passed away.'

"Mr Brooker also faces paying about £500,000 in legal costs. He added: 'It's hard to believe that I've worked with somebody on and off since 1967 whilst they hid such unspoken resentment...'

"Mr Brooker has been granted leave to appeal. It is the second time in 18 months that the band's bank balance has felt the pinch from claims by former members. Mr Brooker reached an out-of-court settlement with Ray Royer, a former guitarist, and Jonathan Weston, a former manager, who claimed royalties for their contribution to 'A Whiter Shade Of Pale'," concluded Bannerman in her *Times* feature.*

Some press reports inferred that Fisher had received legal aid. "What I got in 2005 was a Conditional Fee Agreement with Jens Hills & Co," Fisher clarified, "because by that time legal aid had been abolished for that kind of claim. Hugo Cuddigan (the junior barrister) waited until witness statements had been exchanged before committing himself to a 'CFA'. He wanted to be sure Gary wasn't going to claim not to remember what happened back in 1967 – as that would have been a difficult defence to fight. Iain Purvis came on board soon afterwards... Gary's killer defence would have been to claim that he didn't remember who wrote the organ part. Any high street lawyer could have told him that."

Brooker, Reid and Onward Music opted to take the case to the appeal courts. "Whiter Shade of Pale battle resumes," announced *The Times* on October 3, 2007. This time the hearing was to last just two days. In her *Times* article the following day Lucy Bannerman announced that "Procol Harum singer wins royalty battle over 'Whiter Shade Of Pale' ... Lord Justice Mummery said that the High Court had been right to find that Matthew Fisher made a creative contribution to the work and to grant a declaration of co-authorship, but that it was wrong to allow him a share of the earnings from the musical copyright. His delay in making the claim made it unconscionable and inequitable for him to seek to exercise control over the commercial exploitation of the copyright..."

Lord Justice Mummery's key points were set out as follows, "Matthew Fisher is guilty of excessive and inexcusable delay in asserting his claim to title to a joint interest in the Work. He silently stood by and acquiesced in the defendants' commercial exploitation of the Work for 38 years. His

---

* In 2003 Jonathan Weston issued a claim against Onward Music for his share of royalties obtained from 'A Whiter Shade Of Pale's' movie soundtrack usage [aka 'synchronisation royalties' or 'sync rights'], winning him vast back-royalty payments in an out-of-court settlement, which went to 'arbitration', according to the song's music publisher Simon Platz.

acquiescence led the defendants to act for a very long period on the basis that the entire copyright in the Work was theirs. They controlled the commercial exploitation of the Work without any reference or reward to him... His acquiescence has made it unconscionable and inequitable for him to seek to exercise control over the commercial exploitation of the copyright in the Work."

Six months later the 'Pale' case was in the news yet again. *The Daily Telegraph* (April 4, 2008) reported that: "Mr Fisher's solicitor, Mike Shepherd, said he had applied for permission to appeal against this latest ruling in the House of Lords. He said: 'We will apply to the House of Lords on various grounds, including that it is unreasonable for him not to have a future share of royalties. The court has accepted the decision that he co-wrote it, which was the primary issue for Matthew. But he is disappointed about the future royalties. It seems to us that if someone contributed a significant part to a composition, why shouldn't they get the future income?'"

The *Telegraph* also made mention that Brooker was still in dispute with Fisher over who would foot the estimated £500,000 legal costs of the action.

Shortly after the judgment was sent out to all parties on April 1, 2008 Fisher posted this on his website: "Now it has been set in stone ... 'A Whiter Shade Of Pale' Brooker/Fisher/Reid ... The Court of Appeal has after six months deliberation finally issued their judgment regarding the 'Whiter Shade Of Pale' lawsuit. They have basically upheld all of Mr Justice Blackburne's findings, with one exception – by a two to one majority they have ruled that although I am a writer and copyright owner, I should not be entitled to receive any remuneration arising from the exploitation of that copyright.

"This is a most peculiar judgment that will please nobody. It raises more questions than it answers. Having demolished every single argument advanced by Gary Brooker's legal team, Lord Justice Mummery suddenly produced an argument of his own, like a magician producing a rabbit out of a hat.

"This argument is so obscure and oblique as to defy comprehension. It had never been anticipated, either by the two legal teams concerned, or by the many legal commentators who have written about the original trial. It will be interesting to hear the reactions of other specialist copyright law firms such as Clintons or Davenport Lyons.

"Nevertheless, from my point of view this case was never about money – it was about getting my name on the song to which I contributed the most commercial and essential feature ..."

Brooker simply said in a statement. "For nearly three years this claim has been a great strain upon myself and my family. I believe the original trial was unfair and the results wrong. Justly, the decisions of the Court Appeal have gone some way to putting this right and I would hope that, now, we can all get on with our lives."

"An end to the 'A Whiter Shade Of Pale' dispute?" wondered Chris Cook in an email to *Beyond The Pale* [the Procol Harum website] dated May 7 2008. "The appeal court judges have rejected Matthew Fisher's request for permission to take the matter to the House of Lords. They also elected not to make any order for costs. This effectively means that both sides will have to pay their own costs."

The above assertion vis-à-vis the permission to take the matter to the House of Lords was in fact in error. The case ended up there on April 22 and 23, 2009.

With the British press having given Procol Harum more publicity throughout the course of the hearings of November 2006 and April 2008 than they had had during their entire 1967 heyday, the Law Lords' ruling was finally pre-empted with a mere whimper of media anticipation. The notable exception to this was Jane Fryer's double page spread in *The Daily Mail* of April 23. Her feature headlined "A Darker Shade Of Pale" went on to report that "the pair" [sic] the claimant Fisher versus the defendants Brooker and Onward Music Ltd, "have rattled through nearly £1 million in legal costs and have slogged it out in the High Court, the Court of Appeal and, today are back in the House of Lords for a final ruling on who's entitled to what." Fryer also anticipated that, "The Law Lords will also set some guidelines for how long a person can wait before bringing *any* case to court. Mathew Fisher waited 38 years."

In an attempt to describe key differences between Fisher and Brooker,

Fryer elected to point out that "one has an estate [in Surrey] the other a shabby house in Croydon [south London]."

The Law Lords' ruling came on April 30, 2009. However, their decision was 'officially' announced some three months later on July 30 when it was leaked to BBC TV news bulletins. Five years of conflict were summed up with this: "According to the lawyers, the case marked the first time the Law Lords had been asked to rule on a copyright dispute involving a song … And the final result: Fisher's original claim has been upheld by the Law Lords, reversing the Court of Appeal's decision. Fisher has won!"

The *only* British newspaper to fully report the actual salient facts was *NME* of July 30. "Procol member Matthew Fisher has won a court case to be named the official co-writer of the band's classic 1967 song 'A Whiter Shade Of Pale'. Fisher claims he wrote the song's organ melody and the Law Lords today ruled that he is entitled to his share of future royalties from the song. In 2006, the High Court ruled that the organist was entitled to 40 per cent of royalties from the song. However, royalties were reverted to Procol Harum frontman Gary Brooker and lyricist Keith Reid in 2008, after the Court Of Appeal ruled that Fisher had waited too long – 38 years – to make his claim."

The Law Lords crucially concluded that the length of time Fisher had waited had no bearing on the legitimacy of his claim – a point which the co-defendants had always seen as the central bone of contention.* **

So had Fisher *really* won in the end? And had Brooker truly lost out? Financially, the pair had run up an almighty debt. Three years on in the summer of 2012 there remains the unresolved matter as to who will foot the bill, who pays what and exactly how much each will contribute. As this biography goes to print, the former defendants – Brooker and Onward Music – have evidently failed to reach an agreement as to how the issue will be resolved.

* The key statements from the large 80 point ruling drawn up by the Law Lord are reproduced in Appendix 5.
** The Law Lords' 'Pale' ruling was their final act of decision making before being replaced by the new British Supreme Court.

So did Matthew Fisher have a future after this long legal battle? This has caused much discussion within 'fan' circles on social media websites ever since. More to the point, however, did Procol Harum have a future without Fisher? The answer is most definitely 'yes' in both cases.

Chapter 19

Beyond The Pale

2004–2013

"Gary Brooker's voice is certainly in the same league as Percy Sledge, but his voice is different. It has its own utterly unique character... The guy could literally sing anything!

Alan Parker in 1997

With the ongoing court case involving 'A Whiter Shade Of Pale' overshadowing anything else that Procol Harum might do, Gary Brooker felt the urge to perform with the group again, minus Matthew Fisher. Josh Phillips returned to the fold after a 10-year absence to replace Fisher, but otherwise the line-up remained as in 2003. So with royalty payments tied up pending the court's final decision, Procol Harum played low-profile concerts in only Verona and Vienna during 2004.

2005 saw 16 European gigs across mainland Europe and Scandinavia, including a special concert at London's Bloomsbury Theatre on March 6 where Keith Reid appeared onstage to recite his section of 'In Held 'Twas In I'. Brooker also undertook a special Tsunami Charity Concert inside Guildford Cathedral with The Chameleon Choir & Orchestra on April 16 and performed another big charity fundraiser on June 11 in Wintershall, Surrey with his 'all star' Band Du Lac.

However the most significant musical event on the Procol calendar in 2005 was the unexpected reformation of The Paramounts.

On December 17, the original line-up of Gary Brooker, Robin Trower, Mick Brownlee and Chris Copping (who flew in from Australia especially for the occasion) reformed for the first time since 1964, playing a one-off at Westcliff's Club Riga, inside the old Cricketers Pub, where they'd started off in December 1960. "The magic's still there," wrote the *Southend Evening Echo*. "It was truly a night to remember – and one which many must have thought they'd never witness."

The reunion was partly instigated by the paper's Rock'n'Roll Years series, looking back to the area's glory days of the fifties and sixties. On the night the event attracted a sellout audience with fans present from the USA, Norway, Rome, Denmark and Germany, as well as all four corners of the UK.

"It was a truly magical night," marvelled [Paramounts original drummer] Mick Brownlee. "I really never thought it would happen, but it did – it was just amazing. All the guys in the band had such a great time and played really well. I've never seen Robin smile so much. He just had this huge grin all night long!" Guests of honour were Trower's parents, Len and (stepmother) 'Blonde Shirley', who ran the Shades coffee bar where The Paramounts often played. "It was wonderful to come across so many people from the old days, too," Mick added. "It wasn't all that easy to recognise some of them, though – we've all changed a bit over the years!"

Former Procol bassist Dave Bronze, who was there to support his old friends, summed it all up, "An unforgettable occasion. Magic: the only word for it. Forty years on, no rehearsal, and they can still play like that..."

2006 saw Procol Harum perform 14 gigs across six European countries including two very special festival appearances. First up was the Isle Of Wight Pop Festival with Procol returning on June 11 for the first time since 1970. ITV covered the event and 'A Whiter Shade Of Pale' appeared as a part of a late night festival compilation – an inevitable but interesting choice considering the legal situation surrounding the song.

Three IOW tracks also appeared on Procol's 40th Anniversary Salvo Records' DVD *Another View* in the shape of 'The VIP Room', 'Alpha', and 'Kaleidoscope'.

On August 19 and 20 Procol performed with The Danish National Concert Orchestra and Choir in the grounds of Ledreborg Castle. The epic, sold out proceedings were televised and recorded by Danish television and first appeared on the DVD *Another View* followed by the Eagle DVD and CD issues of July 2009 under the banner *Procol Harum In Concert With The Danish National Concert Orchestra and Choir*. Unlike some of Procol's earlier orchestral outings this particular concert sounded good *on the day* as well as on DVD. Huge strides in technology had taken place since Procol had first attempted an orchestral collaboration at The Stratford Festival, Canada in 1969 when that recording was aborted midway through the concert.

The band was back for a 16-date European tour in 2007 covering six countries. The Italian concerts were made available as an audio download to fans under the title *One Eye To The Future*. Two prestigious Procol Harum '40th Anniversary' concerts took place at St John's Church, Westminster, on July 20 and 21. The first night featured Brooker, Whitehorn, Pegg and Phillips and new recruit drummer Geoff Dunn (born February 26, 1961, Clapham, London) whom manager Chris Cook brought in to replace Mark Brzezicki. Dunn had previously drummed with various soul acts, including Terence Trent D'Arby, Shalamar and Jermaine Stewart, as well as jazz band Spyro Gyra and Georgie Fame. He had also played with Jimmy Page, Eric Burdon and Van Morrison. Dunn had a background in funk and this would help to push Procol in a more dynamic direction in years to come.

Procol Harum's 40th Anniversary Concert took place in the sedate and acoustically friendly setting of St John's Church in Smith Square, Westminster, which is situated around the corner from the Houses of Parliament. The first evening showcased some Procol favourites and rarities while the second featured two bands made up of old friends covering unissued Brooker/Reid songs and outtakes that had seldom been played live in an evening dubbed Procol Rarum. These two bands were grouped as 'Kings' – Tim Renwick (guitar), Martin Wright (drums), Dave Bronze (bass) and Frank Mead (saxes) – then 'Queens' – Geoff Whitehorn (guitar), Martin Wright (drums), Matt Pegg (bass), Josh Phillips (Hammond organ) and special surprise guest Dave Ball (guitar) for one blues number.

The band were off the road in 2008 and only six European gigs were undertaken the following year, four of which – Hagen, Germany; St Petersburg, Russia; Drammen, Norway, and The Brønnøysund Festival in Norway – were made available for fans to download. *The Spirit Of Nokken* would later be issued as a CD in October 2010.

A 20-date tour of North America in 2010 marked Procol's 25th US visit there, alongside gigs in four European countries. Three very special orchestral collaborations took place that year. The first pair of gigs were the 40th Anniversary Reunion Concerts with The Edmonton Symphony Orchestra & The Da Camera Singers at the Jubilee Auditorium in Edmonton, Canada on November 9 and 10 and an epic gig with The Delaware Symphony Orchestra & Delaware Opera Chorus in Wilmington, Delaware, on December 4, which turned out to be Procol's first American orchestral collaboration since the L.A. Philharmonic concert in 1973 at the Hollywood Bowl. In between both orchestral gigs Procol managed to fit in an appearance at Tallinn, Estonia on November 18 – their first show there since headlining the Rock Summer Festival of 1993.

2011 found Procol's popularity in Scandinavia remaining undiminished with four sell out nights with The Danish National Orchestra & Choir. Procol also planned a North American tour for 2012 – their biggest undertaking since 2003.

In the week of the Queen's Jubilee celebrations Gary Brooker was invited to an exclusive party at Buckingham Palace where he was photographed wearing his MBE beside the Kinks' Ray Davies. On May 28, 2012, Procol Harum flew to Cape Town, South Africa to perform at two huge festivals alongside The Moody Blues and King Crimson. The following night the band celebrated Brooker's 67th birthday. To the surprise of many the story hit the international news media, but with an unfortunate twist. Radio bulletins were first to pick it up: "Gary Brooker, lead singer of the British rock band Procol Harum, was rushed to intensive care in a Cape Town hospital, suffering from a fractured skull following on from his birthday celebrations earlier that evening. The situation is apparently critical. Procol Harum have had to cancel their South African appearances as a result.

The next day manager Chris Cook made the following statement: "Gary is still sedated, but I will see him before lunch tomorrow, and the band will be seeing him in the afternoon, before we return to London." Meanwhile, Brooker's wife, Franky, immediately flew out from England to be at his bedside. Remaining sedated for some days the truth behind the full story began to emerge. Gary hadn't just fallen over in Cape Town, and the incident had since become a police matter pending a full investigation. From the statements of those able to report the night's events, it became evident that Gary had had his drink spiked in his hotel bar, and the assumption is that the motive was robbery. Franky said, "People don't realise what he went through. To end up in an intensive care unit for a mugging that went wrong."

Back in England on June 26, it appeared that Brooker was on the mend and, despite this injury and loss of weight, he had every intention of undertaking a huge tour of America throughout the whole of July and August when Procol Harum would be supporting Yes. Franky Brooker added, "Gary and I went to London today to sort out Gary's visa for the US tour. We had to be there at 8am which is so early; we left home at 5.45am. He still gets easily tired due to the medication that he must take for a while. He's doing really good and he's in great spirits. Next week Gary's getting the boys down for a rehearsal in the barn, to test his head. It was a nasty fracture."

In July, Procol Harum flew to Skagen in Denmark for their warm-up concert prior to the American trip, followed by a long flight to Atlantic City to begin Procol's tour. Arriving in America and opening for Yes, it soon became apparent that Gary Brooker was back on top form, and vocally undiminished. The band were also getting louder applause than Yes, according to many social media websites, as well as plenty of good reviews. Procol's 26th tour of the USA was, and continues to be, a runaway success at the time of writing.

Despite now featuring only one original member, Procol Harum appear to have a great musical kinship and they have retained their quirky sense of humour. This is clear for all to see. American photographer Bert Saraco summed this up with these comments, "One of the wonderful things about Procol Harum is that these are five men who simply get together and play great music. No 'costumes', hair extensions, pandering or pretentiousness. The grand thing that happens is the music. The show is the music. The power is the music. We're just lucky that this great music is produced live onstage by people who obviously have [that] affection and respect for one another and are enjoying themselves immensely."

Across 2010 and 2011 engineer-producer Dennis Weinreich captured the current line-up of Procol which, for those who don't already know, is actually five years old this year. Recording the band as a live unit with no overdubs, edits or frills, using old school microphones, analogue technology and incorporating valve amps in the off-lay to CD, Weinreich has captured the vibe that Bert Saraco described so well in his review of the 2012 US tour.

Featuring three new Brooker-Reid songs, the line-up on the 2012 CD entitled *MMX Live* shows a return to pre-Procol roots. The R&B influences are there for all to see. The dynamism of The Paramounts has bubbled back to the surface and Brooker and chums seem to have come full circle. The soul-funk partnership of Pegg on bass and Dunn on drums has pushed the band into a cool groove, and the organ playing from Josh Phillips is solid and assured next to Procol's mainstay guitarist, the ever dependable Geoff Whitehorn, who continues to outshine *any* guitarist that might be waiting in the wings.

November 2012 marks Whitehorn's 21st anniversary with Procol, making him their longest serving guitar player; Matt Pegg will have been with the band for some 19 years, making him Procol's longest serving bassist; organist Josh Phillips has been playing with the band for seven years – although he first gigged with the band almost 20 years ago; and Geoff Dunn has been on the drum stool for five years.

Gary Brooker, the rock upon which Procol Harum was formed some 45 years ago, is now an elder statesman of rockin'-blue-eyed-soul, yet he is also something of a state secret, while remaining strangely familiar. However, to his aficionados and peers, he is simply a national treasure.

The band that Gary Brooker formed in 1967 have a new vigour that one might not expect from a band of their vintage. They remain unique and special.

Afterword

If you were alive in 1967 you will probably remember where you were when you first heard those sonorous descending organ chords that ushered in 'A Whiter Shade Of Pale'. And then that voice, all yearning and regret, bluesy yet English – like a fusion of Syd Barrett and Steve Winwood but with more cutting edge. I was at school, and the boys just stopped running down the corridor, put down their books and listened. There had been nothing like this before. Ever.

In a world where qualified failure is the norm, it was amazing that this beautiful song should have become first the hit and then the classic it deserved to be. Equally surprising is that none of the superlative albums the band went on to produce in the next decade were met with anything like the acclaim or sales you would have expected.

Take the tunes, the pure melodies... 'A Salty Dog', 'Broken Barricades', 'Fires (Which Burnt Brightly)', 'Magdalene', 'Pilgrim's Progress', 'Grand Hotel', 'A Rum Tale', 'Homburg', 'Conquistador', 'Nothing That I Didn't Know', 'As Strong As Sampson'... For simple melody, there were very few songwriters who could match Gary Brooker. Lennon/McCartney in this country or Brian Wilson, Burt Bacharach and Carole King in the USA... Not many more. Keith Reid's words undoubtedly fired Brooker up, moving as they did from the psychedelic, through the pretentious and into masterly lyrical vignettes. Reid could do sea shanties, nostalgia, spite, post-battle tristesse, nightmare, love, neurosis, humour, booze and poetry. And Brooker seemed to have a heartbreaking new melody for each one.

Or take the sound. There was the distinctive Hammond organ, so beautifully played by Matthew Fisher and then by Chris Copping (the solos on 'Nothing That I Didn't Know' or 'A Rum Tale' are effective because they are so modest, like a George Harrison guitar solo). Against the organ is Gary Brooker's melody-defining piano. In addition to the unusual keyboard counterpoint you also have one of England's best rock guitarists, Robin Trower. Sometimes he sounds like an angry wasp, caught in the cage of the two keyboards; then he breaks free on a track like 'Whaling Stories' or 'Repent Walpurgis' and the release is all the greater.

If that's not enough for you, add BJ Wilson's drumming. This is more than time-keeping; this is an additional instrument, wittily played – as witness the solo on 'Power Failure'. I watched BJ from the side of the stage once at Bristol and I felt exhausted after about ten minutes. Every other band seemed to want to steal him. And finally that magnificent voice. I've mentioned Winwood, Barrett, Lennon and McCartney. Add Jack Bruce and maybe Eric Clapton. If there were other British singers as good as Gary Brooker I seem to have missed them. When Keith Reid's words verged on the portentous Brooker either seemed to inject a note of humour or – as on 'A Salty Dog' – just gave it the works.

So, given the fact that on paper they had the songs and the musicians, the drive and the cohesion (not many personnel changes) to be the biggest act in Britain, why weren't they? Why weren't Procol Harum as big as The Beatles or Led Zeppelin or Pink Floyd? Perhaps there wasn't one killer album in which every track was a knock-out. Some songs on *A Salty Dog* seem a bit weak; there are some lesser tracks on *Grand Hotel*. But there is not much wrong with *Home* or *Shine On Brightly*. And in any case, no bands made albums without a few duds; the early Beatles records are full of them; half the Stones' output was padding.

Perhaps Procol Harum were difficult to place – almost literally in those days of vinyl discs in wooden bins at high street record shops. Pop? Rock? Progressive? Orchestral? They were putting out their best work at a time when music seemed to find a new direction every week. Record buyers tended to be young and fashion-conscious; pop journalists, like all reporters, are addicted to labels. Perhaps there was never a fashion-badge that could be attached to Procol that would reassure young fans. For folk-rock you could buy Fairport Convention; for heavy metal Led Zeppelin and Deep Purple; for prog-rock King Crimson and Yes; for singer-songwriters Dylan and Joni Mitchell; for stadium pomp Genesis or Emerson Lake & Palmer. Where did *Broken Barricades* quite fit in? Sometimes the R&B roots gave muscle to the melodic ambition in a happy tension; perhaps at other times there was something unresolved. How well did 'Souvenir Of London', a busking song about picking up the clap, really sit with 'In Held 'Twas in I'? Did a certain modesty and sense of humour sometimes undercut the grandeur?

The only other reason you could imagine was that they disappointed when they played live. But that was not the case. Their most successful album was indeed a live one, with the Edmonton Symphony Orchestra. It seemed to revive their career and in 'Conquistador' gave them the first hit single they had had for years. I must have seen them a dozen times and they were never less than good; sometimes they were sublime.

So that's the mystery of Procol Harum, though perhaps it's only really a mystery if you expect life to be fair.... But meanwhile, people can remember them with joy: they were a prodigiously good band and you can still get their songs on CD and catch a glimpse on You Tube. Thank you for everything, boys. And Gary Brooker still performs.

© 2012 Sebastian Faulks

Acknowledgements

Procol Harum's music has woven a thread throughout my life. I first heard 'Conquistador' forty years ago when it played out over the closing credits of BBC TV's *Top Of The Pops* in 1972. As a youngster it reminded me of themes for Spaghetti Westerns. The song also alluded to *Don Quixote* which, as a reluctant schoolboy, I'd been forced to read repeatedly.

A year later Procol Harum made their Edinburgh debut when they played at The Usher Hall. I was allowed to go to the concert on the basis that I would be accompanied by some *older* friends. When Gary Brooker sang 'Homburg' I heard a familiar chuckle from the row behind me. Somehow my old man had been allowed in to the gig free of charge. To my overwhelming embarrassment he was sat there wearing a Homburg hat and a long overcoat.

Four years later Procol made their final appearance in my home town at Edinburgh University's famous Refectory. After six encores consisting of r 'n' r covers Procol struck up the familiar opening bars of 'A Whiter Shade Of Pale'. I was seated precariously on top of three piled tables. The jostling crowd nudged me from my perch and I tumbled amidst the crashing furniture into a sea of bearded students."You got the biggest applause of the night," laughed Procol's drummer BJ Wilson shortly afterwards. Some months later it was all over. Procol had split-up in the wake of disco and punk.

Scottish blue-eyed soul singer Frankie Miller was an Edinburgh hero. 'The Miller' was managed by Procol's lyric writer Keith Reid. I can recall the first time I gate crashed back stage with my pal Julian Wyllie. "You'ze chancers ponks?" said 'The Miller' in his Glaswegian tones, before adding, "Am no havin' ponks gobbin', right!" A bemused Reid quickly intervened, "Oh don't worry about them, Frankie. They're Procol Harum fans!" 'The Miller' fixed us a menacing stare and hissed, "Well dig thi-sss. When I wiz yer age we did 'The Devil Came Fae Kansas'." He then broke into a menacing grin, shook our hands firmly and eyeballed us with a parting shot, "Nae danger. Gid luck tae yuz." I got to know Keith Reid shortly after this.

In 1979 I wrote a tribute to Procol Harum as a fanzine called *Shine On* which was inspired by Pete Frame's and John Tobler's *ZigZag*. By then Procol's Gary Brooker had already embarked on a solo career and Keith Reid kindly got me some Chrysalis quids so I might include an advert for Brooker's debut disc. More Brooker-Reid meetings occurred and I tape recorded the lot.

A year later, Gary Brooker rolled into the Edinburgh Odeon as the Hammond organ player with Eric Clapton's band while I was working as a 'production unit runner' on the movie *Chariots Of Fire*. "What happened to *Shine On* Issue 2?" enquired Brooker as a bemused Clapton signed an autograph.

Some 11 years later, in 1991, Procol Harum reformed and I finally produced Issue 2. By then I was working in music documentaries following on from a stint at film school. At that point I was a researcher on an ITV programme about the Elton John tribute album *Two Rooms* which featured famous rock stars covering Elton's hits. "Why not pay the newly reformed Procol Harum to cover an Elton song?" I suggested to the disinterested executives, before adding, "Elton and Bernie cited 'Homburg' as a favourite, you know." Elton's co-manager Steve Brown was decidedly unimpressed and quickly vetoed my idea. But as a kind of thank you for my efforts, Procol's manager Kellogs invited me on a mini tour with Procol, which took in Tallinn, Estonia, and Southend-

On-Sea. I later went to California with the band, taking in Los Angeles and San Francisco.

In 1994 RCA hired Gary Brooker and The LSO for the recording *The Long Goodbye - The Symphonic Music of Procol Harum*. I was enlisted to videotape the recording of 'A Whiter Shade Of Pale' and 'A Salty Dog' for an Electronic Press Kit, but in-house difficulties at RCA in New York coupled with the costs of the LSO musicians' payments meant that the footage never saw the light of day. Instead I suggested to Kellogs that I might be able to organise a one-off concert with The LSO at London's Barbican.

I met up with Clive Gillinson, who was the Director of the LSO, and he promptly made the booking there and then in August 1995. On February 8, 1996, Procol Harum, The LSO and The Chameleon Arts Chorus performed the new symphonic versions of Procol Harum's songs to a full house and a standing ovation at London's Barbican followed by a rave review in the *Guardian* newspaper.

Procol celebrated their *30th Anniversary* in 1997 and I was invited to screen a documentary I had made about 'A Whiter Shade Of Pale', which was later shown at London's National Film Theatre. I also MC'd the first half of the show and dedicated *that* part of the proceedings to the memory of the late BJ Wilson and Frankie Miller who was in attendance, but in a wheelchair. I later reminded Frankie about our first meeting way back in 1977 and we shook hands firmly in recollection.

After having worked on 11 *Classic Albums'* documentaries back-to-back over a three year period, I co-produced *Punk Attitude* directed by Don Letts. At this juncture I put it to Gary Brooker that it might be a good idea for me to produce a film about Procol Harum's upcoming 40th Anniversary as a career celebration.

I produced a 75-minute film in 2004, but once again had to put it on ice due the costs of the audio-visual copyrights, funds not being forthcoming, and because of the upcoming 'A Whiter Shade Of Pale' court case. Hearing about the temporary shelving of this documentary, David Barraclough – the Commissioning Editor at Omnibus Press – suggested in 2011 that I should write this biography in the interim.

Gary Brooker has always been supportive and helpful. Four significant Brooker interviews play a part here: two tape recorded conversations spanning a total of six hours from 1979 and 1992, alongside videotaped interviews from 1994 and 2004, and much correspondence. Many members of Procol Harum have given wholly exclusive interviews for this book. In particular I would like to single out Chris Copping, Matthew Fisher and Keith Reid for their tireless attention to detail. Thanks also go to the following band interviewees: Dave Ball, Mark Brzezicki, Mick Grabham, Robin Trower and Geoff Whitehorn. Procol Harum's managers have also been helpful, especially Chris Cook, Doug D'Arcy, John 'Kellogs' Kalinowski, Diane Rolph and Derek Sutton. I'd also like to thank Procol's surviving record producers, Matthew Fisher, Chris Thomas, Tony Visconti and Dennis Weinreich, for their collective input.

Many musicians have played their part in this book, including Pete Brown, Mick Brownlee, Jimmy Jewell, Mickey Jupp, Jimmy Page, Phil Wainman and Kenny White. Alongside these good folk many top writers and journalists have been significant in the telling of the history of Procol Harum. I would like to single out and thank the following: Richard Amey, Max Bell and Johnny Black, Mike Butler, Paul Carter, Chris Charlesworth, Pete Frame, Nick Hasted, Patrick Humphries, Jim Irvin, Paul Kendall, John McFerrin, Angus MacKinnon, Barry Miles, Bud Scoppa, Paul Sexton, Tony Stewart, Ronald L. Smith, Adam Sweeting, John Tobler, Chris Welch, Paul Williams and Richard Williams.

Procol Harum's website *Beyond The Pale* is probably the best website of its kind in the world. Thanks go out to its founders Roland Clare and Jens Anders Ravnaas for their collective help throughout the writing of this biography. Special thanks also go out to Onwards Music publisher and Fly Records' MD Simon Platz and Fly Records' label manager Ronen Guha for their combined assistance.

Numerous unseen and unpublished photographs of Procol Harum are appearing here for the first time. In particular I would like to single out the 1968 San Franciscan photographs of Ron Sanchez and the 1969 Washington DC photographs by William Hatfield. Special thanks go to John Paige and Lorie Leavy for their assistance and to thanks photographers Andrew Kent and Bert Saraco.

Many thanks go to Southenders John Howard, Barry Sinclair and Tony Wilkinson for shedding light on The Paramounts' early days within a Southend context. Thanks also go to Jeff Dexter, Bob Harris and Diane Stevens for providing insights into early Procol days. I'd also like to give a nod of appreciation to former Chrysalis Records' executive Ann P. Munday for putting me in touch with some valuable contacts vis-a-vis 'The Chrysalis Years'.

Thanks also to the following contributors: Carol Fisher, Sandra Simons and The Right Honourable 'The Lord Howard of Lympne' CH PC QC.

A special thanks goes out to Ray Connolly, Eric Kulberg, Pia Meijer, Pedro Mercedes, David Pelletier, Andy Starke, Peter Thomas and Pete Tombs for their continued support during this past year.

At Omnibus Books I would like to thank Helen Donlon and Charlie Harris for excellent press liaison; Jacqui Black for helping to get me some great images, and for the numerous times we re-jigged the illustrations in order to get it *just* right; and finally extra special thanks to my editor Chris Charlesworth for his considered comments, his input throughout, and for his overall dedication towards overcoming the obstacles during this lengthy process.

Extra special thanks go out to Will Birch and John Denton for being consultants vis-a-vis The Paramounts. Thanks also to Will for tirelessly proofing and indexing this lengthy tome. Exclusive consultation on all matters Procol Harum has been undertaken with Frans Steensma of *OOR Magazine* and *The Pop Encyclopaedia* Holland. Frans knows more about Procol Harum – and music journalism – than anyone on the entire planet.

Considerable gratitude goes out to Sebastian Faulks, Sir Alan Parker and Martin Scorsese.

Henry Scott-Irvine, August 18, 2012

Discographies

THE PARAMOUNTS

UK DISCOGRAPHY
(excluding compilations and reissues)

Poison Ivy/I Feel Good All Over
December 1963; Parlophone R5093

Little Bitty Pretty One/A Certain Girl
February 1964; Parlophone R5107

I'm The One Who Loves You/It Won't Be Long
June 1964; Parlophone R5155

**Poison Ivy/I Feel Good All Over/Little Bitty Pretty One/
A Certain Girl**
May 1964; Parlophone GEP 8908

Bad Blood/Do I
November 1964; Parlophone R5187

Blue Ribbons/Cuttin' In
March 1965; Parlophone R5752

You Never Had It So Good/Don't You Like My Love
October 1965; Parlophone R5351

PROCOL HARUM

UK SINGLES DISCOGRAPHY
(Including DVDs and MP3 Downloads but excluding compilations and all reissues, chart positions in brackets)

A Whiter Shade Of Pale/Lime Street Blues
May, 1967; Deram 126 (1)

Homburg/Good Captain Clack
October, 1967 **October;** Regal Zonophone RZ 3002 (6)

Quite Rightly So/In The Wee Small Hours Of Sixpence
March, 1968; Regal Zonophone RZ 3007 (50)

A Salty Dog/Long Gone Geek
May, 1969; Regal Zonophone RZ 3019 (44)

Your Own Choice/About To Die
July, 1970; Regal Zonophone SPSR 328 (withdrawn)

Conquistador/Luskus Delph (both live)
July, 1972; Chrysalis CHR 2003 (22)

Robert's Box/A Rum Tale
April 1973; Chrysalis CHR 2010

A Souvenir Of London/Toujours L'amour
August 1973; Chrysalis CHR 2015

Nothing But The Truth/Drunk Again
March 1974; Chrysalis CHR 2032

Pandora's Box/The Piper's Tune
July 1975; Chrysalis CHR 2073 (16)

The Final Thrust/Taking The Time
October 1975; Chrysalis CHR 2079

As Strong As Samson/The Unquiet Zone
January 1976; Chrysalis CHR 2084

Wizard Man/Backgammon
February 1977; Chrysalis CHR 2138

UK ALBUMS DISCOGRAPHY
(Include DVDs and MP3 Downloads but excluding compilations, chart positions in brackets)

Procol Harum (mono only)
January 1968; Regal Zonophone LRZ 1001

Shine On Brightly (mono & stereo)
November, 1968; Regal Zonophone LRZ 1004 + SLRZ 1004

A Salty Dog
June 1969; Regal Zonophone SLRZ 1009 (27)

Home
June 1970; Regal Zonophone SLRZ 1014 (49)

Broken Barricades
June 1971; Chrysalis ILPS 9158 (42)

Procol Harum Live In Concert With The ESO
April 1972; Chrysalis CHR 1004 (48)

Grand Hotel
March 1973; Chrysalis CHR 1037

Exotic Birds & Fruit
April 1974; Chrysalis CHR 1058

Procol's Ninth
August 1975; Chrysalis CHR 1100 (41)

Something Magic
March 1977; Chrysalis CHR 1130

The Prodigal Stranger
February 1992; BMG-ZOO HH PD 90589

The Long Goodbye: Symphonic Music of Procol Harum
August 1995; RCA Victor 09026 68029 2

One More Time: Procol Harum Live In Utrecht (1992)
June 1997; Gazza Records Gazza CD 003

Ain't Nothing To Get Excited About
(Liquorice John Death, aka Procol Harum) 1998;
Gazza Records gazza 102

Procol Harum: BBC Live In Concert (1974)
June 1999; Strange Fruit CD

Procol Harum Live (In Copenhagen 2001)
February 2002; Classic Pictures DVD

The Well's On Fire
March 2003; Eagle Records EAGCD209

Live At Union Chapel London (2003)
December 2003; Eagle DVD/CD ER DVCD 030

One Eye To The Future – Live in Italy (2007)
September 2008; Strongman Productions MP3

In Concert With The Danish Concert Orchestra & Choir (2006)
May 2009; Eagle DVD/CD EAGCD400

Spirit Of Nokken – Procol Harum Live In 2009
October 2010; Strongman Productions MP3

MMX Procol Harum Live
May 2012; Strongman Productions MP3

US SINGLES DISCOGRAPHY
(Chart positions in brackets)

A Whiter Shade Of Pale/Lime Street Blues
June 1967; Deram 7507 (5)

Homburg/Good Captain Clack
October 1967; A&M Records 885 (34)

In The Wee Small Hours Of Sixpence/Quite Rightly So
April 1968; A&M Records 927

A Salty Dog/Long Gone Geek
May 1969; A&M Records 1069

Boredom/The Devil Came From Kansas (promo)
September 1969; A&M Records 1111

Whisky Train/About To Die (promo)
September 1970; A&M Records 1218

Broken Barricades/Power Failure
May 1971; A&M Records 2128-M2

Simple Sister/Song For A Dreamer (promo)
August 1971; A & M Records 1287

Conquistador/A Salty Dog (both live)
July, 1972; A&M 1347 (16)

Bringing Home The Bacon (edit)/Bringing Home The Bacon (promo)
April 1973; Chrysalis CHS 2032

Nothing But The Truth (promo)
March 1974; Chrysalis CHS 2032

Wizard Man (promo)
March 1977; Warner Brothers CRS 2115

All Our Dreams Are Sold
August 1991; Zoo-BMG Zoo ZP 1026-2

The Truth Won't Fade Away
November 1991; Zoo-BMG ZP17041-2

A Dream In Every Home
May 1992; Zoo-BMG ZP 17051-2

US ALBUMS DISCOGRAPHY
(Including DVDs, MP3 Downloads, but excluding compilations and reissues)

A Whiter Shade Of Pale (stereo only)
September 1968; Deram 18008 (47)

Shine On Brightly (stereo only)
September 1968; A&M Records SP 4151 (24)

A Salty Dog
April 1969; A&M Records SP 4179 (32)

Home
July 1970; A&M Records SP 4261 (34)

Broken Barricades
May 1971; A&M Records SP 4294 (32)

Procol Harum Live In Concert With The ESO
May 1972; A&M Records SP 4335 (5)

Grand Hotel
March 1973; Chrysalis CHR 1037 (21)

Exotic Birds & Fruit
March 1974; Chrysalis CHR 1058 (86)

Procol's Ninth
August 1975; Chrysalis CHR 4335 (41)

Something Magic
March 1977; Chrysalis Warner Brothers CHR 1130 (147)

The Prodigal Stranger
August 1992; BMG-ZOO HH PD 90589

The Long Goodbye: Symphonic Music of Procol Harum
August 1995; RCA Victor 09026 68029 2

The Well's On Fire
March 2003; Eagle Records EAGCD209

Live At Union Chapel London (2003)
December 2003; Eagle DVD/CD ER DVCD 030

One Eye To The Future – Live in Italy (2007)
September 2008; Strongman Productions MP3

In Concert With The Danish Concert Orchestra & Choir (2006)
May 2009; Eagle DVD/CD EAGCD400

Spirit Of Nokken – Procol Harum Live In 2009
October 2010; Strongman Productions MP3

MMX Procol Harum Live
May 2012; Strongman Productions MP3

GERMAN SINGLES

A Whiter Shade Of Pale/Lime Street Blues
June 1967; Deram 126

Homburg/Good Captain Clack
October 1967; Polydor 59122

Quite Rightly So/Rambling On
March 1968; Polydor 59175

A Salty Dog/Long Gone Geek
May 1969; Polydor 59293

Conquistador/All This & More (both live)
May 1972; Chrysalis 6155003

Grand Hotel/Robert's Box
April 1973; Chrysalis 6155012

A Souvenir Of London/Toujours L'amour
August 1973; Chrysalis 6155020

Nothing But The Truth/Drunk Again
April 1974; Chrysalis 6155025

Beyond The Pale/Fresh Fruit
August 1974; Chrysalis 6155034

Pandora's Box/The Piper's Tune
September 1975; Chrysalis 6155048

As Strong As Samson/The Unquiet Zone
February 1976; Chrysalis 6155056

The Truth Won't Fade Away/Learn To Fly
October 1991; ZOO–BMG PB 49159

The Truth Won't Fade Away/Learn To Fly/Into The Flood
October 1991; ZOO–BMG PD 49160

You Can't Turn Back the Page/One More Time/Perpetual Motion
November 1991; ZOO–BMG PD 49092

GERMAN ALBUMS
(Including DVDs + MP3 Downloads, but excluding compilations and all re-issues)

Procol Harum aka **A Whiter Shade Of Pale**
November 1967; Polydor 184115

Shine On Brightly (stereo only)
November 1968; Polydor 184162

A Salty Dog
May 1969; Polydor 184221

Home
June 1970; Polydor 2310 032

Broken Barricades
June 1971; Chrysalis 6499657

Procol Harum Live In Concert With The ESO
May 1972; Chrysalis 6307503

Grand Hotel
April 1973; Chrysalis 6307511

Exotic Birds & Fruit
April 1974; Chrysalis 6307531

Procol's Ninth
August 1975; Chrysalis 6307555

Something Magic
February 1977; Chrysalis 6307593

The Prodigal Stranger
September 1991; BMG–ZOO HH PD 90589

The Long Goodbye: Symphonic Music of Procol Harum RCA
August 1995; Victor 09026 68029 2

One More Time: Procol Harum Live In Utrecht (1992)
June 1997; Repertoire CD

Ain't Nothing To Get Excited About
(Liquorice John Death, aka Procol Harum) 1998;
Repertoire Records gazza 102

Procol Harum: BBC Live In Concert (1974)
June 1999; Strange Fruit CD

Procol Harum Live (In Copenhagen 2001)
February 2002 **February;** Classic Pictures DVD

The Well's On Fire
March 2003; Eagle Records EAGCD209

Live At Union Chapel London (2003)
December 2003; Eagle DVD/CD ER DVCD 030

One Eye To The Future – Live in Italy (2007)
September 2008; Strongman Productions MP3

In **Concert With The Danish Concert Orchestra & Choir (2006)**
May 2009; Eagle DVD/CD EAGCD400

Spirit Of Nokken – Procol Harum Live In 2009
October 2010; Strongman Productions MP3

MMX Procol Harum Live
May 2012; Strongman Productions MP3

GARY BROOKER

UK DISCOGRAPHY
(Excluding compilations, reissues, producer credits and guest appearances)

SINGLES

Savannah/S.S.Blues
May 1979; Chrysalis CHS 2326

Say It Ain't So Joe/Angelina
July 1979; Chrysalis CHS 2347

Leave The Candle/Chasing The Chop
April 1980; Chrysalis CHS 2396

Homelovin'/Chasing For The Chop
May 1981; Mercury MER 70

The Cycle (Let It Flow)/Badlands
April 1982; Mercury MER 94

The Long Goodbye/Trick Of The Night
December 1984; Mercury MER 181

Two Fools In Love/Summer Nights
April 1985; Mercury MER 188

ALBUMS

No More Fear Of Flying
May 1979; Chrysalis CHR 1224

Lead Me To The Water
March 1982; Mercury SRM-1-4054

Echoes In The Night
September 1985; Mercury 824 652-1

Within Our House
December 1996; Gazza Records Gazza CD 001

ROBIN TROWER

UK DISCOGRAPHY

SINGLES

Man Of The World/Take A Fast Train
March 1973; Chrysalis CHS 2009

Too Rolling Stoned/Lady Love
July 1974; CHS 2046

Caledonia/Messin' The Blues
November 1976; CHS 2124

It's For You/My Love/In City Dreams (EP)
September 1978; CHS 2247

It's For You/My Love
January 1979; CHS 2256

Victims Of The Fury/One In A Million
January 1980; CHS 2402

Jack And Jill/The Shout
August 1980; CHS 2423

What Is/Into Money
February 1981; CHS 2497 (BLT)

ALBUMS
(Excluding compilations, reissues and producer credits)

Twice Removed From Yesterday
1973; Chrysalis CHR 1039

Bridge Of Sighs
1974; Chrysalis CHR 1057

For Earth Below
1975; Chrysalis CHR 1073

Robin Trower Live
1975; Chrysalis CHR 1089

Long Misty Days
1976; Chrysalis 1107

In City Dreams
1977; Chrysalis CHR 1148

Caravan To Midnight
1978; Chrysalis CHR 1189

Victims Of The Fury
1980; Chrysalis CHR 1215

BLT
198;1 Chrysalis CHR 1324

Truce
1981 Chrysalis CHR 1352

Back It Up
1983; Chrysalis 4142

Beyond The Mist
1985; Music For Nations MFN 51

Passion
1987; GNP Crescendo 2187

Take What You Need
1988; Atlantic 781-838-1

In The Line Of Fire
1990; Atlantic 82080-2

BBC Radio 1 Live
1992; Griffin/Windsong GCD 336-2

20th Century Blues
1994; Demon, V-12 78857 500012

Someday Blues
1997; Demon, V-12 50020-2

Go My Way
2000; Aezra Media Inc 75766 70600 20

Living Out Of Time
2004; Ruf Records V7500027

Seven Moons (with Jack Bruce)
2008; V-12 Records

RT@R0.08
2008; V-12 Records V-12 501114

Seven Moons Live (with Jack Bruce)
2009; V-12 Records

What Lies Beneath
2009; V-12 Records

Playful Heart
2011; V-12 Records

MATTHEW FISHER

SINGLES

Suzanne/Separation
1973; RCA 2406

Can't You Feel My Love/Only A Game
1979; Mercury 6000 415

Why'd I Have To Fall In Love With You/Just How Blind
1980; Vertigo 6000 455

Take Me For A Ride/She Makes Me Feel
1981; Mercury 6000 699

ALBUMS
(Excluding compilations, producer credits, co-producer credits, engineer credits)

Journey's End
1973; RCA Victor SF 8380 APLI-0195

I'll Be There
1974; RCA Victor APLI 0325

Matthew Fisher
1979; Mercury-Phonogram 9198 652

Strange Days
1980; Mercury-Phonogram 6302 108

A Salty Dog Returns
1990; Promised Land 112152

A Salty Dog Returns (re-issue + 3 bonus tracks)
2012; Angel Air SJPCD389

BJ WILSON

CREDITS
(Excluding The Paramounts and Procol Harum)

Joe Cocker
'**With A Little Help From My Friends**' (single)
1968; Regal Zonophone

Joe Cocker
With A Little Help From My Friends '**WALHFMF**', '**Just Like A Woman**'
1969; Regal Zonophone

Legend
'**Georgia George**'/'**July**' (single)
1969; Bell Records.

Leon Russell
Leon Russell: '**Hurt Somebody**'
1970; Shelter Records

Lou Reed
Berlin: '**Lady Day**', '**The Kids**'
1973; RCA Records

Incredible String Band
No Ruinous Feud: '**Explorer**'
1973; Island Records

Soundtrack
Rocky Horror Picture Show
1975; Capitol Records

The Bonzo Dog Band (untitled and unreleased album)
1977

Frankie Miller
Double Trouble
1978; Chrysalis Records

Tom Petty & The Heartbreakers
Damn The Torpedoes: '**Refugee**' (demo/outtake)
1978; MCA

Slugline
Take Off Your Uniform
1979; MCA

John Hiatt
Slug Line '**Take Off Your Uniform**' (1979)
The Best of John Hiatt
1998; MCA/Capitol Records, 1998

The Hollies
531-7704: **'Harlequin'**
1979; Polydor Records

Joe Cocker Band
German WDR TV concert on *Rockpalast*
1980; Bootleg

Joe Cocker
Live In New York 1980
Concert in Central Park, released in Australia, 1981)
1990; Liberation CD

Joe Cocker
Live In Montreal
Concert televised on American and Canadian TV, 1981

Joe Cocker
German WDR TV concert on *Rockpalast*
1982; Bootleg

Gary Brooker
Echoes In The Night
1985; Mercury-Phonogram

Bob Siebenberg
Giants In Our Own Room: **'Good Man Down'**
1985; A&M Records

Leo Kottke
Paul Bunyan **'Enderlin'**
Recorded in 1987 released 1990; Windham Hill

Frankie Miller
BBC Radio 1 *Live In Concert* (Five tracks recorded in 1978)
1994; BBC Records.

King Biscuit Flower Hour from Poghkeepsie, New York (1982)
1995; King Biscuit Records

Mick Grabham
Mick The Lad (1971/1972, bonus tracks)
1997; Angel Air Records

Liquorice John Death & The All Stars
Ain't Nothing to Get Excited About (1970)
1997; Gazza/Repertoire CD

Joe Cocker
Standing Here (Live in Denver May 2, 1981)
2001; Burning Airlines/NMC Music Ltd

Appendices

Appendix 1:

The Paramounts' Anthologies – 1983 & 1998

In 1983 Demon/Edsel Records – run by lifelong Paramounts fan and rock manager/impresario Jake Riviera – released the first ever Paramounts compilation entitled *Whiter Shades Of R 'n' B*. The album featured four unreleased covers, including Mingus' 'Freedom'.

It was not until 1998, some 32 years after The Paramounts had split-up, that all 22 Paramounts recordings were finally made available on EMI's *The Paramounts At Abbey Road* courtesy of EMI's Nigel Reeve and *EMI At Abbey Road* series compiler-producer Tim Chacksfield. With a track for track breakdown and insightful liner notes from Southend writer/songwriter/musician Will Birch (The Flowerpots, The Kursaal Flyers, and The Records) The Paramounts significant contribution to the UK R&B scene was at last made available to a wider public. Unreleased highlights were 'Chills And Fever' from January 15, 1964 and 'Stupidity' from March 11, 1964, later covered by Southend's legendary Dr Feelgood on their UK number 1 album *Stupidity* some 22 years later.

Appendix 2:

The Paramounts' Re-Union Gig: 2005

On December 17, 2005 the original Paramounts line-up reformed for the first time in Southend's Westcliff district at *Club Riga* situated inside the old Cricketers Pub where they first started playing in December 1960. The *Southend Echo* of December 23, 2005 reported the show with the following review:

> *"The magic's still there. It was truly a night to remember – and one which many must have thought they'd never witness. After 43 years, the four original members of legendary Southend band, The Paramounts, were back together on Saturday night on the stage of Westcliff's Club Riga. Rock legends Robin Trower and Gary Brooker, who became huge international stars with Procol Harum, joined original drummer Mick Brownlee and (former Paramounts and Procol Harum) bassman Chris Copping who flew from his home in Australia especially for the reunion. The show came about as a result of the interest stirred by readers' letters, photos and stories, remembering the coffee-bars of the Fifties and Sixties, featured in our rock'n'roll years series. Believe it or not, your reminiscences have won a worldwide readership, courtesy of the official Procol Harum website, which has been reproducing online. And the sellout audience in Riga reflected that – with fans present from the USA, Norway, Rome, Denmark and Germany, as well as all four corners of the UK.*
>
> *"'It was a truly magical night,' said drummer Mick Brownlee. 'I really never thought it would happen, but it did – it was just amazing. All the guys in the band had such a great time and played really well. I've never seen Robin smile so much. He just had this huge grin all night long!'*

Guests of honour were Robin Trower's parents, Len and (step mum) Blonde Shirley, who ran the Shades coffee bar where The Paramounts often played. 'It was wonderful to come across so many people from the old days, too,' Mick added. 'It wasn't all that easy to recognize some of them, though – we've all changed a bit over the years.' Southend bass player Dave Bronze (Dr Feelgood, Eric Clapton, Tom Jones) summed it all up, 'An unforgettable occasion. Magic: the only word for it. 40 years on, no rehearsal, and they can still play like that...!'"

Courtesy of *The Southend Evening Echo* (2005)

Appendix 3

The original *Procol Harum* album recording sessions

For the first time we are able provide details about the aborted studio sessions featuring Bobby Harrison and Ray Royer that were withdrawn and sent to the vaults. These have *never* been officially released.

May 17, 1967 Olympic Studios 2 – Barnes, London.
Engineer: Eddie Kramer
She Wandered Through The Garden Fence
A Christmas Camel
Salad Days (Are Here Again)
Something Following Me

May 24, 1967 Olympic Studios 2 – Barnes, London.
Engineer: Eddie Kramer
Repent Walpurgis
Conquistador
Morning Dew
Mabel

May 29, 1967 Advision Studios , London.
Engineer – Gerald Chevin
Salad Days (Are Here Again)

June 19, 1967 Olympic Studios 2 – Barnes, London.
Engineer: Eddie Kramer
Outside The Gates Of Cerdes
Understandably Blue (Vocal only)

June 26, 1967 Olympic Studios 2 – Barnes, London.
Engineer: Eddie Kramer
Kaleidoscope
In The Wee Small Hours Of Sixpence

Appendix 4

Shine On Brightly
recording sessions

October 13, 1967 – Olympic Studios – Barnes, London.
Producer: Denny Cordell
Engineer: Glynn Johns
Shine On Brightly

December 6, 1967 – Advision Studios – New Bond Street, London.
Producer: Denny Cordell
Engineer: Gerald Chevin
Rambling On

December, 14 1967 – Olympic Studios – Barnes, London.
Producer: Denny Cordell
Engineer: Terence Brown
Skip Softly My Moonbeams

January 18, 1968 – De Lane Lea Studios – Kingsway, London
Producer: Denny Cordell
Engineer unknown
A Robe Of Silk (unreleased)

January 29, 1968 – Olympic Studios – Barnes, London.
Producer: Denny Cordell
Engineer Terence Brown
Quite Rightly So

March 10, 1968 – Olympic Studios – Barnes, London.
Producer: Denny Cordell
Engineer: unknown
MacGregor (unreleased until 1997)

March 15–16, 1968 – Olympic Studios – Barnes, London.
Producer: Denny Cordell
Assistant Producer: Tony Visconti
Engineer: Glynn Johns
Glimpses of Nirvana★
'Twas Teatime At The Circus★ (Producer Tony Visconti)

March 17, 1968 – Olympic Studios – Barnes, London.
Producer: Denny Cordell.
Assistant Producer: Tony Visconti
Engineer: Glynn Johns.
In The Autumn Of My Madness★
Look To Your Soul★

March 19, 1968 Olympic Studios– Barnes, London.
Producer: Tony Visconti
Engineer: Glynn Johns
Wish Me Well
Magdalene (My Regal Zonophone)

March, 1968, Advision Studios – New Bond Street, London.
Producer: Denny Cordell
Engineer: unknown
Grand Finale★

April 17 till end of April 1968. Olympic Studios – Barnes, London.
Mixing and Mastering Tony Visconti & Glynn Johns
In Held 'Twas In I (as defined by ★)

Appendix 5

The House of Lords Appeal hearing re A Whiter Shade Of Pale, July 30, 2009

The Appellate Committee comprised of Lord Hope of Craighead, Lord Walker of Gestingthorpe, Baroness Hale of Richmond, Lord Mance, and Lord Neuberger of Abbotsbury. The key highlights of a large 80 point statement drawn up by these Law Lords are reproduced below:

LORD HOPE OF CRAIGHEAD
I also agree with the comments of my noble and learned friend Lord Walker of Gestingthorpe …

2.   Re Lord Justice Mummery's statement: One of its most striking features is Matthew Fisher's extraordinary delay in making his claim for a share of the musical copyright. In para 82 of his judgment Mummery L J described the fact that Mr Fisher had waited for 38 years, with knowledge and without reasonable excuse, as unconscionable behavior.

3.   Delay in itself is no bar to these proceedings. There is no statutory limitation period that applies in English law to claims to copyright delayed for so long, that the respondents had to address this part of their argument.

5.   As the judgments below have shown, this was not an easy task. The respondents' main defence to the claim when the case was before the trial judge was that Mr Fisher was not entitled to any share of the musical copyright at all.

8.   A person who has a good idea, as Mr Fisher did when he composed the well-known organ solo that did so much to make the song in its final form such a success, is entitled to protect the advantage that he has gained from this and to earn his reward. These are rights which the court must respect and which it will enforce if it is asked to do so.

9.   The majority in the Court of Appeal were, for understandable reasons, reluctant to offer the court's assistance to someone who had delayed for so long in asserting his claim. But it appears that, when they decided to deny him these further declarations which were designed to give effect to the rights that flowed from his co-authorship of the work which was found on unassailable grounds to have been established by the trial judge, they overlooked this fundamental distinction. I agree with my noble and learned friend that, leaving equity on one side as one must, there were no grounds in law for setting these declarations aside.

BARONESS HALE OF RICHMOND

20. I agree that, for the reasons given by my noble and learned friend, Lord Neuberger of Abbotsbury, supplemented by those of Lord Walker of Gestingthorpe, this appeal should be allowed and the declarations made by the trial judge restored. As one of those people who do remember the sixties, I am glad that the author of that memorable organ part has at last achieved the recognition he deserves.

21. I wish only to add a footnote, prompted by the information which we were originally given, that Matthew Fisher was aged only 20 when Procol Harum recorded "A Whiter Shade of Pale" in April 1967. These days, it is easy to forget that the age of majority was 21, until it was reduced to 18 by section 1(1) of the Family Law Reform Act 1969 as from 1 January 1970. Any member of the band, or indeed their manager, who was under the age of 21 at the relevant time was therefore an "infant" to whom the complex and confusing rules relating to infants' contracts applied

LORD MANCE

33. On 16 May 1967, the five members of the band, effectively acting through Mr Reid (therein "the manager") entered into a further contract ("the recording contract") with Essex. The effect of this contract was to enable Essex to exploit any recording made by the band over the period of a year (subject to renewal by Essex a maximum of four times).

35. In his evidence, Mr Fisher said that, during 1967, he had raised the question of his having a share in the rights in respect of the music with Mr Brooker and Mr Reid, but had been rebuffed or ignored by them. He explained that he had not wanted to push his claim as he feared that, if he did so, he would be asked to "say goodbye to a career in … a number one pop group". In 1969, however, Mr Fisher did indeed leave the band, which by then had accrued certain debts. A relatively informal agreement was reached whereby the remaining members agreed to release (or, more accurately, I think, to indemnify) Mr Fisher from any liability in respect of such debts in return for his waiving any right to certain specified royalties (not including any copyright royalties in respect of the work).

36. Despite leaving the band, Mr Fisher was invited to play with them at various functions from time to time between 1969 and 2003. On a couple of occasions during that period, once in 1971 and once in 1991, Mr Fisher contended that he was entitled to certain royalties which he was not receiving, but he never suggested that he was entitled to any money in respect of the exploitation of the work.

37. In or about 1993, Essex's rights under the assignment and the recording contract were purportedly assigned to Onward Music Ltd ("Onward"), and Onward was registered with the PRS and MCPS as the owner of the copyright in the work. Meanwhile, the first recording was proving very successful, resulting in substantial royalties, which were collected by the PRS and MCPS and distributed to Essex (or their successors), as they were registered with the societies as owners of the copyright, and Mr Brooker and Mr Reid were then paid their shares under the terms of the assignment.

38. Quite apart from the first recording, the work has been extraordinarily successful over the 38 years since it was first released. It has been the subject of many articles and interviews, and has a dedicated following, as can be seen from the number of websites devoted to the work and the band. There are over 770 versions of the work performed by other groups, and themes of the work (especially the introductory bars) are available, and popular, as mobile telephone ring tones. Mr Fisher began proceedings on 31 May 2005, and they came before Blackburne J, who gave a judgment which was largely favourable to Mr Fisher – [2005]

40. The judge had to decide a number of issues, only some of which are now raised in your Lordships' House. First, there was the question whether a fair trial was possible, bearing in mind the passage of time between the composition of the work and the issue of Mr Fisher's claim. Although the judge rightly described Mr Fisher's silence about his claim between 1967 and 2004 as "remarkable" and "quite extraordinary", he concluded that a fair trial was possible – [2006]

41. Consequently, he held that "Mr Fisher qualifies to be regarded as a joint author of the work" – concluded that "Mr Fisher's interest in the work should be reflected by according to him a 40% share in the musical copyright" – ibid, para 98. Rightly, the Court of Appeal had little difficulty in dismissing the respondents' appeal on this issue – [2008] Bus LR 1123, para 44. The respondents do not seek to appeal further on this issue.

42. The third issue was whether, nonetheless, Mr Fisher had no right to claim a share of the musical copyright owing to the circumstances in which he made his contribution to the work. In effect, the respondents argued that, given that the song in its original form had been recorded, and the musical copyright in it had been assigned to Essex, in March 1967, Mr Fisher impliedly assigned to Essex any interest he acquired in the musical copyright in the work. The judge rejected that argument – [2006] EWHC 3239 Ch, para 63. However, the Court of Appeal, or at least the majority, left the point open – [2008] Bus LR 1123, para 100. This "implied assignment" argument is raised by the respondents by way of cross-appeal.

45. The sixth issue at first instance was whether Mr Fisher could claim his share of the monies paid out by the PRS and the MCPS in respect of the work during the six years before the issue of proceedings (it being rightly accepted by Mr Fisher that any claim going further back would be time-barred). The monies collected by the societies had been paid to Essex, or, since 1993, Onward, as the copyright owner registered with the societies, and the appropriate share in accordance with the assignment had then been paid to Mr Reid and Mr Brooker. The judge rejected this claim, on the basis that "for so long as Mr Fisher chose not to make ... his claim [and] allowed the societies to account to the [respondents], ... he must be taken to have gratuitously licensed the exploitation of his copyright" – [2006]

47. However, the judge granted declarations in these terms:

1. [Mr Fisher] is a co-author of ... 'A Whiter Shade of Pale' as recorded by ... Procol Harum ('the work' and released as a single on 12 May 1967.
2. [Mr] Fisher is a joint owner in the musical copyright in the work, with a share of 40%.
3. The [respondents'] licence to exploit the work was revoked on 31 May 2005".

52. Secondly, the fact that the recording contract was only entered into on 16 May 1967, about a month after the work was first recorded, and four days after the release of the recording, undermines the notion that, before that date, Mr Fisher had impliedly assigned his interest in the musical copyright to Essex. The date of the recording contract shows that, as one would have expected, the members of the band were content to leave it to Essex, an experienced record and publishing company, to produce the relevant documentation for them to execute as and when appropriate.

LORD WALKER OF GESTINGTHORPE.

By delaying his claim for nearly forty years, Mr Fisher appears to have lost a great deal of money, which has been received by the respondents. Mr Lord Justice Blackburne said in 2005 that "it would... be a wholly extravagant and unjust result to deprive Mr Fisher for the [future] of his interest in the work's musical copyright

71. The respondents argue that Mr Fisher's failure to raise his claim to a share of the musical copyright during the negotiations leading to the financial agreement when he left the band in 1969 deprive him of the right to raise it subsequently. It is well-nigh impossible to see how Essex or Onward could rely on these negotiations, as they were not involved in them in any way. Mr Brooker was a party to the agreement, Mr Fisher's delay in bringing his claim means that "he could dictate his terms and put the [respondents] in a weaker bargaining position than they would have been in, had he made his claim in, say, 1967 or 1969" (para 88).

77. As for the change in the bargaining position of the parties between 1967 and 2005, that was neither pleaded nor argued before the Judge. In any event, there was no evidence that Essex or the respondentswould have acted any differently from the way in which they did if Mr Fisher had pressed his claim in 1967 or in the ensuing few years.

79. I have also referred, that Mr Fisher's very long delay in asserting his claim has been of considerable financial benefit to the respondents, effectively outweighing any disadvantage to them resulting from the delay.

CONCLUSION

80. In these circumstances, essentially for the reasons given at first instance by Blackburne J and in the Court of Appeal by David Richards J, I would reject all the respondents' arguments based on equitable principles.

DISPOSAL

81. It follows from this that I would allow Mr Fisher's appeal, dismiss the respondents' cross-appeal, and restore the two declarations set aside by the Court of Appeal save that the third declaration may require to be amended to keep open the issue whether Essex's rights under the recording contract have been validly assigned to Onward. I understand that your Lordships and Ladyship are of the same view, and accordingly I would suggest that the parties have 14 days to make submissions in writing as to the order that this House should make in relation to the costs in your Lordships' House.

Source Notes

1. From Daniel A. Muise's *Gallagher-Marriott-Derringer-Trower-Chronicles*. Published by the Hal Leonard Corporation Inc (2002)
2. From John Denton's liner notes for the vinyl edition *Whiter Shades of R&B* issued by Demon-Edsel Records. Courtesy of John Denton and Jake Riviera. (1982)
3. From Will Birch's exclusive liner note interview with Gary Brooker for the CD re-issue of *Whiter Shades of R&B* issued by Demon-Edsel Records. Courtesy of Will Birch and Jake Riviera. (1983)
4. From Bill Wyman' *Rolling With The Stones* by, Dorling Kindersley Books (2002)
5. From Will Birch's 1998 exclusive liner note interview with Gary Brooker for *The Paramounts At Abbey Road 1963–1970*. (1998) EMI Records. Courtesy of Will Birch.
6. From Sandie Shaw's *The World At My Feet – A Personal Adventure* Published by Harper Collins (1991)
7. From Paul Kendall's *Procol Harum Unveiled Part 1: The Thin End of the Wedge* from *ZigZag* 60, May 1976. Courtesy of Paul Kendall, Kris Needs, and Pete Frame. (2012)
8. From Paul Carter's interview with Keith Reid from *Shine On* www.procolharum.com (1997)
9. From Claes Johansen's *Procol Harum- Beyond The Pale* by SAF publishing (1999):
10. From Nick Hasted's *The Making of A Whiter Shade of Pale*. Uncut Magazine by (February 2008)
11. From Johnny Black's *The Ultimate Experience* Published by Barnes & Noble (1999)
12. From Russell Newmark's *Welcome to the Pete Best Club*. Mojo Magazine Published by Beyer Media April (1998)
13. From an Interview with Elton John & Bernie Taupin from *Elton John To Be Continued* (Liner notes.) Published by MCA Records (1989)
14. From an interview by Angus MacKinnon with Keith Reid in *Streetlife*. Issue 15 (May 15–28 1976)
15. From Mike Ober's interview with Matthew Fisher in *Then Play On* (1992)
16. From John Tobler's interview with Tony Visconti in *The Record Producers*. BBCTV Publications (1982)
17. From Chris Welch's interview with Keith Reid for Repertoire Records, Germany (1997 & 2002)
18. From Tony Visconti's autiobigrahy *Bowie, Bolan & The Brooklyn Boy* by Harper Collins (2007)
19. From Eric *Clapton's Clapton – The Autobiography*. Published by Broadway Books Inc (2007)
20. From J.P. Bean's *The Authorised Biography – Joe Cocker*. Published by Virgin Books (2003)
21. From *Lives Of The Great Songs* edited by Tim De Lisle – 'A Whiter Shade Of Pale' by Mike Butler. Published by Pavilion Books (1994)

Index